BUSINESS
DISPUTE
RESOLUTION

BEST PRACTICES, SYSTEM DESIGN & CASE MANAGEMENT

THOMAS D. CAVENAGH

Director, Dispute Resolution Center
North Central College

WEST **WEST LEGAL STUDIES IN BUSINESS**
Thomson Learning™

Australia • Canada • Denmark • Japan • Mexico • New Zealand • Philippines
Puerto Rico • Singapore • South Africa • Spain • United Kingdom • United States

Business Dispute Resolution by Thomas D. Cavenagh

Vice President/Publisher: Jack W. Calhoun
Acquisitions Editor: Scott D. Person
Developmental Editor: Thomas S. Sigel
Marketing Manager: Michael W. Worls
Production Editor: Kara ZumBahlen
Manufacturing Coordinator: Charlene Taylor
Cover Design: Rick Moore
Printer: WebCom

Printed in Canada
1 2 3 4 5 02 01 00 99

For more information contact South-Western College Publishing, 5101 Madison Road, Cincinnati, Ohio, 45227 or find us on the Internet at http://www.swcollege.com

For permission to use material from this text or product, contact us by
• telephone: 1-800-730-2214
• fax: 1-800-730-2215
• web: http://www.thomsonrights.com

Library of Congress Cataloging-in-Publication Data
Cavenagh, Thomas D.
   Business dispute resolution / Thomas D. Cavenagh. – 1st ed.
      p. cm.
   ISBN 0-324-01597-6 (softcover : alk. paper)
   1. Dispute resolution (law)—United States. 2. Compromise (Law)—United States.
   3. Sales—United States. 4. Business law—United States. I. Title.
   KF9084.C38 2000
   346.7307'0269—dc21   99-30343

This book is printed on acid-free paper.

TABLE OF CONTENTS

Preface v

Foreword: Mark E. Holstein, Counsel, Amoco Oil Corporation xi

Chapter 1: Introduction to Corporate ADR 1

       Stages of the American Civil Lawsuit 1
       Overview of Alternative Dispute Resolution 7
       Advantages of Alternative Dispute Resolution 10
       Disadvantages of Alternative Dispute Resolution 12
       Designing Business Dispute Resolution Programs 14

Section One: Internal Employee ADR Programs

Chapter 2: The United States Postal Service 17

Chapter 3: Sandia National Laboratories 39

Chapter 4: Darden Restaurants 59

Chapter 5: Dollar General Corporation 79

Section Two: External Civil Law ADR Programs

Chapter 6: Air Products and Chemicals, Inc. 101

Chapter 7: BP Amoco PLC 125

Chapter 8: Georgia-Pacific Corporation 147

Chapter 9: Snapshot ADR Profiles 167

       Whirlpool Corporation 167
       Baxter International Inc. 169
       National Association of Manufacturers 175
       Johnson & Johnson 176
       Hanford Nuclear Site 179

Chapter 10: Conclusion 185

Appendix 1: ADR System Development Checklists for Business   193

Appendix 2: Resources for Business ADR System Design   197

Selected Bibliography in Dispute Resolution   203

Index   213

PREFACE

Companies of all sizes and from virtually all business sectors are faced with mounting expenses and difficulties related to the resolution of a vast array of disputes with customers, vendors and competitors. Legal fees to resolve such matters are often prohibitively high and traditional judicial processes can take years to complete, even without appeals. Beyond the costs and time associated with a formal trial, there are risks of considerable consequence in litigating a business dispute. A jury may unexpectedly rule against a company despite meritorious defenses to the claims made against it. Trade secrets or proprietary information may be revealed in the very public setting of the trial courtroom. Businesses are searching for approaches to dispute resolution that reduce these liabilities; many believe they have found it in the range of opportunities collectively referred to as *alternative dispute resolution* (ADR).

The CPR Institute for Dispute Resolution, a major national provider of alternative dispute resolution services, reports that more than 4000 U.S. companies have committed to a policy statement obligating signatories to consider the use of alternatives to litigation when those companies face a business dispute. These companies range from the very large to the local. Fortune 500 companies are widely represented on the list: 17 of the top 20 Fortune 500 companies have signed the statement.[1] Companies of much smaller net worth and revenue also appear on the list of signatories. Virtually every major American industry, from Aerospace (Boeing) to Waste Management (Browning-Ferris) is represented on the list.

Not surprisingly, at the same time companies are committing to the use of alternative dispute resolution, law firms are signing a similar CPR pledge. Indeed, 1500 law firms doing business in the United States and abroad have subscribed to a statement obligating them to provide to their business clients, lawyers who are knowledgeable about ADR. In addition, these firms have committed to discussing alternative methods of business dispute resolution with clients at the outset of any representation.

Researchers regularly find that business executives prefer alternative dispute resolution processes to litigation. Courts have initiated voluntary and mandatory programs to shift portions of their dockets to court-annexed and private providers of ADR. State legislators have implemented and funded ADR initiatives across the country. The U.S. Congress has passed several laws in recent years calculated to steer matters away from courts and toward ADR.

Alternative dispute resolution, a series of rapid, private, predictable, party-driven processes used to resolve a wide range of business problems, is here to stay. While ADR processes are not suitable for all business disputes, corporate attorneys and managers are pursuing settlement through ADR more frequently than ever

---

[1] Figures are based on information taken from the 1998 Fortune 500 list contained in the April 27, 1998, issue.

before. Successful companies have worked to create systems for both internal and external dispute resolution utilizing a variety of public and private facilitative and adjudicative processes.

This book tells the reader how they have done so. More specifically, this book lays out for the reader the details of the programs in place at nine highly successful companies specifically designed to bypass litigation. These companies operate in a range of business sectors and have sought to creatively address business dispute resolution; for many companies in-house documents actually used to employ the processes are provided to the reader. In addition, the book describes the reasons for creating these programs in the words of the people who were responsible for the design and implementation of the programs. Finally it assesses the programs and offers predictions about trends in the law and business related to ADR. "Briefing points" throughout the book provide additional supporting information to the reader in the form of short statements of statistical fact or industry custom.

Preceding the examination of company ADR programs, an introduction describes the American civil lawsuit, which these processes seek to avoid. It then describes each alternative dispute resolution process, highlighting strengths and weaknesses. In addition, the introduction briefly reviews the corporate offices normally responsible for designing and implementing corporate ADR programs and policies. Finally the introduction explains the key aspects of business ADR program design and implementation.

The remainder of the book is presented in the following fashion: Company programs are broken into two sections, internal and external. Internal programs are those designed to address employee disputes with one another and with the company itself. These programs are typically created to avoid litigation or outside intervention into internal employee matters. External programs are those programs created to resolve matters involving entities outside the company, typically civil lawsuit plaintiffs. These programs also seek to limit the use of litigation to resolve such difficulties. In the sections on internal and external programs, the chapters begin with the more limited programs and move to the more comprehensive.

The company programs are covered uniformly and each chapter presents a company's approach, including these sections:

- **Due Diligence** – a brief listing of company financial facts;

- **Company Story** – a concise recounting of the development of the company, including the formal corporate name, web address, principal executive officers, current market position and nature of the company.

- **ADR Program** – a detailed explanation of the ADR program in use at the company, many supported by appendices containing ADR program documents provided by the company;

- **Assessment** – a brief appraisal of the strengths of the particular ADR program;

- **Forms & Materials** – actual company documents used to train for and operate the various ADR programs; and,

- **Key Decision** – an edited state or federal court ruling related to the type of ADR program employed by the company.

Two final chapters conclude this overview of business dispute resolution efforts. A chapter of snapshot ADR profiles provides a brief review of particularly interesting features of ongoing programs of four additional companies. A closing chapter draws several broad conclusions about company ADR planning and predicts trends, both legal and business related. Finally, appendices providing additional ADR resources are provided. The reader will find, in short, a wealth of ADR information based on real company experiences.

ACKNOWLEDGMENTS

I would like first to thank my splendid editors at West Educational Publishing: Jack Calhoun & Scott Person, for their faith in pursuing work in this emerging field; Thomas Sigel, who patiently provided absolutely indispensable assistance throughout the duration of this project and without whom it simply could not have been completed; Kara ZumBahlen for working me through the many difficult layout and formatting matters we faced; and, Carol Koletsky for her copy editing efforts.

I would also like to acknowledge the research assistance of and thank the following students each of whom provided invaluable assistance to me in preparing this book:

Dean Frieders
Rick Guzman
Dawn Lockwood
Phillip Perkins
Kim Sluis

Thomas D. Cavenagh, JD
Associate Professor of Business Law & Conflict Resolution
Director, *North Central College Dispute Resolution Center*

For Yasmin, my wonderful wife, and Sean, Ben & Gillian.

ABOUT THE AUTHOR

Thomas D. Cavenagh, JD is Associate Professor of Business Law and Conflict Resolution at North Central College in Naperville, Illinois. He teaches courses in law, ethics and conflict resolution. In addition, he is the founder of and directs the North Central College *Dispute Resolution Center*. He graduated from Trinity College with a B.A. in philosophy, magna cum laude. His J.D. is from DePaul University College of Law. He is co-author of the book <u>Alternative Dispute Resolution for Business</u>, with Lucille Ponte, published by West Publishing Company and a contributor to <u>Teaching Leadership: Essays in Theory and Practice</u>, published by Peter Lang; he has been widely published in a variety of professional journals including *Mediation Quarterly*. He is the 1999-2000 Chair of the *Illinois State Bar Association Council on ADR*, the founding co-chair of the *Academy of Legal Studies in Business Section on Alternative Dispute Resolution* and served as a Consultant to the *Commission of Inquiry into the Rationalisation of the Provincial and Local Divisions of the Supreme Court of South Africa.*

He is the recipient of the *North Central College Dissenger Prize for Faculty Scholarship* and the *North Central College Clarence F. Dissenger Distinguished Teaching and Service Award.* He was named to the *Illinois Leading Attorneys List* in 1996.

FOREWORD

I learned nothing about mediation or other forms of alternative dispute resolution in law school. Then and now, it struck me as odd that the law school curriculum placed so much emphasis on evidence and trial advocacy - this in spite of the fact that 90% or more of all civil cases in the court system settle before trial. But it was fine with me. I wanted to be a trial lawyer.

I went to work for a small insurance defense law firm in 1986, first as a law clerk while I was still in school and then, after graduation in 1987, as an attorney. We handled the traditional portfolio of personal injury lawsuits - automobile accidents, slip & falls, construction accidents and product liability lawsuits. I took depositions, filed motions, prepared cases and engaged in all of the activities I was trained to do. But still, the overwhelming majority of my cases settled, often after 6 or 7 years of expensive litigation.

I first became aware of mediation when it was recommended by an insurance adjuster responsible for one of my cases. She couldn't really articulate what it was, but home office was requiring her to submit a certain percentage of her cases to mediation. I was skeptical. Mediation was, as a method of resolving lawsuits, in its infancy. A few pioneers were found speaking at seminars. Undoubtedly, some home office type attended one of these seminars. It became the cost cutting technique "du jour."

The insurance carriers' view of mediation was unfortunate and rather self-serving. They viewed mediation as a forum to badger the plaintiff into seeing it their way. It was a place to advocate the correctness of their position while remaining absolutely rigid in their own view of the case. As willingness to bargain is generally considered a fundamental requisite of successful mediation, this was not an ideal introduction to the process.

Yet, in spite of this inflexible approach, a surprising thing happened: cases settled. For me, this was an eye opening experience. It wasn't too great a leap to conclude that if cases settled under these less than ideal conditions, mediation could be a powerful tool in cases that were approached in good faith by both parties.

In 1990, I joined the Litigation and Claims Division of the Law Department at Amoco Corporation, currently known as BP Amoco PLC. Now, in addition to handling a certain percentage of my cases directly, I was also supervising a talented and diverse collection of outside law firms throughout the United States. I was no longer just a player. Now, I was a "coach" too.

Back then, Amoco did not have an alternative dispute resolution policy. To be sure, my colleagues were mediating cases, but these examples were few and far between. Truthfully, nobody thought much about it. I decided to call the mediation play in a number of my cases.

One thing that surprised me at the time was the resistance I encountered from my outside lawyers. They came up with dozens of rationalizations for avoiding mediation and other forms of alternative dispute resolution. With the benefit of hindsight, I believe this resistance was based on concerns for self-preservation (a settled case generates no fees) and a lack of familiarity with the process.

Of course, as "coach," I could and did insist. Now, one of my criteria for the selection and retention of outside counsel is their willingness and ability to participate in alternative dispute resolution. It has taken a little time, but most law firms have figured out that this is important to their business clients. They have developed alternative dispute resolution skills (and sometimes, in true law firm fashion, ADR Departments), and now often actively promote ADR as an alternative to traditional litigation.

Not surprisingly, cases I submitted for ADR (usually mediation) settled. As of this writing, I have mediated dozens of BP Amoco lawsuits. I can count on one hand the cases that did not settle. Mediation has allowed me to settle these cases earlier than the traditional litigation process would have allowed. This results in real savings. The courtroom limits the available resolutions to a dispute, usually to money. ADR has no such limits. Anything to which the parties agree is fair game. Mediated settlements often result in promises to take certain actions or promises to refrain from certain activities. Sometimes a mediated settlement may include something as mundane, but as powerful, as an apology. I even settled one case by offering the plaintiff a significant supply of free gasoline.

It is important to keep in mind that litigation dollars are heavily leveraged. The amount in controversy can often exceed in multiples, the cost of litigation. The key for me is to achieve results as good, or better, than the result I would have achieved through traditional litigation.

I think Amoco's experience mirrored my own. Through the 1990s, as mediation and other forms of ADR became popular, the Amoco Law Department was mediating (and settling) more and more cases. But we had no formal policy and no management directive. Some attorneys felt comfortable with the process and championed it; others did not.

Those who follow Fortune 500 companies generally, and energy companies like BP Amoco in particular, know that the 1990s were a period of intense cost scrutiny. Corporate downsizings occupied the front pages of the newspapers, but this was only the beginning of the story. Cost reduction was being pursued with a quasi-religious fervor throughout our companies. Litigation was not exempt. Law Departments were being held directly accountable for their costs and therefore sought new and creative ways to reduce expense without sacrificing results. ADR surfaced as a powerful way to accomplish this goal.

BP Amoco wanted to take ADR even further, and recently decided to adopt a more formal approach to ADR, with a specific focus on mediation. Our general counsel appointed a task force that looked at the approaches taken by other companies and created a policy that is discussed in Chapter 1 of this book. I had the pleasure of working on this project. It differs from the approach of several companies (including the insurance carrier I reference above) in that it avoids a "one size fits all" policy. We recognized that alternative dispute resolution would not work in every case. But we also recognized that alternative dispute resolution should be strongly considered in every dispute we face. We should be willing to risk occasional failure in a case, in favor of increasing the overall use of ADR. The potential cost savings are too significant to continue to be ad hoc in making this decision.

I think this is the place that most business people find themselves. We recognize the need to take alternative dispute resolution seriously, but are not entirely sure how to be systematic in applying the concepts to our business disputes. While there is a lot of literature available, much of it is too basic or too academic to be of value.

By focusing on real world stories of companies that have succeeded with their own ADR programs, this book will provide you with a practical guide to the use of ADR in your business pursuits. Whether you are part of a Fortune 500 organization or the proprietor of a small family business, you will find in these pages valuable ideas for reducing your cost and exposure when faced with a lawsuit. The companies that are featured here have done the legwork and share their ideas, successes and failures. Undoubtedly, at least one of the companies here will have a culture and philosophy similar to your own. A policy that is working at BP Amoco may not work in your business. By collecting these stories in one place, Professor Cavenagh provides us with a practical resource and guide. I wish that I had this book several years ago.

A word about your author. Tom and I were law school classmates. We worked together as moot court partners, competing on regional and national teams, winning a few and losing a few more. Even then I was impressed by Tom's intelligence, but more importantly, by his creative "out of the box" solutions to even traditional legal problems. Tom's "win/win" approach began to emerge before graduation.

To this day, I remain impressed by Tom's dedication to the field of ADR. While Tom's career began as mine did, engaged in the practice of trial law, it was clear to me that Tom's heart wasn't in it. The winner take all, adversarial approach to resolving disputes that is litigation did not square with Tom's ideas of justice and fairness. In my opinion, Tom found his true calling as a professor and Director of the Center for Dispute Resolution at North Central College. Here, his passions for learning, teaching and professional growth flourish.

Tom's ideas about this subject have inspired me to think about ADR in new and different ways. In his first book, Alternative Dispute Resolution in Business, Tom and his co-author, Lucille Ponte, share the nuts and bolts of ADR as well as their thoughts on the subject. Here, Tom has the wisdom to allow the practitioners to speak to us. I'll be listening.

Mark Holstein
Counsel
BP Amoco Corporation

CHAPTER 1

INTRODUCTION TO BUSINESS ADR

Alternative dispute resolution is one of the most significant legal developments of the last decade. Courts, lawyers and businesses are all considering the variety of ways they can implement programs to reduce the use of the courtroom to resolve legal difficulties.

This chapter provides the context in which to consider the programs that are described in the remaining chapters of the book. To do so, it describes the American lawsuit, the dispute resolution mechanism for which ADR is a substitute. In addition, the chapter highlights each of the major alternative dispute resolution processes and briefly describes some of the major reasons for using ADR and some of the reasons to avoid it. The chapter concludes with an overview of ADR system design principles.

STAGES OF THE AMERICAN CIVIL LAWSUIT

The American civil justice system is an adversarial, common law one in which a neutral trier of fact, normally a jury, applies the law to questions of fact to reach a conclusion regarding the claims made by the parties. It is important to note that civil cases, those in which ADR is most often used, are very different from criminal cases. The civil standard of proof is called a preponderance of evidence and means essentially that the claims made by the plaintiff must be more likely true than not. It is a radically different measure than the criminal standard of proof requiring certainty beyond a reasonable doubt. It is, consequently, much easier to prevail in a civil trial than in a criminal trial. Second, the civil case seeks to establish liability, while the criminal case seeks to establish guilt. Liability simply means a finding that an error was made; guilt involves a finding of intentional culpability. Third, civil cases are generally resolved through the payment of money damages, criminal cases typically by punishment. Civil money damages may compensate a plaintiff or may include punitive damages to punish or deter a defendant for its conduct. Finally, we think of the civil trial as a private matter between two parties, while we conceive of the criminal trial as a public matter between the state, the 'victim' of a crime, and a defendant.

American civil litigation is a three-phase process. The *pre-trial* phase of the civil lawsuit involves the variety of practices undertaken to prepare a case for presentation to the finder of fact, whether a judge or a jury. The *trial* is a multi-step proceeding involving the presentation of evidence by the plaintiff and defendant and a decision by the finder of fact. The *post-trial* period involves efforts by both the prevailing party and the losing party to implement or prevent the implementation of the judgment through appeals.

Pre-Trial. The costs, duration and risks of litigation are such that some business losses are better ignored than litigated. In the event the matter is litigated, the first phase is the pre-trial phase. This is the lengthiest step in civil litigation, often requiring years to complete, because it is the phase of litigation least supervised by courts. There are several components of the pre-trial phase. Taken in chronological order they are:

1. The initial component of the pretrial stage is *case investigation* during which parties endeavor to ascertain the boundaries of the dispute by determining the exact facts that give rise to the dispute and the damages attendant to those facts to determine whether formal resolution of the case is possible and desirable.

2. Following or simultaneous with case investigation *legal counsel* may be retained. Businesses often use in-house attorneys to consider the initial merits of a case and later retain outside counsel to pursue formal litigation. Initial legal research will focus on two areas primarily: jurisdiction and liability. Jurisdiction involves determining which court has power to hear a case and render a judgment that binds the parties. In addition, parties will need clear legal advice on whether the facts that support liability that can be demonstrated with the existing evidence. While no lawyer can make a perfect assessment of the chances of a judge or jury finding liability, the attorney can research similar cases and predict for a party what law will be applied and whether, after the application of that law, a reasonable likelihood of a finding of liability exists.

3. The formal litigation process is started by the plaintiff's decision to file a *complaint*. The complaint is a document that puts parties on notice of the nature of the claims and a rough estimate of damages. Very few courts require the complaint to recite all of the facts that give rise to an action. Instead, they require what is known as "notice pleading" which obligates the plaintiff to describe the theories of law to be pursued, the facts that support that theory and in very general terms the damages sought.

4. The defendant in turn files an *answer*. The answer essentially admits or denies the allegations contained in the complaint and lists any affirmative defenses to the claim being made. The defendant may also counterclaim, which means sue the plaintiff, or implead other defendants, that is, sue parties not listed by the plaintiff for contribution to any judgment against the principal defendant.

5.   ***Discovery*** is the longest and most complex step prior to trial. Discovery is essentially a court sanctioned investigation of the case through written and oral means. Interrogatories are written requests for information in the form of questions from one party to the other. Parties may also request documents from the other side. Finally, parties may use the deposition to question, on the record, both parties and others with sufficient knowledge to make them potential witnesses. The presiding judge often will assist when discovery disputes arise between litigants.

6.   ***Expert witnesses*** are a particularly interesting and controversial feature of the American trial system. Expert witnesses hold a unique position in most courts, as they are the only class of witnesses (unlike so-called fact witnesses) who can offer opinions on the ultimate issues in the case. Parties hire partisan experts to persuade the trier of fact that the position taken is supported by science or some other objective standard. Expert testimony is controversial because it is rarely, if ever, truly objective. Consider for example the various experts in the litigation regarding the Dow-Corning silicon breast implant device. Scientific experts have testified widely on both sides of the case taking diametrically opposing views of the effects of a ruptured implant. The result is that the trier of fact must observe the testimony and decide which set of experts is more compelling and believable based upon their respective qualifications, experience, ability to substantiate their claims and demeanor.

7.   Legal research, discovery and expert witness input are chiefly designed to fully develop the parties' understanding of their case. The result is that parties who believe they have discovered sufficient evidence to persuade a judge to dispose of the matter without a trial will file ***dispositive motions***. Dispositive motions argue that the facts or the law are so clearly favorable to one party that a trial is unnecessary and a judgment should be entered on the pleadings and accompanying materials. The "motion for summary judgment" is a fact-based motion that can be filed by either party. It argues that as a result of discovered information and documents, reasonable minds could not differ on the question of liability and therefore the trial is unnecessary. The "motion to dismiss" is a law-based motion available to the defendant arguing that there is no case or statutory law to support the plaintiff's claim and thus it should be dismissed without a trial.

8.   In the event the dispositive motions are denied, and they often are, ***trial preparation*** begins. Party witnesses will be prepared for trial, often by rehearsing testimony and participating in mock examinations. Evidentiary and demonstrative exhibits will be created to support and explain the positions taken by the parties. Finally pre-trial motions, called motions <u>in limine</u>, will be filed to define the exact nature of the trial. Motions <u>in limine</u>

are used primarily to exclude certain witnesses or evidence from use at the trial, and usually are filed on the day of trial in order to prevent a meaningful response by the opponent.

Trial. The trial itself is a six-step process. It is normally relatively short, often lasting days or weeks, compared to the pre-trial period that may have lasted years. It is a formal, solemn process played out in front of a judge (the chief officer of the court) alone, or in front of a judge and jury. The judge makes procedural rulings during the trial, and decides which laws apply to the findings of fact made by the jury. The so-called "bench trial" is available only when the right to a jury is waived; the Seventh Amendment of the Constitution provides a jury trial as a matter of right to civil litigants. The bench trial occurs because the parties believe it is a better form of fact-finding in a particular case, perhaps a highly technical or complex case. The components of the jury trial phase in their usual sequence are:

1.   The trial begins with *jury selection* or *voir dire*. The process of jury selection is significant in the civil trial because lawyers may exclude certain jurors through the use of the peremptory challenges and others by requesting that the judge excuse them for cause. The jury theoretically should consist of impartial individuals. Therefore, the judge and the attorneys have an opportunity to interview prospective jurors as to any potential bias or prejudice prior to placing them in a position to decide the case. Jurors who cannot, in the judgment of the court, hear the case without preconceptions or biases are excused.

2.   Following jury selection party *opening statements* are made by all counsel; in most jurisdictions these statements are made first by the plaintiff and then by the defendant. These statements tell the jury what it will hear from each of the parties in terms of evidence and law. They are not designed or permitted to be argumentative; instead they offer the jury a descriptive overview of what the parties expect to prove at trial. Skillful attorneys artfully convey not just the contents of their cases to the jury, but often find ways of inserting some argument into the opening statements.

3.   Following opening statements, the *plaintiff presents a case in chief*. In other words, all of the plaintiff's evidence is presented to the jury first. As a result of the discovery phase of the trial, the parties will be familiar with the evidence by this time, so it is unlikely that any surprises will take place. The defendant is entitled to object to evidence or the method of introduction of evidence, but the trial is in many ways a ritual that is planned long in advance and played out in front of the jury. Defense counsel is permitted to cross-examine, or test, the testimony of the plaintiff's witnesses during this phase of the trial.

4. In the likely event that the motion for a directed verdict is denied, the *defendant then presents a case in chief* as well. The case will consist of all of the evidence that tends to show that the defendant is not liable for the injuries or damages suffered by the plaintiff. As such, defense experts will likely testify, documents rebutting those presented by the plaintiff will be introduced and the defendant may testify. Unlike the criminal trial, there is not a Fifth Amendment protection against self-incrimination, so defendants normally testify, voluntarily or in response to plaintiff's subpoena. Plaintiff's counsel may cross-examine defense witnesses.

5. *Closing arguments* are, as the name suggests, the opportunity for the lawyers to sum up and interpret the evidence that has been offered to the jury during the trial. Unlike opening statements, these are intended to persuade, not simply to inform, and normally include a specific request for a verdict for each side and some support for that request.

6. *Jury deliberations* follow the closing arguments. These are conducted in a secluded room, off limits to the judge, lawyers, parties the press or the public. The jury receives detailed instructions from the judge, ordinarily prior to beginning deliberations. These instructions will guide the jury through the process of reviewing the case and reaching a decision. They are prepared by the parties, but with significant judicial supervision. The deliberating jury may request any piece of evidence offered during the trial for review, including testimony by transcript. Frequently, state civil trials do not require a unanimous jury decision.

Post-Trial. Litigation does not always end with the trial. Indeed, the post-trial period can be very costly and time-consuming. It consists of the following components:

1. The losing party at trial has the opportunity to request that the judge set aside the verdict as inconsistent with the evidence. This is usually done through a *motion for a judgment notwithstanding the verdict*. The motion is only granted in rare circumstances when a judge believes a jury has acted against the overwhelming weight of evidence. Because the finding of a trier of fact is a relatively sacrosanct notion in the system, judges normally expect that an appellate panel will remedy any wrongs in the trial and accordingly deny the motion.

2. The losing party who does not prevail in a motion to set aside the verdict may *appeal*. On appeal that party may ask that a panel of higher court judges decide that errors of law were made in the trial such that a new trial or other relief is warranted. It is important to note that an appellate court rarely will substitute its judgment for that of the trier of fact by considering

the weight of the evidence. Indeed, no new evidence is introduced at all at the appellate level. Instead, appellate courts hear arguments from counsel that the legal procedure used to reach the verdict was flawed. An appellate court may simply affirm the lower court's judgment, or it may reverse the judgment and remand for additional proceedings, perhaps a new trial. Further, a higher court may dismiss an action as relief, but may not award damages.

3.   When all appellate avenues have been exhausted, a successful plaintiff, will move to collect the judgment. This often involves a court order called a *perfection or enforcement of judgment* if assets are held in another jurisdiction.

BRIEFING POINT 1.1
A 1997 Deloitt & Touche survey of in-house counsel and private attorneys practicing primarily as outside corporate counsel found that 71% of all respondents believe that ADR makes the resolution of claims and disputes easier than traditional litigation.

It is important to note that the American legal system is one in which good lawyering is frequently rewarded. Indeed, cases that lack merit can be won by effective lawyering and sufficient resources - good lawyers with ample resources can win bad cases. For many, this miscarriage of justice is the principle reason to distrust the legal system. For others, it is a necessary byproduct of a system that provides free access to the courts and allows parties significant latitude in proving their cases.

The civil trial has other disadvantages as well, five of which are worth noting in the context of a discussion of alternative dispute resolution. The economic *cost* of civil litigation is a very significant fault. Though some estimates range as high as $100,000 to defend the typical civil suit, meaningful average litigation costs are nearly impossible to compute given the tremendous range of case types and the confidential nature of the attorney-client relationship. What can be said with great certainty is that litigation costs represent a major business liability, one that clearly affects corporate decision-making in many significant ways.

In addition, the length of *time* required to resolve a case, even one not appealed following a verdict, is unreasonably long. In many metropolitan areas, litigants may wait many years for a trial in state court; the wait for a federal court trial while shorter, remains considerable. While they wait, in part due to crowded court dockets and in part due to very lengthy pre-trial work by their attorneys, businesses see their expenses mount. John Lande puts it this way in the *Harvard Negotiation Law Review*,

> The essence of adversarial litigation is procedure. We define justice in procedural terms ... When we want to improve our judicial system we pass a procedural reform, which invariably means elaborating old procedural rules or adding new ones – rules that govern the presentation of evidence

and arguments, rules that create opportunities to investigate and to prepare evidence and argument, and rules that are designed to regulate the use of the procedures that are available to investigate, prepare and present evidence and argument.   The upshot is a masterpiece of detail, with rules on everything from special appearances to contest the jurisdiction of the court, to the use of exhibits during jury deliberation. But we cannot afford it. As litigants, few of us can pay the costs of trial; as a society, we are unwilling to pay even a fraction of the cost of the judicial apparatus that we would need to try most civil cases. We have designed a spectacular system for adjudicating disputes, but it is too expensive to use.[1]

Moreover, after the time and expense of preparing for trial, parties relinquish control over the outcome of the case and *risk* that a jury will interpret the facts or law in unexpected ways or even ignore the law and do as they see fit. Indeed, no case is so strong that an absolute guarantee of success at trial can be made. One lawyer in John Lande's survey describes trial risks frankly: "[I]f I come in and tell you, 'Look the odds we're going to win this case are a toss-up. I mean we're before a California jury. It should be a $200,000 case, but it's a California jury so it could be $2 million. Or, we can settle it for $300,000.' I mean there's not a businessman in this world who's going to say, 'let's gamble.'"

Lawyers may have *different interests* in and perceptions of the trial system than their clients. While Lande's survey found that 76% of outside counsel and 57% of in-house counsel were satisfied with the results in their experiences with litigation, only 25% of business executives were satisfied. Not surprisingly, more than 85% of outside counsel saw increased litigation as beneficial for their compensation and 72% of inside counsel saw augmented litigation as increasing their prestige within their firm.

Perhaps the most significant problem with litigation from the businessperson's perspective is the almost inevitable *loss of the business relationship* one may have established or continued with the other party. In a very substantial number of cases, litigants are also current or potential business partners. It is very difficult, if not impossible to do business with a person or company who has sued you or forced you to sue them. Alternative dispute resolution offers processes that avoid these difficulties.

OVERVIEW OF ALTERNATIVE DISPUTE RESOLUTION

There are myriad ways of addressing conflict in the business world. The major dispute resolution processes can, however, be divided into two main classes: processes focusing the authority to resolve a case on the parties themselves, and processes in which a third party is given the authority to decide the matter for the

---

[1] "Failing Faith in Litigation: A Survey of Business Lawyers' and Executives' Opinions," Lande, John, 3 Harvard Negotiation Law Review 1, Spring, 1998.

parties. The former class includes negotiation, mediation, the summary jury trial and the mini-trial. The latter is reserved for arbitration, private judging and a hybrid mediation process called mediation-arbitration. Often, parties will attempt to resolve a matter through a process that they control before turning the case over to a third-party decision-maker.

The first four processes we will define briefly are the party-driven settlement processes. We will begin with the least formal process and arrange the others according to their increasing formality.

Negotiation is the most widely used process for the resolution of disputes. It is simply the process of refining and agreeing to the issues requiring resolution and establishing a range of compromise options from which to choose. Negotiation is often done directly, without legal representation. Negotiation is the most private of all dispute resolution processes as it normally does not require the introduction of third parties into the case. It also can be risky, as there are no external rules or protection for the parties.

Mediation is facilitated negotiation using a specially trained, neutral third party to assist the disputants in presenting their positions and in generating and evaluating options to resolve the dispute. Mediation is a more formal process than negotiation since it involves the intervention of a third party and because it is often conducted pursuant to rules agreed to by the parties. Like negotiation, it may be done either through legal representatives or directly with one's adversary. The process is virtually always voluntary and private.

BRIEFING POINT 1.2
The Deloitt & Touche survey found that mediation is the ADR process of choice for in-house attorneys. 65% of in-house attorneys prefer mediation to arbitration.

Mini-trials allow parties to carefully structure a process blending negotiation, mediation and litigation. In the process, attorneys for each side make a semi-formal presentation of the case to representatives, often members of senior management, of each party. The length, content and nature of the presentations are agreed upon by the parties in advance so that the representatives will hear a balanced and meaningful presentation of the case. Parties normally are permitted to engage in limited discovery prior to the presentation. Next, the representatives negotiate directly or with the assistance of a mediator; often the mediator will have presided over the presentation of the cases by the parties. The mini-trial process is voluntary and generally private.

The *Summary Jury Trial* allows parties the opportunity to litigate their dispute in an abbreviated and mock courtroom proceeding designed to demonstrate the strengths and weaknesses of each side's case and to lead to negotiation based on the advisory result rendered by the jury. In the typical summary jury trial process, a six member jury is impaneled to hear the case <u>without</u> being advised that it will render a non-binding and advisory verdict. Prior to the 'trial,' parties have the opportunity to engage in discovery, often including depositions and document requests. After the parties present an abbreviated version of their respective cases, the jury deliberates and presents its verdict. On the basis of the jury's verdict, the parties then endeavor to negotiate an outcome to the dispute. Like the minitrial, the summary jury trial is designed to preface negotiations with an objective review of the evidence.

There are three processes used widely by parties for resolution of disputes that entail a decision, generally binding, made by an impartial third party. The first, *Arbitration*, is a private version of the public courtroom trial. The process is based on the presentation of evidence, rather than a negotiated understanding of the facts. It results in a third party judgment by an arbitrator who is normally experienced in the subject matter of the case. Because arbitration involves both presentation of evidence, sometimes through witnesses and on the record, and third party decision-making, it is less private than other ADR processes. In addition, arbitration is normally governed by either statutory or private rules. In either event, the parties will have agreed on the exact regulations for the procedure prior to commencing the hearing. It is often a mandatory process due to agreements between the parties, as in collective bargaining agreements, though parties may, and often do, submit cases for arbitration without any obligation to do so.

Mediation-arbitration is a mixture of mediation and arbitration in which parties endeavor initially to reach agreement with the assistance of a mediator. In the event that they are unable to do so, the case is immediately transferred to arbitration for a binding judgment by a neutral. Often, the same neutral works as both mediator and subsequently as arbitrator. Med-arb allows parties the advantages of a party-driven, informal process, while at the same time providing the parties with absolute certainty about the timeframe within which their dispute will be resolved. In addition, this process, developed primarily in the labor context, motivates parties to settle through mediation so that they can avoid the neutral rendering a judgment after witnessing their failure to agree.

Numerous states provide litigants with the opportunity to have their case heard and decided by a privately hired judge. *Private judging* allows parties to purchase the procedural expertise of a retired state or federal court judge to hear testimony and review evidence and render a decision in a dispute. The private judging statutes in several states allow for juries to be impaneled, and decisions to be appealed, though very few parties actually appeal. Private litigants benefit from much quicker resolution of cases, though there is likely to be little economic savings as the process is essentially identical to public litigation once commenced. Disputants are generally free to 'rent-a-judge' in states that do not have authorizing statutes. They do not, however, have the right to appeal the decision to a state court. Nor do they have the same certainty of the enforceability of the decision reached in the process as they would with a conventional legal judgment.

ADVANTAGES OF ALTERNATIVE DISPUTE RESOLUTION

While all non-litigation dispute resolution processes have unique benefits and detriments, some general observations can be made about the advantages of alternative dispute resolution.

Speed. As we have previously said, it is not uncommon to wait years for a trial in state court and many months in federal court. Most alternative dispute resolution processes provide closure far more rapidly than litigation. Less time is spent between occurrence and resolution due to the avoidance of vastly overcrowded court dockets and lengthy pre-trial procedure. In addition, ADR processes can begin as soon as parties have prepared their cases. Finally, the investment of time throughout the resolution process itself is likely to be less significant in a non-litigation forum where such things as motions, witness preparation and appeal are not necessary.

Cost. The expense of most alternative dispute resolution processes can be substantially less than litigation. While a complete arbitration proceeding is not likely to save a party much, mediation, for example, can significantly reduce the cost of resolving a dispute. There are several reasons for the diminished expense of ADR: The processes take less time to prepare for and complete, so attorney fees are reduced. Indeed, companies may in some instances proceed without attorneys. The use of expert witnesses is far less likely in most ADR processes, so the expense of retaining such individuals is limited or avoided. Moreover, in cases involving substantial potential economic exposure, it is not uncommon for litigants to expend considerable sums on jury selection assistance. In virtually all ADR processes such an expense is unnecessary because juries are not used or are used in an advisory capacity only. Finally, both pretrial motion practice and discovery may be curtailed in the processes that focus on negotiated outcomes rather than evidentiary decisions.

BRIEFING POINT 1.3
Deloitt & Touche also found that ADR is often used by large companies in cases involving considerable potential exposure. 57% of cases sent to ADR by companies with values in excess of 1 billion dollars had more than $500,000 in possible exposure.

Individually Tailored Outcomes. Many alternative dispute resolution processes provide negotiated outcomes likely to enhance business relationships in a fashion not possible in a trial setting, because courts are generally able to award only money damages. In ADR processes there is no such limitation and the negotiated resolutions resulting from ADR are more likely to comport with the individual needs and interests of the parties than the 'one size fits all' approach taken in litigation. Indeed, many cases are resolved in negotiated settings for types of compensation that are simply unavailable through a trial. In addition, the level of acrimony and confrontation that the trial is likely to produce is avoided in most ADR processes, so settlements are likely to work.

Control. Trials are highly specialized procedural affairs in which lawyers take center stage and parties observe. A noteworthy strength of ADR that is closely related to tailored and creative outcomes is the heightened control parties have over the case. While legal representation is the rule rather than the exception in most ADR settings, the nature of the processes is such that vastly increased input from the parties during the process, particularly regarding the outcome, is possible and encouraged. Exercising this control, especially in settlement oriented processes, not only allows for outcomes more closely aligned with mutual party interests, it all but eliminates the risk of a third-party decision maker ruling in an unexpected and potentially harmful fashion in a given case.

Confidentiality. ADR processes are usually private, allowing businesses to resolve disputes without creation of a public record or public response. Companies concerned about public confidence in their products or services will be attracted to processes that allow them to negotiate an outcome without a public trial. Similarly, companies faced with the possibility of revealing trade secrets or proprietary information in the course of litigation will see significant advantages in using processes that allow them to avoid such disclosure. Finally, companies seeking to avoid the creation of legal precedent that may later harm them will benefit from processes that are not subject to appeals through which legal precedent could be established and generalized.

Flexibility. Most alternative dispute resolution processes can be customized by the parties. For example, arbitration can be advisory or binding, by panel or individual arbitrator, with limited evidence or with unlimited evidence. Mediation can be done in a single session or a series of conferences with either one or two mediators. In short, while there are several broadly defined processes available, they are all subject to refinement to meet the needs of the particular participants. Conversely, the trial is governed in all state and federal courts by virtually inflexible rules of procedure, providing parties with a high level of certainty relative to process, but virtually no ability to mold the process to the particular dispute.

Internationalization. Businesses are competing on an international level with increasing regularity. As a result, they are often involved in disputes with companies from foreign countries. These sorts of disputes are among the most difficult to resolve because jurisdiction, the law governing which court may hear the case, is very complicated, and concomitantly expensive to resolve. In addition, companies in other countries often have negative perceptions of the American court system and regard defending a suit in the courts as a profoundly unpleasant experience. Moreover, the individuals managing foreign companies may have cultural orientations that suggest that negotiation, rather than litigation, is not simply the preferable fashion for resolving business disputes, but the only way, if a business relationship is to be continued. ADR offers the opportunity to resolve international disputes with many of the same advantages listed above, speed, economy, flexibility, etc. It also allows American businesses the very favorable opportunity to resolve disputes in a fashion consistent with the cultural expectations of many foreign businesspersons.

DISADVANTAGES OF ALTERNATIVE DISPUTE RESOLUTION

Like the civil trial, ADR processes have several drawbacks. The civil and criminal court systems at both the state and federal levels are governed by *due process* requirements rooted in the Fifth and Fourteenth Amendments to the United States Constitution. Due process is essentially the obligation to create laws and the procedures by which they are applied that are fair and reasonable. To assure parties that they receive due process at trial, carefully constructed rules of both civil and criminal procedure have been developed. For example, due process prohibits courts in criminal proceedings from requiring a defendant to make self-incriminating statements. In addition, it provides the right to present evidence, to confront one's adversaries and to cross-examine hostile witnesses.

Most alternative dispute resolution processes are informal and private. They are not, therefore, governed by due process principles in any meaningful way. The parties may draft rules of procedure for themselves on a case by case basis or rely voluntarily on model rules promulgated by professional associations. As a result, parties waive certain due process rights and protections they may have had at trial when they agree to use an alternative dispute resolution process instead. It should be noted however, that due process requirements create longer and more difficult proceedings. In addition, due process as we know it in the United States is rooted in the adversarial system of evidentiary justice. Parties seeking amicable resolutions to disputes rarely find them through the trial.

Equal Protection. Equal protection rights assure all individuals and businesses that they will receive similar, if not identical, treatment at law. Equal protection prohibits government from closing the courts to the indigent, while allowing access to the wealthy. In addition, it guarantees the same level of consideration to all litigants once in court. In short, it provides a day in court for all who have a legal issue for resolution, irrespective of their social or economic status. Because certain claims of minimal economic consequence have become subject to mandatory ADR, the courthouse has been effectively closed to some disputants. As a result, some argue that the rights of those forced to use ADR are violated.

Enforcement. A more practical concern for many businesses considering the use of ADR is enforcement of agreements reached through settlement processes or awards made in adjudicative processes. While courts generally are very supportive of ADR processes and protective of the results reached in those processes, executives occasionally express concern that the results reached may not be as readily enforceable as a court judgment. While there are rare cases in which courts review and reject arbitration awards or mediation contracts, it is safe to say that the vast majority of all ADR outcomes have an enforceability that is essentially equivalent to that of a legal judgment. Furthermore, parties are far less likely to contest ADR outcomes than trial outcomes, particularly those reached in settlement processes like mediation, because they are far more invested in the processes they have created.

Public Access. Because public access to private ADR processes is very limited, some argue that the processes are subject to abuse when the public interest may be circumvented by participants. This is an argument made more frequently regarding private mediation of criminal matters than civil cases, but is worth considering briefly. The public arguably has an interest in the adjudication of some corporate matters, perhaps those involving antitrust or pollution questions that stand to affect their interests. However, the ethical obligations of the attorneys representing businesses in these matters to avoid illegal agreements is, in all likelihood, a sufficient protection for the public. In addition, the laws regulating corporate conduct are sufficiently broad and detailed to prevent private settlements that jeopardize public interests in the sorts of cases resolved privately.

Regulation. Finally, but significantly, executives and attorneys alike convey concern with an ADR system that in many states is completely unregulated and in the remaining states only very loosely regulated. While the parameters of arbitration are fairly well defined by statute in many states and in the federal law, arbitration stands as the exception to the rule. Most ADR processes are not described or defined in state or federal law in any meaningful fashion, and some ADR practitioners resist such efforts at standardization. In addition, very few states regulate the credentialing and practice of the individuals providing private ADR services. While most ADR providers maintain memberships in voluntary professional associations, virtually all of which have promulgated codes of conduct, formal licensing or certification with regulatory oversight offering aggrieved consumers a remedy against an ADR practitioner is nearly non-existent.

ADR practitioners argue that the absence of regulation of either practice or practitioner allows for the very flexibility that consumers of ADR seek. However, it is clear that those same consumers wish for the security afforded by some form of general regulation in the area. Indeed, a recent study of private, Illinois attorneys found that a leading reason to avoid ADR processes was the absence of regulation and training requirements.[2] Efforts are underway in many quarters to address this

---

[2] "A Quantitative Analysis of the Use and Avoidance of Mediation by the Cook County, Illinois Legal Community," Cavenagh, Thomas D., 14 Mediation Quarterly 4, at 353, Summer, 1997.

concern, primarily at the state level, and legislation to bring a measure of consistency in training, ethics and process parameters is likely in the near future.

DESIGNING BUSINESS DISPUTE RESOLUTION PROGRAMS

A final area in which general background information is necessary prior to reviewing several corporate ADR programs is corporate ADR system design. A significant body of literature has evolved on the topic, some of which is summarized in appendix 1 and more of which is cited in the bibliography following this text. At this juncture examination of several crucial, but fairly general principles in system design will suffice. The company profiles that follow will illustrate the application of these principles in much greater detail. As are so many business decisions, the approach to system design is a two-step process that addresses planning and implementation.

Planning. Designing a system of ADR initiatives within the corporation generally requires several different steps. Taken in chronological order those planning steps are:

1. ***Predict the Problems.*** Understanding the nature of the disputes likely to face the company is the threshold area of analysis. A careful examination of the company's legal history and business objectives will provide insight into the types of cases, both internal (involving employees) and external (involving clients, partners, vendors and others), that the company has addressed and can expect to address in the future. One must be clear about what one needs to resolve before one can construct a system to do so.

2. ***Assess the Procedural Risks.*** Different case types present different procedural risks. Cases involving highly technical and proprietary information require different approaches than those involving facts to which the public has or may have access. Successful business ADR systems are tailored in company-specific ways to avoid identifiable and predictable procedural risks.

3. ***Quantify the Desired Outcomes.*** Consider and prioritize the company's short and long term interests in terms of case management. Many possible outcomes including reduction of legal expenses, protection of trade secrets, reduction of suits through vigorous legal response and preservation of economic relationships are likely. Tailor the resulting dispute resolution system to achieve outcomes of particularly substantial value to the company.

4. ***Allocate Resources for Success.*** An ADR system will be successful only to the extent interested parties from upper management through entry-level

employees understand, endorse and participate in it. Indeed, money spent on training, marketing and staffing the program may reap returns beyond simply reducing legal liability and cost. ADR programs can change a corporate culture by conveying a company-wide commitment to addressing difficulties and disputes of all sorts in non-adversarial ways.

5. ***Formalize Program Goals and Policies.*** Because a variety of people ranging from employee disputants to outside legal counsel will be required to comply with the dictates of the program, clearly written and widely disseminated program policies and goals are clearly need. Use of the employee handbook as well as special policy documents improve the likelihood of program success.

6. ***Seek Multi-level Support for the Program.*** No corporate program can thrive, indeed survive, in the absence of support from all levels of the company. Particularly important to the success of an ADR program is the participation and support of the in-house legal staff who will be charged with day-to-day case assessment and management. Equally important is the unequivocal support of the senior management to whom the legal staff reports. To the extent that staff counsel believe litigation improves prestige and advancement in the company, they must believe that successful use of ADR to meet company goals also provides such career benefits.

Implementation. Execution of the corporate ADR program also requires a variety of initiatives. Again, in chronological order, those steps include:

1. ***Require Rigorous and Systematic Case Evaluation.*** The importance of consistent and thorough evaluation of each claim for resolution in a fashion consistent with the formal company ADR policy is difficult to overstate. Not only does such an approach reinforce the centrality of the program to the company's overall objectives, it makes meaningful the evaluation of the program itself.

2. ***Condition Advancement on Participation.*** Communication to key employees that successful use of ADR to resolve company claims will be a favorable career advancement indicator cements commitment to the program. In light of the voluntary nature of most ADR processes and the possibility of participation that is simply calculated to fail with the long-term view of returning the case to litigation, particularly when outside counsel will often encourage such an approach, company staff need tangible reasons to make ADR work. Employees should be told that successful use of ADR may enhance their performance evaluations within the company.

3.   ***Train Key Players Extensively.*** The mere suggestion that ADR will lead to favorable review is insufficient to guarantee success.   Comprehensive training for those charged with case evaluation and management increases the probability of overall program success. Provision of awareness training by way of a brief overview of company efforts in ADR for all employees also can significantly improve program quality.

4.   ***Construct Effective Methods of Program Evaluation.*** ADR is a bottom line matter, and methods of program evaluation that account for all the potential savings and benefits, as well as losses and liabilities resulting from its use are crucial. The difficulty in constructing such accounting methods is that ADR is intended to provide intangible values in addition to its simple economic cost-cutting benefits.   Clearly one can, and should, measure incremental change in in-house legal expense, outside legal expense, resolution expense in terms of settlements and judgments as well as the process costs to achieve those results. ADR also offers less easily measured benefits like goodwill and preserved business relationships.   While one cannot, in all likelihood, place fixed dollar amounts on the importance of such things, program success depends on acknowledgement of these benefits.

5.   ***Alter the Program to Improve Outcomes.*** No program is likely to achieve success without constant refinement and revision. Companies should solicit the input of the staff charged with implementing the program, as well as consult the results of the accounting suggested above to make changes calculated to improve the program.

The companies considered in the chapters that follow have each developed programs designed to widely use ADR to address business disputes. Each has in some fashion done all of the things suggested in the planning and implementation sections above – some more successfully than others. The remaining chapters in this book offer the reader the opportunity to learn from the successes and failures of these companies that have pioneered the use of ADR in the business setting.

CHAPTER 2

UNITED STATES POSTAL SERVICE

"Resolve Employee Disputes Reach Equitable Settlement Solutions Swiftly"

DUE DILIGENCE[1]

United States Postal Service
475 L'Enfant Plaza, SW
Washington, D.C. 20260
202.268.2284
www.usps.gov

Sam Winters, Chairman
William J. Henderson, Postmaster General/CEO
Michael S. Coughlin, Deputy Postmaster General
Clarence E. Lewis, Jr., Executive Vice President/COO
M. Richard Porras, Senior Vice President/CFO

Total assets exceeding $53 billion
Net income of $1.264 billion
Total liabilities of $53 billion
Total Equity N/A

COMPANY STORY

The United States Postal Service, an independent governmental entity headquartered in Washington, D.C., needs no introduction. As the principal carrier of mail and packages in the country, readers are, no doubt, familiar with the public operation of the Postal Service. Indeed, if the Postal Service were a private, for-profit company, it would be the tenth largest in the country. To provide a context for the employee ADR program that follows, however, more detailed information on the size and management structure of the Postal Service is useful.

The Postal Service operates every hour of every day at 38, 019 post offices and 331 mail processing plants. 130 million delivery addresses and 18 million post office boxes receive 107 billion pieces of first class mail annually, 3.4 billion weekly.

---

[1] Year ended September 30, 1998

The Postal Service is the largest <u>consumer</u> of commercial shipping services in the United States, sending over 2.7 billion pounds of mail on over 15,000 commercial airline flights. In addition, the Postal Service maintains a fleet of nearly 193,000 vehicles that travel, collectively, 1.1 billion miles annually. The Postal Service handles 41% of the world's mail volume; Japan is the second largest mail volume handler at 6%.

The Postal Service is the nation's largest civilian employer. More than 765,000 career employees and 127,699 part-time, temporary and other non-career employees make a total workforce of nearly 900,000, a very substantial number of whom are covered under union collective bargaining agreements. That 900,000 includes over 234,000 letter carriers.

The 1970 *Postal Reorganization Act* established the current form of governance under which the Postal Service is operated. A governing board that consists of nine governors and is very similar to a corporate board of directors runs the Postal Service. Governors are appointed to nine-year terms by the President and may be removed following appointment only for cause. No more than five governors may be members of the same political party, and none may be representatives of special interests of any sort. The nine governors select a Postmaster General who becomes a governor and serves at the pleasure of the Board. The Board directs the exercise of the many powers of the Postal Service, controls its monetary expenditures, reviews its employment and operating practices, conducts long-range planning and sets policies on all postal-related matters. Control of day-to-day operations is vested in local and regional Postmasters.

The Postal Service is not required to file a financial report with the Securities and Exchange Commission. They do, however, produce a detailed annual report from which the "Due Diligence" numbers above are drawn.

ALTERNATIVE DISPUTE RESOLUTION PROGRAM

We begin this text with review and analysis of a fascinating program created by the U.S. Postal service. "R.E.D.R.E.S.S." (**R**esolve **E**mployment **D**isputes **R**each **E**quitable **S**olutions **S**wiftly) is an internal employee equal employment opportunity mediation program. The program was created as a result of a class action lawsuit settlement in the northern district of Florida, and began with just three pilot sites in 1994. The program expanded to select cities across the country shortly thereafter. The Postal Service commenced a national roll-out of the program in 1998, and is now close to offering postal employees in every "performance cluster" in the nation access to REDRESS mediation for resolving EEO disputes. By the year 2000, REDRESS will be available to every employee in every district in the Postal Service.

The REDRESS program has several features that make it an appropriate starting point for an assessment of best system design practices in dispute resolution. First, it is a program premised on the idea that effective employee conflict resolution can transform a workplace, making that workplace more efficient and profitable.

The Postal Service program is the only large and well-publicized employee dispute resolution program explicitly to adopt a form of mediation calculated not simply to resolve cases, but to address underlying causes of conflict and thereby improve the work environment. That form of mediation is called "transformative mediation" and is covered at greater length below.

Second, the Postal Service program provides a comprehensive approach to managing workplace conflict by substantively training not just select employee mediators or facilitators, but its entire workforce in effective communication and dispute resolution techniques. We will revisit this point below.

Third, the Postal Service has developed a helpful set of mediator *Standards of Practice* for its outside mediators that will function as a very useful introduction to and reference on mediator ethics in the programs that follow; those *Standards* are provided in the "Forms & Materials" section of this chapter.

Finally, the Postal Service program has been more thoroughly reviewed by an external organization than any other program discussed in this book. As a result, the reader is provided early with a sense of how effective a well-planned employee dispute resolution program can be in terms of participant satisfaction levels and cases closed.

The mission of the REDRESS program is to provide mediation of EEO disputes by qualified outside mediators to all employees seeking it in a timely and effective fashion. The program further seeks to address employee disputes in a fashion that will ultimately make a positive difference in the climate of the Postal Service workplace by improving employee communications and workplace relationships. At a meeting of the Postal Service's Board of Governors, former Postmaster General Marvin Runyon stated: "REDRESS offers a unique way to manage the conflict aspect of employee issues," Runyon said. "These new methods have been well tested in the postal work place and they work. They rely on mediation to promote communication instead of confrontation."

The program is completely voluntary. In addition, neither party in the dispute surrenders her right of access to other forums by submitting a case for REDRESS mediation. Finally, either party may refuse settlement or withdraw from mediation, without any prejudice to her claim, at any time.

Since REDRESS was introduced in North Florida in 1994, it has been pilot tested in more than 25 cities. More than 70 percent of the cases mediated have been resolved. Senior Vice President and General Counsel Mary Eicano told the Board in a presentation on REDRESS, "In an effort to improve workplace relationships in the Postal Service, we needed an approach where better communication comes first and litigation comes last. We have created a better way to handle EEO disputes through REDRESS, which has proven to be an effective Alternative Dispute Resolution mediation program." Eicano also stressed that REDRESS gives employees alleging discrimination access to speedy and effective mediation. Employees and supervisors are given an opportunity to meet face-to-face to resolve workplace conflicts within approximately 14 days of a request for REDRESS mediation.

Moreover, participants in the REDRESS program seem satisfied, telling of improved working relationships. The majority of employees surveyed reported better opportunities to be heard, while the majority of supervisors surveyed reported improved ability to address workplace conflict. Since the program began in Kansas City, for example, EEO informal contacts have been reduced by 26% and formal complaints reduced by 41%.

BRIEFING POINT 2.1

Companies may find participation in ADR processes obligatory. Federal law often requires the use of ADR to resolve claims involving government agencies. In addition, courts at the federal level are empowered to mandate ADR mechanisms when they deem them appropriate.

REDRESS Process Overview. The REDRESS process is employee initiated. After first contacting an EEO office, employees are given the option of going to REDRESS mediation instead of using the standard EEO counseling approach. Mediations normally take place within two weeks of employee agreement to mediate and are confidential to the extent the law permits them to be. The REDRESS style mediation conference starts with a joint session between the aggrieved employee and the supervisor during which the mediator will explain how the mediation process works and answer questions. Both parties will outline fully the nature of the dispute. The mediator likely will ask questions at this juncture to clarify the issues to be resolved by the parties. In most mediation conferences the mediator will also meet with each party separately, in a caucus, to discuss the dispute further and to seek a range of options for resolution. If an agreement is reached, the mediator prepares a writing memorializing the settlement terms. (the form for drafting REDRESS agreements is included in the "Forms & Materials" section) The agreement is final and binding on all participants, and the EEO dispute is withdrawn as a result of the settlement. If a settlement is not reached in mediation, employees are permitted to enforce EEO rights by filing a formal complaint.

REDRESS Mediators can be counselors, attorneys, or other professionals with training and experience in mediation. The Postal Service pays these private practitioners to provide mediation services to its employees. Before mediating a Postal Service EEO dispute under the REDRESS program, a mediator must complete a three-step process. First, applicants must complete and submit to REDRESS headquarters an *ADR Provider Survey* to determine whether they meet minimum requirements, which include a minimum of 24 hours of formal mediation training and performance as lead mediator in at least 10 mediations. If these threshold qualifications are satisfied, mediators are required to attend an additional two-day training sponsored by the Postal Service. Following that training, applicants may be required to mediate one case pro bono for evaluation purposes. The Postal Service may require subject matter or legal expertise prior to mediating certain more complicated disputes, though mediators never dispense professional advice to REDRESS clients.

Postal Service employee materials suggest the following reasons for choosing mediation under the REDRESS program rather than other approaches to resolving employment-related claims:

- **Mediation is fast:** It gives you a chance to meet face-to-face with your supervisor soon after the dispute arises.
- **Mediation is informal:** No witnesses are called, nobody testifies under oath, and no complicated procedures and technicalities get in your way.
- **Mediation allows representatives:** You are entitled to bring a representative of your choice to the mediation; however, the process is designed for people who are handling the problem themselves.
- **Mediators do not make decisions or force decisions on you:** Mediators are trained to work with all parties to help them find solutions to their dispute. An agreement crafted by the people involved is almost always more satisfying and more lasting than one dictated by an outside third party.
- **Mediators are impartial:** They are trained, experienced, third party neutrals.
- **Mediation is free:** There is no cost to you for mediation.
- **Mediation is confidential:** What you tell the mediator when you are alone is kept between the two of you unless you agree to let the mediator share it with your supervisor. After the mediation is over, the mediator destroys all notes of discussions with you.

Extensive Dispute Resolution Training. A first, crucial feature in the REDRESS program is the extensive training and educational opportunities made available to a variety of audiences. Prior to REDRESS program implementation in any geographic area, there are several training initiatives for the many constituencies involved in the program. These initiatives include a one-day *Conflict Resolution Overview* for all employees. The *Conflict Resolution Overview* provides a summary of mediation principles and the advantages of using mediation in the workplace during a one-day course usually attended by employees and supervisors from postal plants and distribution facilities. A three-day basic mediation skills class offers the fundamentals of mediation through an interactive course to EEO professionals, human resources personnel, union officials, labor relations staff and other interested stakeholders as well as in-house mediator volunteers. A two-hour conflict resolution and REDRESS workshop for supervisors and stewards, a variety of semi-formal presentations, and an all-employee mailing further promote employee awareness and understanding of the program. As part of the expansion of REDRESS, thousands of postal employees are, therefore, receiving specially designed training in communication skills, mediation, and conflict resolution. In addition, outside mediators are required to attend a two-day Postal Service REDRESS mediation training session irrespective of any prior training or mediation experience they may have.

Facilitative Mediation Approach. A second noteworthy REDRESS feature is the type of mediation it offers participants. Conventional facilitative mediation offers the disputants a third-party neutral to the disputants for the purpose of aiding them in negotiating mutually acceptable outcomes to a current and readily identifiable dispute. The facilitative mediator does not decide the merits of the case or give advice to the parties on professional matters, like law or psychology. Furthermore, the mediator's role in a facilitative conference normally is to attempt to settle only the case currently troubling the parties. The emotional well-being of the parties following the mediation is not a principal concern of the facilitative mediator.

REDRESS mediation employs a transformational approach to employee conflict resolution, "giving participants, rather than the mediator, the power to decide whether and how issues can be resolved." The mediator still facilitates the negotiations between the parties in a transformative mediation rather than determining which party is blameworthy. However, and very significantly, in addition to resolving the instant dispute, the transformative mediator will endeavor to uncover and address underlying issues and to improve overall workplace climate. The emotional well-being of the parties is vitally important to the transformative mediator, who is as interested in empowering and building the self-esteem of the parties as in settling the case.[2]

BRIEFING POINT 2.2
Federal courts must make efforts to use ADR in resolving cases on their dockets. The *Alternative Dispute Resolution Act of 1998*, for example, obligates all United States District Courts to "authorize . . . the use of alternative dispute resolution processes in all civil actions" and to encourage and require its use wherever it is feasible to do so."

Detailed Program Analysis. A third important aspect of the REDRESS program is the nature of the review to which it is currently subject and already has undergone. The Postal Service has participated in an evaluation process that no other company discussed in this text has. The Indiana University School of Public Administration and Environmental Affairs is tracking and evaluating the program's success on an on-going basis. The results[3] suggest that the program is working. A majority of

---

[2] Transformative mediation is not without controversy. The seminal book on the transformative mediation process is Bush, Robert & Folger, Joseph. The Promise of Mediation: Responding to Conflict Through Empowerment and Recognition. San Francisco: Jossey-Bass Publishers, 1994. See also, Cavenagh, Thomas. "The Promise of Mediation: Responding to Conflict Through Empowerment and Recognition, a Review" *In The Alternative,* Illinois State Bar Association (Vol. 2, No. 4) June, 1995.

[3] See Bingham, Lisa. "Mediating Employment Disputes: Perceptions of REDRESS at the United States Postal Service." 20 Review of Public Personnel Administration: Spring, 1997 and Bingham, Lisa and Anderson, J. "Report to the United States Postal Service: What Participants Say About the REDRESS Program and its Effect on Workplace Conflict" (n.d.).

EEO informal complaints mediated under the REDRESS program settled shortly after the employee's initial contact with an EEO mediator. In addition, the number of EEO informal complaints that usually become formal complaints has dropped significantly. Interviews reveal that supervisors who have been through the mediation process are managing workplace conflict more effectively. Furthermore, the Bingham findings reveal that there is no meaningful difference in satisfaction rates between supervisors and employees when asked about the mediator, the outcome of the mediation, and the mediation process itself. This is true despite the apparently unequal negotiating power between supervisors and employees at the start of the mediation process. Bingham argues that process satisfaction translates to a more contented employee whose energy can be positively channeled back to work obligations. Finally, Bingham found that the amount of monetary settlements achieved in REDRESS mediation do not appear to affect employee's satisfaction with outcomes.

The following charts display the some of actual numbers associated with some the Bingham study results. The first chart depicts national case closure rates and shows a very significant move toward mediation resolution.

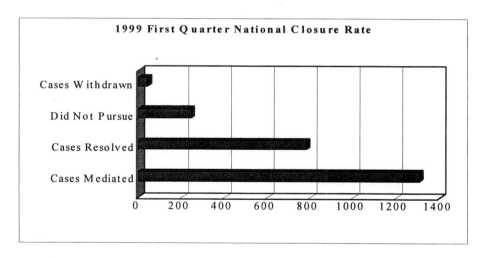

The next pair of charts compares participant satisfaction with the mediation process.

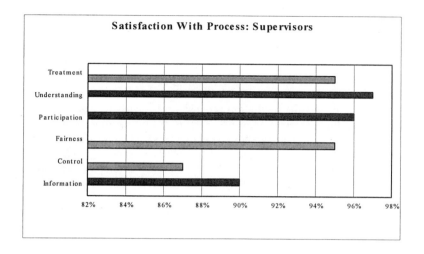

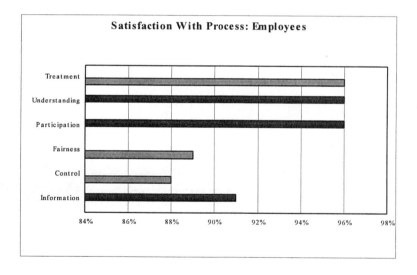

Satisfaction with the mediator is also high in the REDRESS program among both surveyed constituencies.

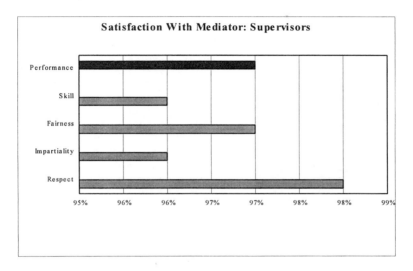

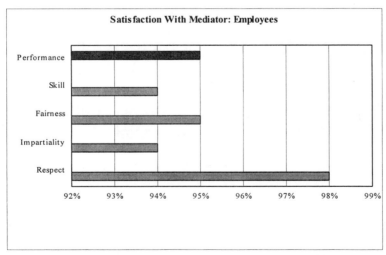

Finally, satisfaction with the outcomes reached in mediation is high in the REDRESS program among both surveyed constituencies.

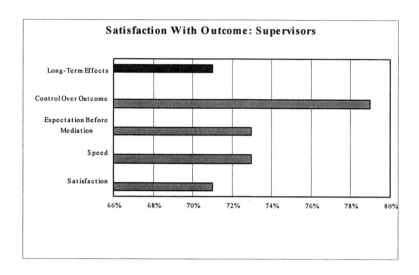

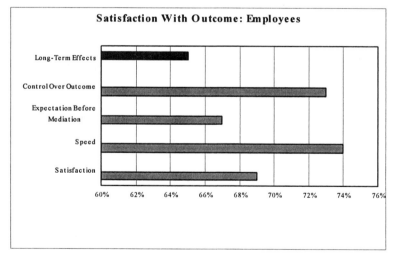

ASSESSMENT

A discussion of the Postal Service REDRESS program is an appropriate starting point for a text on best practices in ADR system design and practice, because it works. Well-trained participants, an interesting and effective mediation model, as well as careful professional evaluation of the program are three key reasons for its success.

A potential weakness in the program is noteworthy, however. Parties who expect help settling their cases may resent mediators trying to reach beyond that specific goal to accomplish challenging, and perhaps questionable objectives like 'empowerment' or 'recognition.' While it is laudable to attempt to resolve broad, underlying social, emotional or psychological issues in the transformative model, parties likely want rapid results in concrete cases first, and transformation second, if at all. Moreover, mediators trained in and competent at facilitative mediation may feel excluded from participation in the REDRESS program, costing the Postal Service needed talent at a time of program expansion. Indeed, the key indicators of success described above (process, mediator and outcome satisfaction) are all matters unrelated to a transformational approach. Because the transformational approach runs the risk of giving the parties more than they might wish from the mediation process, the Postal Service may be wise to revisit its terminology on the mediation process to emphasize settlement and the related benefits it offers, rather than empowerment or recognition.

U.S. POSTAL SERVICE FORMS & MATERIALS

Standards of Practice for Postal Service Mediators

Purpose of the Standards

The purpose of these standards is to provide a guide for mediators when mediating Postal Service disputes. These standards are intended to be instructional and to provide assistance when mediators are faced with dilemmas. These standards are drawn from several existing codes, particularly the code developed by Professor Robert A. Baruch Bush in his *The Dilemmas of Mediation Practice – A Study of Ethical Dilemmas and Policy Implications,* and the "Model Standards of Conduct for Mediators" developed jointly by the American Arbitration Association and the Society of Professionals in Dispute Resolution.

The Mediation Process and the Mediator's Role

Mediation is a process in which an impartial third party, with no decision-making authority or power to impose a resolution, helps the disputing parties explore and, if possible, reach a mutually acceptable resolution of some or all of the issues in dispute.

The mediator's role is (1) to encourage and assist the parties in deciding whether and how to resolve their dispute and (2) to promote the parties' mutual understanding of each other's positions, interests, and perspectives, despite their conflict.

Standard I: Competency

Mediators shall maintain professional competency in mediation skills and, where lacking the skills necessary for a particular case, shall decline to serve or shall withdraw from serving as mediators.

Comments:

- A mediator must meet the Postal Service's criteria before mediating a Postal Service case.
- The Postal Service maintains the right to require a mediator to have subject matter expertise prior to mediating certain disputes.
- A mediator should maintain and upgrade skills and substantive training appropriate to his or her area of practice.
- A mediator should disclose to the parties the limits of his or her skills or substantive expertise wherever this may be relevant to the handling of the case.
- Beyond disclosure, a mediator should exercise his or her own judgement regarding whether his or her expertise or skills are sufficient to meet the demands of the case and, if they are not, should decline to serve (or, if the case has begun, withdraw from serving) as the mediator.

Standard II: Impartiality

Mediators shall, in word and action, maintain impartiality toward the parties and the issues in the dispute and, where their impartiality is in question, shall decline to serve or shall withdraw from serving as mediators.

Comments:

- The concept of impartiality is central to the mediation as it directly affects a mediator's ability to facilitate a neutral and balanced process.
- Impartiality means absence of favoritism or bias – i.e., expressed sympathy or antipathy – toward any party or any position taken by a party to a mediation. In addition, it means a commitment to aid all parties, as opposed to a single party, in exploring the possibilities for resolution.
- To ensure not only the fact but the appearance of impartiality, a mediator is obligated to disclose to the parties, at the earliest moment, any conflicts of interest, any present or prior relationship, personal or professional, between the mediator and any party or party representative.

- A mediator is obligated to decline to serve (or, if the case has begun, withdraw from serving) as the mediator, if:

  1. as a result of disclosure of relationship, any party (or representative) objects to the mediator's serving;
  2. the mediator's own judgement is that a relationship with a party will compromise impartiality, or appear to do so, even after full disclosure to the parties; or
  3. the mediator or any party believes that, apart from relationships, the fact or appearance of impartiality is compromised, either by the mediator's personal reaction to any party (or party position) or by the mediator's background or experience.

Standard III: Confidentiality

Mediators shall, subject to statutory obligations to the contrary, meet the reasonable expectations of the parties regarding the confidentiality of all communications made within the mediation process.

Comments:

- Apart from statutory or regulatory duties to report certain kinds of information, a mediator is obligated not to disclose to a nonparty, directly or indirectly, any information communicated to the mediator by a party to the mediation process.
- Where a case is referred to mediation from any agency, a mediator must limit the information given to the referring agency to the sole fact of whether or not a settlement was reached.
- Absent statutory or regulatory duties, a mediator must not disclose, directly or indirectly, to any party to a mediation, information communicated to the mediator in confidence by any other party unless that party gives permission to do so.
- Where confidential information from one party might, if known to the other party, change the second party's decision about whether to accept or reject certain terms of settlement, a mediator should encourage the first party to permit disclosure of the information; but absent such permission, the mediator must not disclose it.
- A mediator cannot ensure the confidentiality of statements parties make to each other or of any memoranda, documents, or other tangible evidence shared during the mediation.

Standard IV: Consent

Mediators shall make reasonable efforts to ensure that all parties understand the mediation process and the options available to them, and that the parties are free and able to make whatever choices they desire regarding participation in mediation generally or regarding specific settlement options.

Comments:

- A mediator is obligated to explain the mediation process to the parties, including the role and function of the mediator, and to inform the parties of their right to refuse any offer of settlement and to withdraw from mediation at any time and for any reason. This obligation continues throughout the mediation of any case.
- A mediator is obligated to avoid exerting undue pressure on a party – whether to participate in mediation or to accept a settlement. Nevertheless, the mediator may and should encourage parties to consider both the benefits of participation and settlement and the costs of withdrawal and impasse.
- Where a party appears to be acting under coercion or fear, or without capacity to comprehend the process, issues, or options for settlement, a mediator must explore the circumstances with the party and, unless the party objects, discontinue the mediation. If the party insists on continuing, the mediator may do so, but should continue to raise the question and check for willingness to proceed.

Standard V: Self-Determination

Mediators shall respect and encourage self-determination by the parties in their decision to resolve their dispute, and on what terms, and shall refrain from being directive and judgmental regarding the issues in dispute and options for settlement.

Comments:

- A mediator must leave to the parties full responsibility for deciding whether, and on what terms, to resolve their dispute. The mediator may and should assist them in making informed and thoughtful decisions, but should never substitute his or her personal judgment for that of the parties, with regard to any aspect of the mediation.
- Subject to the above and Standard VI below, a mediator must raise questions for the parties to consider regarding the acceptability, sufficiency, and feasibility, for all sides, of proposed options for settlement – including their impact on affected third parties. Furthermore, the mediator may make neutral suggestions for the parties' consideration. However, at no time is the mediator allowed to make decisions for the parties, or directly express his or her opinion about or advise for or against any proposal under consideration.
- Subject to Standard VI below, if a party to mediation declines to consult an attorney or counselor after the mediator has raised this option, the mediator is obligated to permit the mediation to go forward according to the party's wishes.

- If, in a mediator's informed judgment, an agreement desired by the parties could not be enforced because of illegality, unconscionability, or any other reason, the mediator is obligated to so inform the parties. If the parties insist on that agreement, a mediator must discontinue the mediation in such circumstances, but should not violate the obligation of confidentiality.

Standard VI: Separation of Mediation From Counseling and Legal Advice

Mediators shall limit themselves solely to the role of mediator, and shall refrain from giving legal or therapeutic information or advice and from otherwise engaging in counseling or advocacy during mediation.

Comments:

- A mediator may, in areas where he or she is qualified by training and experience, raise questions regarding the information presented by the parties in the mediation session, including information about the law.
- Even in areas where a mediator is qualified by professional training and experience, a mediator is never allowed to offer professional advice to the parties or express a professional or personal opinion on an issue or option for settlement, but may offer relevant legal information.
- When a mediator believes a party is acting without adequate information or advice on legal or psychological aspects of the issues presented, the mediator must raise the option of obtaining independent expert advice prior to resolving the issues and must afford the parties the opportunity to do so.
- A mediator must limit his or her role to that of mediator, and must never assume the role of advocate for either party's interests or provide counseling or therapy to either party during the mediation process.

Standard VII: Promotion of Respect and Control of Abuse of Process

Mediators shall encourage mutual respect between the parties and shall take reasonable steps, subject to the principle of self-determination, to limit abuse of the mediation process.

Comments:

- At the outset of mediation, a mediator should remind the parties that they are agreeing to participate in good faith. The mediator is obligated to make reasonable efforts not only to promote a full dialogue and prevent manipulation or intimidation by either party, but also to promote each party's understanding and respect for the concerns and positions of the other, even if they cannot agree.
- Where a mediator discovers an intentional abuse of the process, such as nondisclosure of vital information or lying, the mediator is obligated to

encourage the abusing party to alter the conduct in question. The mediator is not obligated to reveal the conduct to the other party, nor to discontinue the mediation, but the mediator may discontinue the mediation as long as this does not violate the obligation of confidentiality.

Standard VIII: Conflicts of Interest

Mediators shall, as far as possible, avoid conflicts of interest and, in any event, shall resolve all such conflicts in favor of their primary obligation to impartially serve the parties to the dispute.

Comments:

A mediator who is a lawyer must not advise or represent either of the parties in future proceedings concerning the subject matter of the dispute, and the mediator who is a therapist must not provide future therapy to either of the parties or both of them regarding the subject matter of the dispute.

A mediator must not give or receive any commission, rebate, or other monetary or nonmonetary form of consideration in return for referral of clients for postal mediation services.

BRIEFING POINT 2.3

While there is no legal obligation to do so, many ADR providers voluntarily comply with the rules of the major professional associations in the field. It is wise to inquire to which, if any, rules of professional conduct a particular ADR provider will adhere.

REDRESS materials to Postal Service employees provide the following helpful question and answer section:

Redress – It's fast, it's voluntary, it works!

Q: **How does REDRESS work?**

A: Once a complaint contacts an EEO counselor he/she is offered mediation in lieu of counseling. Mediators are trained third-party neutrals outside the Postal Service provided at no cost to employees. Mediations are usually scheduled within a few weeks of a complainant's first contact with an EEO counselor. If a case settles under REDRESS, it is treated like any other EEO settlement. However, if a case does not settle, the complainant is given appeal rights and may continue to pursue his/her EEO complaint.

Q: **How long does mediation take?**

A: A typical mediation usually lasts between 4 to 5 hours.

Q: **Who manages REDRESS?**

A: The National REDRESS Task Force consists of a small staff at headquarters who administers the program with the help of 13 EEO Alternative Dispute Resolution (ADR) Coordinators and 85 EEO ADR Specialists at the area and district levels, respectively. The Task Force is sponsored by the Deputy Postmaster General.

Q: **Who pays for REDRESS?**

A: Mediations are paid for under the national program budget. Most associated training and all staffing costs are funded through the national program as well.

Q: **Where is REDRESS available?**

A: REDRESS is currently available in select cities. During the next two years, REDRESS will be implemented in all 85 Postal Service performance clusters. By the year 2000, employees in every performance cluster will have access to mediation in EEO cases. For more details, contact your area EEO ADR Coordinator. (See the separate listing of coordinators.)

The Postal Service uses the following form to memorialize settlement agreements reached in REDRESS mediations.

SETTLEMENT AGREEMENT FORM

Date: _____

Mediator Case No.: _____

USPS EEO Case No.: _____

District: _____

IN THE MATTER OF MEDIATION BEWTWEEN

Counselee: _____

Management Official: _____

Any alleged breach arising out of the implementation of or compliance with this settlement agreement must be reported in writing to the EEO Office within 30 days of the alleged breach.

THIS AGREEMENT DOES / DOES NOT NEED TO BE APPROVED BY:

_____ (e.g., union official, management official, labor relations, etc.)

AGREEMENT

As a complete and final settlement of the subject matter, and without prejudice to the position of the parties in any other case, and with the understanding that it will not be cited in other proceedings, by the counselee, the counselee's representative (if any), and/or the union, the following resolution has been entered into by the parties. It is mutually agreed between the parties that this matter be resolved as follows:

Initials: _____ Counselee   _____ Mgt. Official   _____ Mediator
          _____ Counselee's Rep.   _____ Mgt. Official Rep.
          _____ Union Rep.

Date: _____
Mediator Case No.: _____
USPS EEO Case No.: _____
District: _____

This agreement constitutes a full and final settlement of all issues arising out of the subject matter.

Management agrees to the contents of this resolution solely in an effort to resolve the counselee's allegation(s), and this agreement should not be construed as an admission of discrimination or wrongdoing on the part of any official of the U.S. Postal Service.

By signing this agreement, the counselee withdraws any and all pending complaints, appeals, or other actions relative to the subject matter contained in this complaint. **If there are other related grievances (beyond Step 1) which the counselee would like to withdraw, a union official must sign below in order to effectuate the withdrawal of the grievance.**

If the terms of this agreement are determined to violate a provision of the applicable collective bargaining agreement, this agreement will be null and void. In the event that this agreement becomes null and void, the complainant will be allowed to either renegotiate the terms of this agreement to be in cOompliance with the collective bargaining agreement OR reinstate his or her complaint.

Everyone signing this document does so fully and without coercion.

_____   _____
Signature of Mgt. Official   Date

_____   _____
Signature of Mgt. Official Rep. (if any)   Date

_____   _____
Signature of Counselee   Date

_____   _____
Signature of Counselee's Rep. (if any)   Date

_____   _____
Signature of Union Official for the Union   Date
(only if grievances are being withdrawn)

_____   _____
Signature of Mediator   Date

KEY DECISION

Use of alternative dispute resolution mechanisms for the disposition of federal statutory claims remains an area of interest to the federal courts. While the following brief opinion relates to a waiver of the right to sue in favor of arbitration, it introduces the discussion of ADR in federal statutory claims cases for the reader.

KUMMETZ v. TECH MOLD, INC.
152 F.3d 1153 (1998)
United States Court of Appeals for the Ninth Circuit.

William Kummetz sued Tech Mold, Inc. for employment discrimination pursuant to the Americans with Disabilities Act. The district court granted the defendant's motion for summary judgment on the ground that Kummetz had waived his right to sue by agreeing to arbitrate any employment-related disputes. We conclude that Kummetz did not knowingly enter into an arbitration agreement.

Tech Mold, a manufacturer of sophisticated steel molds, hired Kummetz as a mold maker in its prototype department. About four months after he started work, Tech Mold attempted to transfer Kummetz from the prototype department to a lower-paying position in the milling department, even though Kummetz had successfully completed a 90-day probationary period. Tech Mold's general manager, Len Graham, stated in an affidavit that the transfer was necessary because Kummetz did not possess the skills of a top mold maker, although he did possess excellent milling skills. Kummetz believed that Tech Mold attempted to transfer him only after it learned that he had previously undergone a kidney transplant. He resigned, but insisted that the transfer and the corresponding reduction in pay constituted a constructive discharge. Consequently, he filed a charge of disability discrimination with the EEOC, secured a right-to-sue letter, and filed his complaint in district court. The district court dismissed Kummetz's action, reasoning that he had waived his right to a judicial forum.

The facts surrounding the purported waiver are not complicated. About a week after he began work, Tech Mold issued to Kummetz an Employment Information Booklet and an Information Booklet Acknowledgement. The Acknowledgement, which Kummetz signed, declared that:

> I understand and agree that I am covered by and must abide by the contents of this Booklet. I also understand and agree that this Booklet in no way constitutes an employment contract and that I remain an at-will employee.
> I understand that the policies, practices and benefits set forth in this Booklet are subject to change at any time and without prior notice at the sole and unlimited discretion of the Company. The Company also reserves the right to interpret any ambiguity or any confusion about the meaning of any term in this Booklet, and that interpretation shall be final and binding.

The Acknowledgement did not mention or imply that the Booklet contained an arbitration provision. The arbitration provision in the Booklet provided that:

> *The Company and the employee shall submit to arbitration, as provided in the Dispute Resolution Policy, any alleged unlawful employment discrimination, termination or employment tort or benefit claim during or following employment. The parties waive all rights to a trial, with or without a jury, for resolution of any dispute covered by this policy.*

The Booklet also stated that employees could obtain a copy of the Dispute Resolution Policy from Tech Mold's accounting office. Neither party alleges, however, that Kummetz did so. The ten-page Policy identified the types of disputes that were subject to arbitration, including those of discriminatory termination and constructive termination. It also set forth the rules of arbitration, which included a six-month limitations period for claims of unlawful discrimination.

The Federal Arbitration Act authorized courts to enforce agreements to arbitrate statutory claims. A particular statute, however, may either preclude or limit the enforcement of arbitration agreements with regard to claims arising under that statute. This court has previously concluded that the ADA requires that agreements to arbitrate disputes arising under the ADA must at least be knowing, which means that the choice must be explicitly presented to the employee and the employee must explicitly agree to waive the specific right in question. The arbitration agreement in the present case is not enforceable because it was neither explicitly presented nor explicitly accepted.

There was no knowing waiver by Kummetz in this case. The Acknowledgement he signed did not refer to the fact that the "Information Booklet" that he had just received included an arbitration clause that waived his right to go to court. It is true that Kummetz acknowledged that he had read the Information Booklet and "agreed to the matters set forth in it," but there was in that Acknowledgement no explicit reference to arbitration or waiver of right to sue. Indeed, the Acknowledgement contained other language negating the idea that the booklet amounted to or included a contractual agreement. The Acknowledgement stated: "I understand and agree that this Booklet in no way constitutes an employment contract and that I remain an at-will employee." It further stated: "I understand that the policies, practices and benefits set forth in this Booklet are subject to change at any time and without prior notice at the sole and unlimited discretion of the Company." The clear implication of these clauses is that the Booklet contained a set of non-contractual policies unilaterally established by Tech Mold.

Because the Acknowledgement failed to alert Kummetz to the fact that the Information Booklet contained an arbitration clause, the presence of the clause in the Booklet is insufficient under Nelson to effect a waiver. Only if Tech Mold had specifically called Kummetz's attention to the arbitration clause in the Booklet would the clause suffice in the face of the uninformative Acknowledgement. We do not mean to suggest that one who is aware that he or she is entering a contract may avoid its effect by failing to read it. Such a rule would undermine reliance on written instruments. The problem in Kummetz's case is that nothing in the Acknowledgement that he signed or the circumstances of record suggested that he was entering a contract. We conclude, therefore, that Kummetz did not knowingly agree to arbitrate his ADA claim.

CHAPTER 3

SANDIA NATIONAL LABORATORY[1]

Using the Ombudsman to Preempt & Control Workplace Conflict

DUE DILIGENCE

Sandia National Laboratories
PO Box 5800
Albuquerque, NM 87185
505.844.9763
www.sandia.gov/

C. Paul Robinson, President & Laboratories Director
Joan Woodard, Executive Vice President & Deputy Director
Bob Kestenbaum, Vice President, General Counsel & Corporate Secretary
Miguel Robles, Ethics Director

Total assets exceeding $ N/A
Net income of $ N/A
Total liabilities of $ N/A
Total equity of $ N/A

COMPANY STORY

Sandia National Laboratories was founded in 1945, in Albuquerque, New Mexico, as "Z Division," part of what is now Los Alamos National Lab. The Lab was created to assist in the "Manhattan Project," the American World War II atomic bomb development effort. In 1949, President Truman requested that American Telephone and Telegraph Company manage Sandia; AT&T accepted and continued in that role for nearly 44 years.

Sandia is now a National Laboratory operated by the Sandia Corporation, a Lockheed-Martin Company. The lab designs non-nuclear components for the nation's nuclear weapons, performs a range of energy research projects, and works on assignments that respond to military and economic national security threats. The Lab does so, in part, by creating partnerships with appropriate U.S. private industry as well as universities to collaborate on emerging technologies. Sandia applies its

---

[1] The author is deeply grateful to Messrs. Don Noack and Wendell Jones, the Sandia Ombudsmen, for their kind and invaluable cooperation in the preparation of this chapter.

own technology as well. Sandia bomb dismantlement experts, for example, were intimately involved in resolving the "Unabomber" case.

The Department of Energy is Sandia's principal customer. The Department's recent strategic plan revises how the Department views its defense mission. The new model, in which Sandia figures prominently, is based on a smaller nuclear stockpile and greater attention to the threat posed by the proliferation of weapons of mass destruction. The Department's *Nuclear Posture Review* outlines the foreseeable requirements of our nation's nuclear forces in the next several years. Sandia will have a major role in implementing the objectives of the *Nuclear Posture Review*. Indeed, after the strategic arms treaties are both implemented, Sandia will remain a primary part of the nation's "technical conscience" for the nuclear weapon stockpile. The institutional memory, the experience base, and the engineering expertise for nuclear warheads as integrated systems will reside at Sandia. In addition, as the Department restructures production, Sandia will assume a larger responsibility for nonnuclear component production. Sandia's energy and environmental programs also reflect changing governmental and industry expectations. Finally, Sandia's work with energy technologies will continue with renewed emphasis on making U.S. industry successful in the global market.

In 1996, Sandia created a set of eight *Strategic Objectives*. Four objectives focus on <u>what</u> Sandia seeks to accomplish:

1.   Ensure that the Nuclear Weapons Stockpile is safe, secure, and reliable and fully capable of supporting our Nation's deterrence policy.
2.   Reduce the vulnerability of our nation to threats of proliferation and use of weapons of mass destruction, nuclear incidents, and environmental damage.
3.   Enhance the safety, security, and reliability of critical infrastructures. The critical infrastructures are energy, information, transportation, and civilian physical systems like water supply.
4.   Develop high impact responses to emerging national security threats. Emerging threats include terrorism and chemical/biological warfare.

Four additional objectives focus on <u>how</u> Sandia will accomplish the foregoing objectives:

1.   Apply excellence as the standard for attracting **people** to join and remain at Sandia and for measuring the performance of teams and individuals.
2.   Pursue "**science** with the mission in mind" and apply the new knowledge to solve customers' technical problems.
3.   Create an **infrastructure** that operates as a system and is a differentiating advantage for our strategic missions.

4.   Maximize the beneficial use of strategic **partnerships**.

Sandia's overarching corporate values are: teamwork, integrity, quality, leadership and respect for the individual. The dispute resolution program at Sandia reflects these values.

ALTERNATIVE DISPUTE RESOLUTION PROGRAM

The Sandia National Laboratories dispute resolution program is an internal program for the prevention and resolution of employee/employee and employee/management disputes. In light of the highly sensitive research and production work done at Sandia, effective management and resolution of such disputes is profoundly important. The central figure in the program is the ombudsman, a company employee whose principle occupation is workplace dispute resolution.

History of the ombudsman. The unusual word *ombudsman* derives from the Old Norse word *"umbodhsmadhr"* which meant a "trusty manager or commissary." In Sweden, where the office has a long history, the ombudsman was a deputy who looked after the interests and legal affairs of a group such as a trade union or business.

Traditionally, there have been two types of ombudsmen. The first is a government or external official who investigates citizen complaints against the government or its functionaries, the citizen's advocate office in the Alaska state government, for example. This type of ombudsman is an advocate empowered to adjudicate matters as a sort of arbitrator. In addition, they may make official policy recommendations. Outside of government several private sector examples of this advocacy role exist. The patient ombudsman in a hospital or retirement home is one such office; the franchisee ombudsman for the "7-11" convenience store chain is another.

The second type of ombudsman is one hears concerns, serves to increase understanding regarding those concerns and mediates agreeable settlements between aggrieved parties such as employees, consumers or students and an institution, an organization, or a company. This private business approach is the Sandia model. It is based on the guidelines for a corporate ombudsman office provided by *The Ombudsman Association*, and there are many companies employing a similar, non-adjudicative ombudsman style including: AT&T, General Electric, UPS, American Express, Upjohn and Sony Corporation of America. Several governmental entities also use this model for in-house dispute resolution, including: The U.S. Secret Service, The U.S. Federal Bureau of Investigation, The U.S. Department of Energy and The World Bank.

The company ombudsman is a unique role in business and dispute resolution. The company ombudsman serves many of the same functions that arbitrators, mediators, judges and attorneys do. Like the arbitrator and judge and unlike the mediator, the private ombudsman has an affirmative duty to seek out and actively encourage resolution of disputes; ombudsmen may even undertake dispute resolution procedures for parties on their own initiative. Like the mediator, the ombudsman is strictly neutral and not permitted to take sides or otherwise align with either company or employee interests. Finally, the investigative role undertaken by some ombudsmen is not unlike the attorney's role in discovery: seeking relevant information useful in the resolution of a dispute. The ombudsman is regarded as an integral part of the organization. The ombudsman is not, however, an employee in the conventional sense of the word, nor a part of the organization's management. Indeed, to be effective, the ombudsman must have the complete support and trust of both management and employees – a very delicate task, calling for a very thoughtful person.

The private ombudsman function has an established, though somewhat mixed legal foundation. State and federal statutes as well as court decisions have acknowledged favorably the role of the ombudsman. The Administrative Dispute Resolution Act of 1990 describes the role of the ombudsman positively, as does Recommendation 90-2 of the Administrative Conference of the U.S. entitled "The Ombudsman in Federal Agencies."   Kientzy v. McDonnell Douglas (one of two cases included in this chapter) is an example of a federal court decision supporting the use of the corporate ombudsman.[2]

The principal way in which the courts and legislatures have fostered the role of the ombudsman is by protecting the confidentiality of the dispute resolution efforts made by the ombudsman. While the courts have not settled on a uniform ombudsman privilege, they have created a fairly easily employed model for establishing and maintaining the confidentiality of the work done by company ombudsman. Consistent with those decisions, the Sandia office has been designed to maximize the likelihood that an ombudsman's privilege will be enforced in favor of its ombudsman's office. The Sandia ombudsman's office conforms to four "cardinal factors" drawn from federal caselaw in order to protect the privilege in the event that litigation follows the ombudsman's intervention:

1.   The communication to the ombudsman was made in the belief that it would not be disclosed;
2.   Confidentiality was essential to the relationship of the parties;
3.   The ombudsman relationship is worthy of being fostered; and,
4.   The injury caused by disclosure of the communication would be greater than the benefit gained in the correct resolution of the litigation.

Promises of confidentiality can be sustained only if all four factors are present. Furthermore, Sandia is a large government contractor, a fact considered very important when the courts assess the social benefits of the ombudsman's offer of

---

[2] The Kientzy case is included in this chapter. Roy v. United Technologies, Shabazz v. Scurr and Wagner v. The UpJohn Company are other useful decisions concerning the role and value of the ombudsman and the nature of the confidential relationship between the ombudsman and his or clients.

confidentiality. Four additional characteristics of the Sandia ombudsman program support confidentiality:

1.   The Sandia ombudsman functions solely as a mediation provider, as opposed to a decision-making office within the company;
2.   The ombudsman remains independent from the human resources department;
3.   The ombudsman has direct access to the company president; and,
4.   The ombudsman adheres to the *Code of Ethics of the Corporate Ombudsman Association*, which requires that records be kept confidentially even from the company.

Ombudsman Ethics. *The Ombudsman Association* identifies three key functions for the ombudsman: listening, counseling and fact-finding. In each of these roles the ombudsman is obligated by rules of conduct that go beyond simply maintaining confidentiality. The *Association's* Code of Ethics is not a binding code, but is the code to which the vast majority of those practicing as ombudsmen adhere. The code can be summarized in three broad statements of ethical obligation:

1.   First, the ombudsman, as a designated neutral, has the responsibility of maintaining strict confidentiality concerning matters that are brought to his/her attention unless given permission to do otherwise. The only exceptions, at the sole discretion of the ombudsman, are where there appears to be imminent threat of serious harm.
2.   Second, the ombudsman must take all reasonable steps to protect any records and files pertaining to confidential discussions from inspection by all other persons, including company management. The ombudsman should not testify in any formal judicial or administrative hearing about concerns brought to his/her attention in his/her official capacity.
3.   Third, when making recommendations, the ombudsman has the responsibility to suggest actions or policies that will be equitable to all parties.

Additionally, and more specifically, the *Association* sets forth a 10 point "Standards of Practice:"

1.   We adhere to *The Ombudsman Association* Code of Ethics.
2.   We base our practice on confidentiality.
3.   We assert that there is a privilege with respect to communications with the ombudsman and we resist testifying in any formal process inside or outside the organization.

4.   We exercise discretion whether to act upon a concern of an individual contacting the office. An ombudsman may initiate action on a problem he or she perceives directly.

5.   We are designated neutrals and remain independent of ordinary line and staff structures. We serve no additional role (within an organization where we serve as ombudsman) which would compromise this neutrality.

6.   We remain an informal and off-the-record resource. Formal investigations – for the purpose of adjudication – should be done by others. In the event that an ombudsman accepts a request to conduct a formal investigation, a memo should be written to the file noting this action as an exception to the ombudsman role. Such investigations should not be considered privileged.

7.   We foster communication about the philosophy and function of the ombudsman's office with the people we serve.

8.   We provide feedback on trends, issues, policies and practices without breaching confidentiality or anonymity. We identify new problems and we provide support for responsible systems change.

9.   We keep professionally current and competent by pursuing continuing education and training relevant to the ombudsman profession.

10.   We will endeavor to be worthy of the trust placed in us.

Reasons to establish an ombudsman's office. The Ombudsman Association notes several tangible and measurable benefits that may result from an ombudsman's office. These benefits include: increased employee productivity, management time savings, reduced employee turnover costs, reduced legal expenses. There are several more particular purposes for maintaining the Ombudsman's Office at Sandia. From a **corporate compliance perspective**, serious concerns are being officially reported more often as required by law. This reduces the possibility that concerns regarding EEO, EAP or other legal areas go unreported and unaddressed.

From a **laboratory interests perspective,** "early warning" is given for issues not yet having a specific formal reporting or resolution channel. In addition, a variety of very difficult issues have an enhanced possibility of being resolved at an early and less emotional stage. Finally, the maintenance of the ombudsman's office explicitly encourages and supports management involvement in issues where communication with the employee is the real and critical issue.

BRIEFING POINT 3.1

Corporations that have developed collaborative conflict management systems report significant cost savings in outside litigation costs:

- Brown & Root reported an 80% reduction;
- Motorola reported a 75% reduction over a six year period;
- NCR reported a 50% reduction and a drop of pending lawsuits from 263 in 1984 to 28 in 1993.

Slaiku, K. & Hasson, R., Controlling the Costs of Conflict: How to Design a System for Your Organization, Jossey-Bass (1998) at 14.

From the **employee's perspective** the ombudsman's office is the safest place to take issues that are sensitive, complicated and/or confusing. Furthermore, the ombudsman's office is an appropriate venue for concerns that don't fit the assignment or role of other corporate resources. In addition, the office provides a safe place to explore a wide range of resolution options in a highly confidential and non-adjudicative setting. There employees have a place to talk about outcomes with a person who has a big-picture view of the company and can act as a sounding-board for the employee before that employee makes a decision.

From a **managerial perspective**, managers, directors and officers have, in the office of the ombudsman, a neutral resource to address and resolve subordinate or organizational concerns without direct intervention and the acrimony with the employee that direct intervention may cause. Furthermore, employees improve key employment skills when they use the office. They communicate better and more freely, for example.

In short, while the ombudsman may not make, change or set aside a policy or management decision unilaterally, she can have a very positive impact on the company. The ombudsman gives employees 'the opportunity to do the right thing for the right reasons.'

BRIEFING POINT 3.2

Managers spend 42% of their time reaching agreement with others when conflict arises. Watson, C. & Hoffman, R. "Managers as Negotiators," Leadership Quarterly (1) 1996. This is not surprising when:

- The turnover cost for an employee is anywhere from 75% to 125% of annual salary, Philips, D., "The Price Tag of Turnover," Personnel Journal, December 1990; and,
- The average jury verdict in wrongful termination cases is over $600,000 and employers lose 64% of the cases filed, "Without Just Cause: An Employer's Practical Guide on Wrongful Discharge," Bureau of National Affairs, 1998.

Use of the Sandia Program. The Sandia ombudsman program can be compared favorably to published research concerning use of corporate ombudsman programs. That literature suggests a normal activity level per 1000 employees of 72 cases annually. Sandia is very near that norm with 78 cases per 1000 employees. The activity level at Sandia has been steadily increasing since the inception of the still relatively new program. Activity now ranges from 30 to 50 appointments per week. This growth in activity is likely attributable to four factors: First, the confidential nature of client appointments encourages employees to trust the office. Second, a growing number of requests from directors and managers to help in resolving conflicts in the organization encourages reluctant employees to participate. Third, the introduction to the program provided to all employees through staff and department meetings, the *Lab News* and other newsletter articles as well as a corporate intranet Office of the Ombudsman page gives vital information to employees considering use of the program. Fourth, regular meetings with executives and program managers, the diversity director, personnel manager, medical director and EAP staff, and the security, investigative and legal staff keep all interested parties involved in and current on the ombudsman program.

BRIEFING POINT 3.3

A recent CPR study covering a five-year period found that 652 responding companies that implemented CPR sponsored ADR processes and programs saved over $200 million; the average company saved $300, 000.

The Sandia program addresses a wide variety of employee and management concerns ranging from employee benefits to corporate policy implementation. In fact, there is virtually nothing that an employee or management cannot bring to the ombudsman's office, at least initially. If a more appropriate venue for dispute resolution is available, the ombudsman's office will provide the employee with information to use it effectively.

A significant cluster of employee concerns addressed through the ombudsman's office is described as "management concerns." This broad category represents everything from work and team assignments to performance and salary reviews. The following chart shows the types and numbers of these cases on an annualized basis for fiscal 1997.

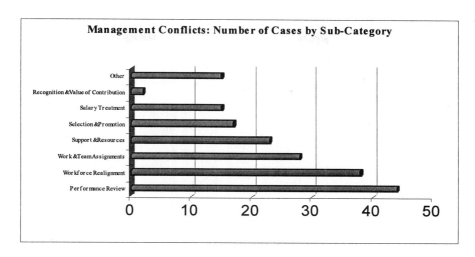

Interpersonal conflict represents nearly three-quarters of all cases addressed by the ombudsman's office. Interpersonal conflict cases involve disputes with a colleague or conflict with an on-site contractor. The following chart shows the types and percentages of these cases for the same year.

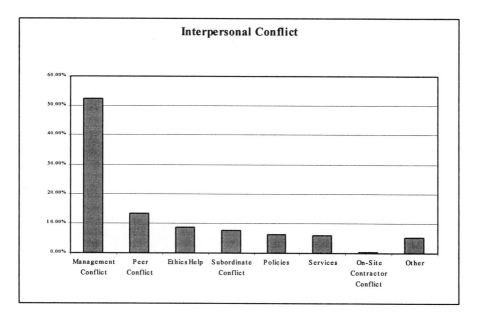

Like many companies, Sandia operates an ethics advisory office. Significantly though, Sandia makes an effort to distinguish the function of the *Ethics*

Office from that of the *Ombudsman's Office*. The following table, created by the Sandia Ombudsman's Office, compares the two offices and shows the major ways in which the they are distinct:

The Defining Principles of the Ethics & Ombudsman Programs Compared

	Ombudsman Program	Ethics Program
Is an "Official" Reporting Place	No	Yes
Conducts Official Investigations	No	Yes
Testimony Available to Corporation & Plaintiffs	No	Yes
Records Available to Corporation & Plaintiffs	N\A	Yes
Makes Official Recommendations	No	Yes
Reports Aggregate Trends & Statistics	Yes	Yes
Is Friendly, Helpful & Trustworthy	Yes	Yes
Exercises "Legal Privilege"	Yes	No
Is Neutral in all Situations	Yes	No
Works as a Pre-reporting Resource	Yes	No

It is also important to note that beyond the differences in the principles that govern the two offices, the ombudsman's office pursues different tasks in the company. The following table, also created by the Sandia Ombudsman's Office, compares the missions of each office.

Ethics & Ombudsman Program Tasks Compared

Usual & Frequent	***	Rarely Done	*
Commonly Done	**	Never	

	Ombudsman Program	Ethics Program
Supervises Investigations into Allegations of Wrongdoing		***
Conducts Audits for Waste, Fraud & Abuse		**
Provides Documented Investigations to Insure the Corporation Benefits from Sentencing Guidelines		***
Looks out for the "Little Guy" with HR Concerns		*

Chapter 3: Sandia National Laboratory

	Ombudsman Program	Ethics Program
Listens to all Concerns (Beyond Allegations)	***	*
Recommends Policy Changes	*	*
Works Toward & Encourages Win-Win Solutions	***	*
Engages in Privileged Prior to Official Reporting	**	
Works with Managers & Staff to Resolve Organizational Disputes	**	
Focuses on Repairing Broken Relationships	***	

The Ombudsman Association handbook suggests several reasons why company ombudsman offices are effective. **First, the ombudsman office legitimates the idea that it is acceptable to raise questions.** Indeed, because there is almost no cost or risk associated with contacting an ombudsman, people with questions and problems often come in early, when most disputes are more easily resolved. Ombudsman offices are especially useful with respect to whistleblowing. In the course of informal problem solving, ombudspeople almost never identify a client without permission. They are, therefore, often in a position to act as a buffer for a legitimate whistleblower, and can talk with that person to gather details useful to management in addressing the complaint.

Second, ombudsmen will likely support disputants in choosing negotiated dispute resolution approaches if it is appropriate to do so. Settlement processes are far less costly and acrimonious than adjudicative ones. The ombudsman is in a unique position to encourage and employ these approaches where it is appropriate and will benefit the parties to do so. The ombudsman is also an effective screen for cases that require a more formal intervention. Furthermore, the chance for an employee to choose or custom-tailor a dispute resolution process or settlement option is likely to be appealing to a complainant. An ombudsman may be able to help fashion unusual processes or remedies which fit unusual circumstances.

Third, ombudsmen often fill in for parts of a dispute resolution system that are not functioning effectively. The ombudsman may, for example, substitute for an established complaint procedure that may not be helpful in a particular case.

Fourth, ombudsman users refer new clients. As is the case with private mediation, users of ombudsmen appear to be satisfied with the opportunity to cooperatively resolve a problem, and to learn new problem-solving skills. There is as a result, a growing pool of people who practice and teach others these skills.

Fifth, ombudsmen provide low-cost data collection for the company by tracking their caseloads and conducting surveys. Ombudsmen, for example, collect important data identifying problems that may be new to the organization and for which policies and procedures do not yet exist.

Sixth, ombudsmen deal effectively with unusual issues, with difficult people, and with cross-cultural issues. Ombudsmen become adept at understanding hidden agendas and managing chronic complainers. They may also play an important role in sensitive areas like recommending assistance or medical help to people who have not yet sought it themselves.

ASSESSMENT

The Sandia National Laboratory Ombudsman Office is a very attractive example of an all-purpose, in-house dispute resolution and conflict management provider. The office supplies a service that has a proven track-record in repairing and maintaining employee-employee, employee-manager and manager-manager relationships, in providing early warning of potentially disruptive difficulties and trends and in conveying to employees the high level of importance placed on preemptive conflict management. Moreover, Sandia has very talented people in the office possessing a thorough understanding of the role they play for the employee and the company who have the confidence of senior management. Finally, Sandia endeavors to assess the impact of the office on the company in ways that are both tangible and meaningful.

The Sandia program could be augmented in a very favorable manner by the addition of a well-structured program for managing disputes originating outside the company. Such matters are, generally, outside the purview of the in-house ombudsman, but confront the company with costs and risks similar to those presented by in-house cases. Further, confidentiality could be protected to a greater degree by drafting an enforceable document signed by users of the office prior to the provision of services. Such a document would waive the right of the employee and the company to ask for documents or discovery of any kind in any subsequent action on the matter. The company could make a similar, but more general commitment in writing as well, perhaps in the employee handbook section describing the Ombudsman Office. Agreements to Mediate making similar claims have been enforced, and there is every reason to believe that such a document would enhance the arguments made in favor of confidentiality if the above factors also are addressed. Finally, Sandia would benefit from formal mediative and adjudicative processes to which an aggrieved party might turn in the event the informal efforts of the ombudsman were unsuccessful. The system of outside mediators retained to resolve in-house claims at the U.S. Postal Service is a program of this nature as is the three-step program at Darden Restaurants.

SANDIA FORMS & MATERIALS

Sandia company materials describe the Ombudsman role at Sandia carefully and in non-legal and user-friendly fashion. The following is the contents of the pamphlet provided to employees describing the role of the ombudsman office at Sandia Laboratories.

What is an Ombudsman?

The word "ombudsman" has roots from Scandinavia where they pioneered the idea of a neutral party to champion for a fair process concerning citizen complaints. At Sandia the definition of the ombudsman is expanded to include confidential and informal assistance regarding any work-related issue. The ombudsman is a designated neutral and not an advocate for an employee nor an advocate for management. The ombudsman adheres to the National Ombudsman Association's Code of Ethics and CPR 001.2.2.

"In addition to being a resource in your individual decision-making process, the ombudsman also serves as a neutral resource for project groups or committees in their decision-making process."

Why have an Ombudsman?

It is Sandia's commitment to its employees to improve the hospitality of the workplace environment. Adherence to Sandia's Corporate Values plays a vital role in fostering our workplace environment. Yet sometimes issues and problems arise that test the policies and procedural framework that support these values.

When these ethical dilemmas, personal conflicts and gray areas appear, it may not be obvious what options are available to resolve them.

The ombudsman provides a safe, confidential option outside of formal reporting channels to help address these issues.

Mission of the Ombuds is:

To provide an avenue for all Sandians to confidentially voice and/or resolve concerns, issues, and barriers; the process aims to improve the hospitality of Sandia and complements existing resources.

Who can contact an Ombudsman?

The Ombudsman is available to all Sandia employees of any classification, including managers, staff, technicians, administrative support, union represented, student and special program employees, independent contractors and vendors. If the issue has anything to do with Sandia or Sandians, an ombudsman can be contacted.

When should I contact an Ombudsman?

You can contact an ombudsman at anytime, regardless of the stage where your concern or issue resides.

Contact an ombudsman if:

♦ You are uncertain about taking your problems through other normal or formal channels.
♦ You're not sure who to see.
♦ Previous attempts to resolve a concern haven't worked out.
♦ You want to take early and informal action.
♦ You need a neutral and impartial perspective.

Is the Ombudsman confidential?

Confidentiality is the rule. No formal written records are kept. No action is taken without your permission. If the ombudsman is not allowed to take action on your behalf, Sandia itself will be unaware of your complaint and unable to respond or assist you. The only exceptions to confidentiality are where there appears to be imminent threat of serious harm to yourself or others, or a breach of National Security.

What should I expect from the Ombudsman?

An Ombudsman Does:

♦ Listen to your concerns.
♦ Remain impartial to all individuals.
♦ Keep your information confidential.
♦ Follow up on each person's request for assistance.
♦ Provide information on options for resolving the concern.
♦ Improve communications by providing an alternate communication channel.
♦ Recommend necessary changes in policies.
♦ Provide unfiltered feedback to management by reporting issues and trends without disclosing names.

An Ombudsman Does Not:

♦ Take sides.
♦ Breach confidentiality.

- Conduct formal investigations.
- Make Sandia policy.
- Make formal management decisions to resolve the concern.
- Resolve non-work related concerns.
- Take action on a concern without permission.

May I remain anonymous?

Yes. Remaining anonymous may limit the options available to you in seeking resolution to a problem, but the ombudsman will respect your decision.

Who does the Ombudsman report to?

The ombudsman directly reports to general trends and unfiltered feedback to the President and Executive Vice President without breaking confidentiality. This provides an "early warning system" to help senior management identify underlying concerns that if addressed may have a greater positive effect on the Lab. Problems that continue without resolution can weaken the entire Laboratory.

What is the difference between the Ethics Center and Ombuds Program?

Both the Ethics Center and the Ombuds program share a common mission in improving the hospitality of the organization and providing an environment that fosters and encourages adherence to corporate and ethical values.

The Ethics Center uses a formal process to respond to employee concerns and will perform formal investigations to clarify these concerns. The Ombuds Program uses informal and nonescalating approaches, and is completely confidential.

The National Ombudsman Association's Code of Ethics

The ombudsman, as a designated neutral, has the responsibility of maintaining strict confidentiality concerning matters that are brought to his/her attention unless given permission to do otherwise. The only exceptions, at the sole discretion of the ombudsman, are where there appears to be imminent threat of serious harm.

The ombudsman must take all reasonable steps to protect any records and files pertaining to confidential discussions from inspection by all other persons, including management. The ombudsman should not testify in any formal judicial or administrative hearing about concerns brought to his/her attention.

When making recommendations, the ombudsman has the responsibility to suggest actions or policies that will be equitable to all parties.

KEY DECISIONS

Confidentiality is critical to the office of the ombudsman. The two cases that follow present both sides of the argument regarding an ombudsman privilege. While both cases, ironically, involve the same company and ombudsman, they reach very different conclusions on the establishment of a privilege assuring confidentiality. The U.S. Supreme Court has not addressed the question, so there remains some uncertainty among companies and ombuds regarding the extent to which they can assert that a matter the ombudsman has managed will be treated as confidential by the courts.

KIENTZY v. McDONNELL DOUGLAS CORPORATION
133 F.R.D. 570 (1991)
United States District Court, E.D. Missouri, Eastern Division.

Mary Kientzy alleges in this action that McDonnell Douglas Corporation terminated her from employment as a security officer on account of her gender. This matter is before the Court upon the motion of Therese Clemente for an order, under Federal Rule of Civil Procedure 26(c)(1), protecting from pretrial discovery, by both plaintiff and defendant, the communications she received in her position as a company ombudsman of defendant McDonnell Douglas. McDonnell Douglas argues in support of Clemente's position. Plaintiff argues that any such ombudsman privilege should not include the information sought.

Plaintiff has noticed Therese Clemente for deposition and would depose other company personnel about their statements to ombudsman Clemente. The record has established that Clemente is employed by defendant as a Senior Staff Assistant in the Ombudsman Program of defendant's subsidiary McDonnell Aircraft Company. Clemente has been employed in the McDonnell Aircraft Ombudsman Office since the ombudsman program began in 1985. The purpose of the ombudsman program and office is to mediate, in a strictly confidential environment, disputes between employees and between employees and management.

Plaintiff argues that the information received by Clemente is relevant to the trial of the action and is discoverable, on two grounds. First, she argues that the statements made to Clemente by defendant's personnel may evidence discriminatory animus in the decision to terminate her. Second, she argues that the ombudsman program is a company procedure for appealing her dismissal and that the ombudsman thus participated in the final decision to terminate her.

Rule 501 requires that this Court assay the ombudsman's claim of privilege by interpreting the principles of the common law "in light of reason and experience." Four cardinal factors have been discerned for this purpose: (1) the communication must be one made in the belief that it will not be disclosed; (2) confidentiality must be essential to the maintenance of the relationship between the parties; (3) the relationship should be one that society considers worthy of being fostered; and (4) the injury to the relationship incurred by disclosure must be greater than the benefit gained in the correct disposal of litigation.

First, ombudsman Clemente received the subject communications in the belief that they would be kept confidential. The McDonnell Aircraft ombudsman office is constituted as an independent and neutral entity. It has no authority to make company policy. Its head has the position of company vice-president, independent of the company's human resources and personnel offices. The office has direct access to the company president. Ombudsman Clemente is bound by the Code of Ethics of the Corporate Ombudsman Association, which provides for the confidentiality of communications. The office has adopted procedures to assure such confidentiality. The McDonnell Aircraft Ombudsman Office has given its strict pledge of confidentiality to all employees and to the company. All new employees are so advised and defendant has repeatedly restated to its employees that they may rely on the confidentiality of the ombudsman's office. Since it opened in 1985, the McDonnell Aircraft ombudsman's office has received approximately 4800 communications. Defendant has sought, but has been refused, access to the ombudsman's files and records regarding plaintiff. The company has indicated it will not request them in the future.

Second, confidentiality of communications is essential to relationships between the ombudsman's office and defendant's employees and defendant's management. The function of the McDonnell Aircraft ombudsman's office is to receive communications and to remedy workplace problems, in a strictly confidential atmosphere. Without this confidentiality, the office would be just one more non-confidential opportunity for employees to air disputes. The ombudsman's office provides an opportunity for complete disclosure, without the specter of retaliation that does not exist in the other available, non-confidential grievance and complaint procedures.

Third, the relationship between the ombudsman office and defendant's employees and management is worthy of societal support. The Court takes judicial notice of the fact that McDonnell Aircraft are very large federal government contractors in the aircraft, space, and other industries. It is important that their employees have an opportunity to make confidential statements and to receive confidential guidance, information, and aid to remedy workplace problems to, benefit themselves and possibly the nation. This is true in spite of the possibility that such actions may be perceived by an employee to be against company or fellow employees' interests.

Fourth, the harm caused by a disruption of the confidential relationship between the ombudsman's office and others in plaintiff's case would be greater than the benefit to plaintiff by disclosure. A successful ombudsman program resolves many problems informally and more quickly than other more formal procedures, including court actions. A court order that Clemente disclose the information communicated to her in confidence, or that her informants disclose what they told her in confidence about plaintiff, would destroy the reputation and principle of confidentiality that the McDonnell Aircraft ombudsman program and office now enjoys and needs to perform its function. The utility of that program and office, in resolving disputes in this workplace and thus diminishing the need for more formal resolution procedures, is founded on the confidentiality of its communications to and from company officials and employees. Federal Rule of Evidence 408 has recognized the utility of confidential settlement discussions. The societal benefit from this confidentiality is paramount to plaintiff's need for disclosure.

CARMAN v. McDONNELL DOUGLAS CORPORATION
114 F.3d 790 (1997)
United States Court of Appeals for the Eighth Circuit.

In October 1992, McDonnell Douglas Aircraft Corporation laid off Frank Carman as part of a reduction in force of its management staff; Carman then sued McDonnell Douglas. In June 1994, Carman requested 54 sets of documents from McDonnell Douglas. Including a request for all notes and documents reflecting data known to Clemente a company ombudsman concerning the plaintiff, a number of other individuals, and various topics including meeting notes regarding lay-offs in Plaintiff's Division and meeting notes regarding Plaintiff Frank Carman. McDonnell Douglas with regard to documents known to Therese Clemente because her activities as an 'ombudsman' were considered confidential and any information and documents relating to her activities are immune from discovery. In response, plaintiff filed a motion to compel production of certain documents. The Court ruled that "defendant is not required to produce documents protected by the Ombudsman Privilege."

In the context of this case, the term "ombudsman" refers to an employee outside of the corporate chain of command whose job is to investigate and mediate workplace disputes. The corporate ombudsman is paid by the corporation and lacks the structural independence that characterizes government ombudsmen in some countries and states, where the office of ombudsman is a separate branch of government that handles disputes between citizens and government agencies. Nonetheless, the corporate ombudsman purports to be an independent and neutral party who promises strict confidentiality to all employees and is bound by the Code of Ethics of the Corporate Ombudsman Association, which requires the ombudsman to keep communications confidential. McDonnell Douglas argues for recognition of an evidentiary privilege that would protect corporate ombudsmen from having to disclose relevant employee communications to civil litigants.

The first important factor for assessing a proposed new evidentiary privilege is the importance of the relationship that the privilege will foster. The defendant argues that ombudsmen help resolve workplace disputes prior to the commencement of expensive and time-consuming litigation. We agree that fair and efficient alternative dispute resolution techniques benefit society and are worthy of encouragement. To the extent that corporate ombudsmen successfully resolve disputes in a fair and efficient manner, they are a welcome and helpful addition to a society that is weary of lawsuits.

Nonetheless, far more is required to justify the creation of a new evidentiary privilege. First, McDonnell Douglas has failed to present any evidence, and indeed has not even argued, that the ombudsman method is more successful at resolving workplace disputes than other forms of alternative dispute resolution, nor has it even pointed to any evidence establishing that its own ombudsman is especially successful at resolving workplace disputes prior to the commencement of litigation. In recognizing a privilege for the McDonnell Douglas ombudsman's office in 1991, the court in Kientzy v. McDonnell Douglas Corp., found that the office had received approximately 4,800 communications since 1985, but neither the court nor McDonnell Douglas in the present case provides us with any context to evaluate the significance of this statistic.

Second, McDonnell Douglas has failed to make a compelling argument that most of the advantages afforded by the ombudsman method would be lost without the privilege. Even without a privilege, corporate ombudsmen still have much to offer employees in the way of confidentiality, for they are still able to promise to keep employee communications confidential from management. Indeed, when an aggrieved employee or an employee-witness is deciding whether or not to confide in a company ombudsman, his greatest concern is not likely to be that the statement will someday be revealed in civil discovery. More likely, the employee will fear that the ombudsman is biased in favor of the company, and that the ombudsman will tell management everything that the employee says. The denial of an ombudsman privilege will not affect the ombudsman's ability to convince an employee that the ombudsman is neutral, and creation of an ombudsman privilege will not help alleviate the fear that she is not.

We are especially unconvinced that no present or future [McDonnell Douglas] employee could feel comfortable in airing his or her disputes with the Ombudsman because of the specter of discovery. An employee either will or will not have a meritorious complaint. If he does not and is aware that he does not, he is no more likely to share the frivolousness of his complaint with a company ombudsman than he is with a court. If he has a meritorious complaint that he would prefer not to litigate, then he will generally feel that he has nothing to hide and will be undeterred by the prospect of civil discovery from sharing the nature of his complaint with the ombudsman. The dim prospect that the employee's complaint might someday surface in an unrelated case strikes us as an unlikely deterrent. Again, it is the perception that the ombudsman is the company's investigator, a fear that does not depend upon the prospect of civil discovery, that is most likely to keep such an employee from speaking openly.

McDonnell Douglas also argues that failure to recognize an ombudsman privilege will disrupt the relationship between management and the ombudsman's office. In cases where management has nothing to hide, this is unlikely. It is probably true that management will be less likely to share damaging information with an ombudsman if there is no privilege. Nonetheless, McDonnell Douglas has provided no reason to believe that management is especially eager to confess wrongdoing to ombudsmen when a privilege exists, or that ombudsmen are helpful at resolving disputes that involve violations of the law by management or supervisors. If the chilling of management-ombudsman communications occurs only in cases that would not have been resolved at the ombudsman stage anyway, then there is no reason to recognize an ombudsman privilege.

We disagree with the District Court's holding that employee communications to Therese Clemente were protected from discovery by an ombudsman privilege. The judgment is reversed, and the cause remanded for further proceedings consistent with this opinion.

CHAPTER 4

DARDEN RESTAURANTS[1]

Four Steps to Effective Employee Dispute Resolution

DUE DILIGENCE[2]

Darden Restaurants
5900 Lake Ellenor Drive
P.O. Box 593330
Orlando, Florida 32859-3330
407.245.5215
www.darden.com

Joe Lee, Chairman/CEO
James Smith, Senior Vice President
Clifford Whitehill-Yarza, Senior Vice President/Counsel/Secretary
Clarence Otis Jr., Senior Vice President Finance/Treasurer
Linda Dimopoulos, Senior Vice President/Controller

Total assets exceeding $1.9 billion
Revenues exceeding $3.2 billion
Net Income of $101 million
Total liabilities of $964 million

COMPANY STORY

While the name Darden Restaurants may not be familiar to the reader, no doubt *The Olive Garden* and *Red Lobster* are eateries with which the reader is well acquainted. Darden Restaurants is, as owner and operator of these two popular venues, the largest full-service dinnerhouse chain as well as the leading seafood company in North America. Darden, a Fortune 500 company traded on the NYSE, operates more than 1,150 restaurants in 49 states and the District of Columbia. The company also owns and operates 52 food outlets in Canada and licenses 37 restaurants in Japan. The company employs in excess of 115,000 people at its domestic outlets and at its

---

[1] The author is deeply grateful to Clifford Whitehill-Yarza, Darden Restaurants Senior Vice President, General Counsel & Secretary for his kind and invaluable cooperation in the preparation of this chapter.
[2] Year ended May 31, 1998.

corporate headquarters in Orlando, Florida. This year, the company expects to serve more than 100 million pounds of seafood to more than 150 million guests.

The Company was founded in 1968 by restaurant entrepreneur Bill Darden with a *Red Lobster* store in Lakeland, Florida. The five-unit *Red Lobster* chain was acquired by General Mills in 1970. General Mills market research lead to the creation of a second restaurant, *The Olive Garden*; this expansion also included a third new entry named *China Coast*. General Mills provided considerable resources for a rapid nationwide expansion over the next two decades, including conversion of considerable General Mills owned real estate into *Olive Gardens* restaurants. In 1995, General Mills spun-off the entire restaurant division forming Darden Restaurants, Inc., as an independent, publicly traded corporation. Shortly thereafter, Darden closed the *China Coast* chain. A new venture for Darden is the *Bahama Breeze* Caribbean restaurant which began operations in 1996.

The company has always been one that devotes considerable attention and resources to a high quality employee base. Indeed, Bill Darden opened the first *Red Lobster* restaurant stating that the success of the company was directly linked to its employees: "I am convinced that the only edge we have on our competitors is the quality of our employees as reflected by the job they do." The company works diligently to "create an environment that attracts, develops and keeps the best people in the business," with a strong emphasis on training and career growth as well as a very competitive compensation and benefits package. In addition, the company has a very meaningful dedication to building a diverse workforce. There are, for example, over 1000 workers with disabilities working in the *Red Lobster* organization. More broadly, Darden is active in "expanding the role of diversity throughout the restaurant industry." Maintaining a significant and well-conceived program for employee dispute resolution is a critical component of these workforce commitments.

Recently, *Olive Garden* employees created a set of principles both descriptive of and prescriptive for restaurant employees:

1. We are committed to open honest communication, mutual respect and strong teamwork.
2. We are clear on each individual's role, accountabilities and key performance measures.
3. We do not compromise standards in selection, training and job performance.
4. In the process of making change we seek the opinions of those closest to the action, listen and value their ideas.
5. Everyone should expect regular, ongoing training opportunities to sharpen and advance their skills.
6. When accountabilities are not met, we act quickly.
7. We will achieve the results and share our successes.

These principles, focusing as they do on respect, teamwork and 'accountabilities,' convey clearly the culture at Darden and make obvious the need for and centrality to the corporate mission of effective mechanisms for employee dispute resolution.

ALTERNATIVE DISPUTE RESOLUTION PROGRAM

Darden has created a comprehensive dispute resolution program for employee disputes. The Darden program is a multi-step, multi-process approach to the resolution of internal disputes involving employees. It is, significantly, a program in which employees participate, not solely as parties, but as peer review panel neutrals. In addition, the program draws in external ADR practitioners with particular expertise in a given process, whether mediation or arbitration, when in-house, informal processes prove unsuccessful in resolving a matter.

Recognizing that infrequent disputes may arise between the company and employees during or following employment is critical at Darden. Moreover, Darden acknowledges that these differences normally are resolved either very informally or, where an informal procedure does not produce a satisfactory result, that the only recourse for the employee or the company is litigation. Finally, Darden understands that this nothing or all approach can be costly and time-consuming for all parties. Darden believes there is a better method to resolve employee disputes. It does so by adding three additional dispute resolution steps: peer review, mediation and arbitration, which provide a fair and equitable ways to resolve disputes.

BRIEFING POINT 4.1

The EEOC reported a 22% increase in charges of employment discrimination from 1991 to 1993. (Bureau of National Affairs, Daily Labor Report, July 29, 1994 at D20.) In addition, monetary benefits for sexual harassment cases handled by the EEOC between 1991 and 1997 have increased from 7.1 million to 49.5 million – these benefits do not include monetary benefits obtained through litigation. (EEOC statistics at http://www.access.gpo.gov/eeoc/stats/harass.html.)

The Darden *Dispute Resolution Procedure* ("DRP") is used to "resolve claims or controversies as defined in the DRP arising out of an Employee's employment or termination, that an Employee may have against the Company or the Company may have against the Employee." These disputes, which have not been resolved through normal personnel channels or the Darden Open Door Policy, are resolved through peer review, mediation or, if necessary, "exclusive, final and binding arbitration." Therefore, neither the company nor the employee may litigate such claims against each other in a court. In sum, the Darden Restaurants Dispute Resolution Procedure consists of four distinct process options:

1.   Open Door;
2.   Peer Review;

3.   Mediation; and,
4.   Binding Arbitration.

How to use the Darden DRP. The following language from the Darden DRP
Handbook[3] provided to all employees succinctly describes the procedure for
commencing a claim:

> "Any controversy, claim or dispute subject to the DRP which has not been
> resolved through the open door policy must be submitted in writing on a
> Peer Review/Mediation/Arbitration Request Form[4] to the restaurant's
> general manager if the employee works in a restaurant, or to the vice
> president of personnel, within one year from the date the employee first
> learns of his/her claim. Any claims not submitted to DRP during this one
> year period shall be considered resolved and closed and the employee may
> not thereafter pursue the claim through the DRP or seek relief from any
> federal, state or local governmental administrative agency or court, unless
> otherwise provided by law in which event, the one year period shall be
> accordingly extended."

Any issue as to this provision or any other limitation on the use of the
program, is resolved solely by arbitration as described elsewhere in the program
materials. Furthermore, while access to state and federal court is precluded generally
by the DRP, nothing in the DRP limits an employee's independent or concurrent use
of any state or federal administrative agency. Indeed, in the event that a matter is
returned for resolution directly between the parties, a 'right to sue letter,' for
example, it is thereafter processed exclusively under the DRP, which includes
mediation and arbitration to the full extent permitted by law.

What is Covered Under the DRP. Any employee may submit to the *Dispute
Resolution Program* any claims for:

1.   Wages or other compensation due (except as herein limited);
2.   Tort related matters;
3.   Discrimination including but not limited to race, color, sex,
          religion, national origin, disability, sexual orientation, material
          status or age;
4.   Denial of benefits;
5.   Violation of any federal or state law or regulation; and/or,
6.   Other common law matters.

---

[3] A brief employee program pamphlet is included in the "Forms and Materials" section of this chapter.
[4] This form is included in the "Forms and Materials" section of this chapter.

However, the Dispute Resolution Program is not available to review the following types of claims:

1. Performance evaluations;
2. Job elimination or layoff decisions; or,
3. Company work rules, policies or pay rates or increases and decreases in benefits except to the extent such matters relate to statutory or breach of contract claims.

The Employee is notified within fourteen days after he or she submits a claim to the restaurant manager or to the vice president of personnel whether the claim is eligible for resolution under DRP.

Open Door. When notice is given that a claim is eligible for resolution in the DRP, it normally moves through a four-step chronologically arranged sequence of ADR processes. The first, and least formal step, is one or more "**Open Door Meetings.**" At this stage, the goal is for a face-to-face, unstructured meeting to lead to an agreed upon, as opposed to adjudicated, outcome. This step is, of course, simply an articulation of the traditional 'stay first in the chain of command' approach. It is not, however, a dictatorial approach in which managers impose an outcome on employees. Instead, it emphasizes the possibility that a threshold conversation with lawyers and formalities might resolve simple miscommunications before they evolve in to more significant disputes with the attendant likelihood of litigation and lasting acrimony and cost. It is important to note that the aggrieved party may approach a person other than the alleged perpetrator to assist in resolution of the matter.

Darden employee materials summarize the Open Door Meeting in the following way:

Option	What	Who	Why	How
Open Door	A process that allows you to discuss and resolve concerns with various levels of management. ▪ Informal ▪ Covers work-related disputes ▪ Encourages early resolution	Management Chain of Command: ▪ Manager ▪ General Manager ▪ Director ▪ Employee Relations ▪ Senior Vice President	▪ Early solution to problem ▪ Open and flexible ▪ Easily accessible	Present concern in person to manager or Employee Relations.

Peer Review. If the Open Door Meeting process does not resolve the matter, the aggrieved party may choose to drop the matter or move to the next DRP process step. At that level, the employee may present the complaint to a **Peer Review Panel** made up of two co-workers and one manager. This is a completely confidential setting in which the employee is provided the opportunity to make his or her case in a full, frank and more structured evidentiary fashion. It is important to note that the 'defendant,' the manager who made the decision affecting an employee or the co-employee, will also present his or her case in its entirety. The panel may investigate the complaint further and will arrive at and communicate to all parties a final decision regarding the claim.

Within thirty days after the employee's claim is presented to the Peer Review Panel, the Panel issues a written decision. If both the employee and the company are fully satisfied with the decision, both sign a written statement agreeing to the Panel's decision within twenty days. The decision of the Panel shall then be final, binding and enforceable against both parties. If either the employee or the company is not satisfied with the Peer Review Panel decision, the employee or the company may submit the claim, within thirty days, to mediation as explained in the next section. They may also at this point proceed with formal arbitration if they believe that there is no chance that a settlement-oriented process could resolve the matter equitably. A further note on timing of processes is important: the employee and/or the company must either sign the statement agreeing to the Review Panel's decision, or submit the claim to mediation or arbitration within thirty days of receiving the Panel's written decision. If either party fails to take any action, it means that party has accepted the Panel's decision, and that decision becomes final, binding and enforceable against both parties.

Darden employee materials summarize the Peer Review Panel in the following way:

Option	What	Who	Why	How
Peer Review	A process that allows you to bring your concerns to a three member in-house panel for resolution. ■ Informal ■ Covers most work-related disputes ■ If both parties agree, produces written decision	Three member panel: ■ Two trained employees ■ Includes managers or general manager ■ A general manager you choose facilitates the process	■ Fresh perspective from those outside the issue, but within the company ■ Quick, in-house resolution of the problem.	If Open Door is not successful, submit Peer Review/Mediation /Arbitration Request Form to general manager.

Mediation.   Mediations, under the DRP, are conducted in accordance with the *Employment Mediation Rules*[5] of the American Arbitration Association ("AAA") in effect at the time the request for mediation is made. To request mediation of a matter not resolved in one of the previous processes, a formal written request for mediation by either the employee or the company is delivered to the AAA. That notice must be sent by certified or registered mail, return receipt requested, with a copy of the request sent in the same manner to the other party. The form for such a request may be secured from any AAA office or online. The mediation will take place in or near the city in which the employee is or was last employed by the company.   The mediator is chosen according to the procedures set forth in the *Employment Mediation Rules* of the AAA or by the company. Significantly, the costs and fees of the mediation conference and the mediator will be paid by the Company to the AAA. Such an arrangement may give rise initially to questions of mediator bias. However, the fact that the fee is paid to the AAA directly, that the mediator is paid as a subcontractor of the AAA by the AAA, and that the mediator is not an employee of Darden in any sense of the word, should put that concern to rest. The value of this provision is that it provides for a genuine commitment to mediation by placing the economic burden of the process on the party likely best able to bear it.

If the dispute is resolved in mediation, the agreement will be reduced to writing, signed by all parties, and become enforceable in a court of competent jurisdiction against either party. Mediation is not always successful. The mediation conference shall be considered terminated without an agreement by a declaration by the mediator that further attempts at mediation are no longer worthwhile or a statement by either party that they desire to terminate mediation. Darden employee materials summarize DRP Mediation Conferences in the following way:

Option	What	Who	Why	How
Mediation	A process that allows you to take your dispute to an outside, neutral third party for resolution through assisted negotiation. ▪ Informal ▪ Covers most work-related disputes ▪ Nonbinding unless parties agree to settle ▪ Legal representation allowed but not required	Mediator from American Arbitration Association (AAA) or other chosen by company.	▪ Benefit of neutral, outside third-party expert to assist in negotiation ▪ You have considerable input to the process ▪ Win-win solution ▪ Fast and inexpensive (no cost to employee) ▪ Helps preserve working relationships	If Peer Review is not successful, submit written notice for Mediation to the company.

---

[5] These rules may be found online at www.adr.org or as an appendix in L. Ponte & T. Cavenagh, <u>Alternative Dispute Resolution in Business</u>, West (1999)

Arbitration. If a mediation conference is terminated without a settlement or the employee or the company has declined to engage in mediation, the claim or dispute may be submitted to binding arbitration in accordance with the *Employment Dispute Resolution Rules*[6] of the American Arbitration Association. The arbitration and any decision or award made by the arbitrator is final and binding on both parties. Arbitration is a far more formal and structured process, one that in many ways resembles a courtroom trial. As a result, the rules for arbitration are longer and more involved. In addition, the rules for arbitration make the process one of last resort for the aggrieved party as it is binding and final and does not allow for litigation in the event a party is not satisfied with the outcome reached in arbitration. Beyond its increased formality, arbitration adds many of the costs, delays and risks associated with trial, and therefore is less effective at preserving workplace relationships than is peer review or mediation. It does, however, provide parties with an external impartial, adjudicative process in the event the in-house or facilitative processes that preceded it are not fruitful in resolving the matter. It is important to note that courts have generally upheld the right of employers and employees to avoid court litigation by using private arbitration. While the <u>Hooters</u> decision in this chapter stands as an exception to this rule, and while other courts have expressed some reticence about the arbitration of federal statutory rights, generally a fair system of arbitration will preclude access to a subsequent trial.

BRIEFING POINT 4.2
Industry-wide ADR initiatives are proliferating. The National Association of Securities Dealers, the National Association of Manufacturers, the National Healthcare Lawyers Association and the World Intellectual Property Organization, for example, all have model programs.

Requirements for Arbitration. Submission of a timely claim under the DRP is a prerequisite to binding arbitration. If the Company or the Employee fails to submit a timely claim for arbitration, the claim is deemed settled. The employee or the company are, as a result, barred from arbitrating the claim under the DRP or from seeking relief from any federal or state court unless further time to do so is required by federal or state law.

To make a timely claim, the company or employee must give written notice of the decision to arbitrate to both the other party and to the AAA by certified or registered mail, return receipt requested, within thirty days following the termination of mediation or of the provision of written notice of the decision not to proceed with mediation. However, if these dates occur within one year from the date the employee first learns of his/her claim, the employee is provided any additional time remaining in the one-year period within which the written notice of the decision to arbitrate must be given. The written notice to arbitrate must identify and describe the

---

[6] These rules may be found online at www.adr.org or as an appendix in L. Ponte & T. Cavenagh, <u>Alternative Dispute Resolution in Business</u>, West (1999)

nature of all claims asserted by the requesting party and the facts upon which those claims are based. In addition, the notice should include the remedy requested by the employee or the company.

The arbitration will be scheduled to take place in or near the city in which the employee is or was last employed by the company. The arbitration is conducted by one arbitrator, chosen according to the procedures set forth in the *Employment Dispute Resolution Rules* of the AAA. The selected arbitrator shall be experienced in law relating to employment disputes.

The Arbitration Hearing. The arbitration hearing will normally start no later than sixty days following the date of the selection of the arbitrator. However, the selected arbitrator may order the hearing rescheduled if mutually agreed to in writing by the company and the employee or if good cause is shown. The arbitration hearing under the Darden rules is limited to two days; each party has one day to present his/her position to the arbitrator. The arbitrator may, for good cause, extend the hearing and adjust the timing of the presentations.

Both the company and the employee have the right to be represented by counsel of their choice and at their own expense before and during the hearing. However, if the employee notifies the company at least thirty days before the date of the hearing that he or she will not be represented by counsel at the hearing, the Company agrees to waive representation by counsel at the hearing as well. As with any conventional arbitration, each party has the right to subpoena witnesses and documents for the arbitration hearing by requesting a subpoena from the arbitrator; any such request must, of course, be served on the other party as well. Objections to the issuance of a subpoena must be submitted to the arbitrator within ten days following receipt of the request.

To facilitate an orderly hearing, at least fifteen days before the start of the arbitration hearing, the employee and the company must provide each other and the arbitrator with a list of witnesses, including any expert witnesses, a brief summary of the testimony of each witness and a list of all exhibits intended to be used at the arbitration. Unless ordered by the arbitrator, witnesses or exhibits which do not appear on these lists will not be allowed to testify or be introduced during the arbitration hearing. The company, at its option and expense, may arrange for and pay the cost of a court reporter to provide a stenographic record of the proceedings; the employee may obtain a copy of the record by paying 25% of the reporter's fee or, if not done by the company, arrange for a court reporter at his/her sole cost. Either party, upon request at the close of hearing, shall be allowed to file a post-hearing brief. The time for filing briefs and the length will be determined by the arbitrator at the hearing.

The arbitrator is required to issue a written decision within thirty days of the conclusion of the hearing. That decision will include a complete statement of the arbitrator's findings of fact, conclusions of law and the remedy ordered, if there is a remedy. The arbitrator is limited in his or her authority in terms of the remedies available to the parties. The Darden policy, like many others, describes the limitations on the arbitrator's authority as follows:

1. The arbitrator has the authority to grant legal and equitable relief, if requested, including both temporary restraints and preliminary injunctive relief, to the same extent as could a court of competent jurisdiction.
2. Unless the claim or controversy alleges a violation of a specific federal or state statute, the arbitrator has no authority to establish wage rates or wage scales or benefits, to establish performance standards, work rules, food quality and service standards, or similar company policies and procedures.
3. The arbitrator has no authority to hear claims which the Employee did not submit to Peer Review, if those claims could have been so submitted.
4. The arbitrator may give any weight to the decision of the Peer Review panel that the arbitrator deems proper under the circumstances.

Either party may bring an action in court to compel arbitration under the Darden DRP or to enforce an arbitration award made in a hearing held pursuant to the DRP.

Arbitration Fees and Costs. The arbitrator's fees and expenses, the costs of the hearing facilities, plus any costs owed to the AAA or the arbitrator are shared equally by both the employee and the company. The employee is not, however, required to pay more than the equivalent of two weeks' salary in his/her current position, or the last position held with the Company; any amount over this limit shall be paid by the Company. Any other expenses incurred by either party during the arbitration process, including attorney's fees, if any, are paid by the party incurring the expense. However, in cases of demonstrated hardship, the company will pay all arbitration expenses and relieve the employee of any of the shared costs. In the event the Employee prevails on a statutory claim which entitles him to attorney's fees, the arbitrator may award fees to the employee under the statute. Darden employee materials summarize DRP Arbitration Hearings in the following way:

Option	What	Who	Why	How
Arbitration	A process that allows you to take your disputes to a neutral third party for resolution by binding decision. ▪ Structured, but less formal than court trials ▪ Covers most work-related disputes ▪ Decision binds you and company ▪ Lawyers allowed, but not required	Third-party arbitrator from AAA	▪ Benefit of neutral, third-party expert to make final decision ▪ Same recovery possible as in trial ▪ Private ▪ Quicker resolution than from traditional litigation ▪ Simpler and more economical; gives you more control than in a trial ▪ Helps preserve working relationships.	If Mediation is not successful, submit written notice for Arbitration to the company and to the nearest office of the AAA by certified mail or registered mail.

ASSESSMENT

This chapter began with the statement that the Darden program was a model because of its comprehensiveness. That observation merits repetition. The Darden program endeavors to limit company exposure to employee claims as well as to provide the company with expeditious approaches to solving disputes with the employee wherein the company is the aggrieved party. It does so with a program that encourages facilitated and organization-building outcomes rather than adjudicative, and perhaps less productive ones. In addition to its comprehensiveness, the Darden program is one that appears to meet the legal tests applied to company efforts to avoid the courtroom. The company does not, for example, shift costs to the employee in ways calculated to discourage participation in the program. The choice of neutral is governed by external rules preventing abuse in the selection of the mediator and/or arbitrator as courts require. Further, the program is consistent with the company's principles. Teamwork, respect and communication are fostered in significant ways in this program that not only solves problems for employees, but allows them a role in solving problems for their colleagues. The goodwill engendered by such an approach is difficult to quantify, but no less valuable than the more tangible time and economic savings offered by the program. Finally, the program emphasizes appropriate sequencing when it starts with the open door meeting and moves progressively toward the arbitration. Such an order is sensible and advisable as it moves gradually from simple to complex, informal to formal, inexpensive to costly, facilitative to adjudicative and from very low risk to far riskier.

Two ways to improve the program might be considered. First, since very few cases are not mediatable, the provision allowing parties to opt out of the mediation process in favor of arbitration could be deleted from the program. Because mediation is the first point in the DRP that introduces an outside agent, trained to settle cases, it is likely that cases that seem intractable may, in fact, be ones that could settle. Allowing the parties to avoid mediation and move directly to arbitration misses the chance to settle and creates a much more significant level of acrimony and expense.

In addition, the two-day limitation on arbitration hearing length may trouble some judges, particularly in a case in which difficult statutory rights are in question. While abbreviated arbitration hearings are common in many court-annexed arbitration programs, they are rarely used for resolution of highly complex cases. The Darden DRP could be improved by allowing for increased hearing length as the nature of the claim or the amount of damages increases. In addition to assuring court approval of the program, such a modification would enhance the reliability of the arbitration outcome considerably.

BRIEFING POINT 4.3

An instrument designed by Daniel Dana to measure the financial cost of organizational conflict can be found at http://www.mediationworks.com/mti/cost.htm

---

DARDEN FORMS & MATERIALS

Darden company materials describe the Dispute Resolution Program at Darden carefully and in non-legal and user-friendly fashion. The following is the complete contents of the pamphlet provided to employees describing the Darden Dispute Resolution Program.

Dispute Resolution
A fair, consistent way to resolve differences

At Darden Restaurants, we strive to treat people fairly and with respect, because every job contributes to our continued success. This philosophy extends to the way we handle problems and disputes in the workplace, because we know that even routine differences can get bigger when there are no resources to help solve them.

Our goal is to resolve all workplace disputes in a way that is effective and fair to all parties. In order to do this, we have developed four ways to resolve workplace problems and concerns, while protecting the legal rights of all parties. These options make up our Dispute Resolution Procedure.

Dispute Resolution covers claims for wages and other compensation, tort claims, discrimination claims, denial of benefit claims, claims for violation of state and federal laws or claims under common law. Dispute Resolution does not cover issues such as performance reviews, benefits, pay, layoffs and job elimination. Company work rules cannot be changed by Dispute Resolution. This folder outlines the basics; for more details, refer to your Dispute Resolution Handbook.

Here's How Dispute Resolution Works:

Open Door Policy

The first step in resolving a dispute is to use our Open Door Policy. This means that if you have a workplace concern or dispute, you can feel free to talk about it with one of the managers in your restaurant. If, for any reason, you don't feel you can talk to any of your managers about the problem, you may discuss it with your director of operations or senior vice president. They will listen and try to help you resolve the dispute. At any time in the process you may also call the toll-free Employee Relations number in Orlando.

Our Open Door Policy remains the first – and often the best – way to resolve a problem or dispute before it becomes a crisis. That's because an open and honest exchange by the people who are closest to the problem provides the best insight and opportunity for resolution. And our Open Door Policy guarantees you can use it without fear of retaliation.

Peer Review

If the Open Door Policy does not resolve your concern, you may choose to air your complaint before a Peer Review panel. This panel consists of two employees and a manager (not from your restaurant) chosen from a pool of trained panelists. Let's say you disagree with a management decision and decide to appeal to a Peer Review panel. A neutral facilitator will set up the review and help you prepare. You will present your side of the issue, and the manager would present her or his side. The panel will listen to both sides, consider all evidence, and make a decision. All proceedings are confidential. You'll find more details on Peer Review in the Peer Review brochure.

Mediation

If you (or the company) are not satisfied with the decision of the Peer Review panel, you may submit your claim to mediation. A mediator is a neutral, outside party who is trained in dispute resolution. All costs of mediation are paid by the company. The mediator listens to the dispute and helps you and the company reach an agreement by opening up communications and suggesting options. If both parties do not agree on a solution (or if you or the company decide to bypass mediation), then you or the company may choose to take the dispute to arbitration for a final and binding solution.

Arbitration

Arbitration is the final step in our Dispute Resolution Program. Like mediation, arbitration uses a neutral, outside party to hear the dispute. In arbitration, however, the arbitrator makes a final and binding decision. Both sides present their arguments at a hearing, which is more formal than mediation and less formal than court. The arbitrator then weighs the evidence and makes a decision. If you win, you can be awarded anything you might seek through a court of law. The costs of arbitration are split by you and the company.

Questions and Answers About Dispute Resolution

Q: Why would I want to use Dispute Resolution instead of going to court?

A: Unfortunately, our court system is overloaded and slow. In some areas of the country, civil litigation   (including workplace disputes) often takes six or seven years to settle. And the cost of litigation puts it out of the reach of most people. Dispute Resolution is much faster and cheaper.

Q: Won't I give up some of my legal rights by using mediation or arbitration?

A: No. Mediation and arbitration protect your rights just like a court of law. In a variety of cases, including discrimination cases, the U.S. Supreme Court has recognized mediation and arbitration as effective ways to resolve disputes.

Q: Who are the mediators and/or arbitrators used in Dispute Resolution?

A: They are trained, neutral experts who belong to the American Arbitration Association, a public service, non-profit organization that offers a wide range of dispute resolution services to business and government. The organization has established accepted rules and procedures to hear and decide cases, and their decisions are recognized by the court system.

Q: Why does the company use Dispute Resolution?

A: We have an obligation to both our employees and our investors. Employee disputes that end up in court are costly and time-consuming for all involved, and after lawyers' fees are paid, generally neither party gains. Dispute Resolution offers a way to settle these claims more quickly and cheaply, while protecting the rights of both parties. In this way, we can devote more of our resources toward improving our business, which benefits employees and investors.

DARDEN RESTAURANTS, INC.
PEER REVIEW/MEDIATION/ARBITRATION REQUEST FORM

We recommend that you read the Dispute Resolution Procedures booklet before completing this form; copies are available from your manager or Employee Relations.

From: Name of employee: _____
          Employee number: _____
          Address: Work: _____
                       Phone: (   ) _____
                       Home: _____
                       Phone: (   ) _____

Indicate where you would like your notifications set: ☐to home   ☐to work   ☐both.

1. Describe the details of your complaint(s) or dispute(s). You may attach a separate statement or relevant supporting documents if you need more space.

_____
_____
_____
_____

2. To the best of your ability, indicate the nature of your dispute by checking the applicable category(s) below:

☐Working conditions	☐Medical Condition	☐Retaliation
☐Age	☐National Origin	☐Sex
☐Disability	☐Race	☐Sexual Harassment
☐Marital Status	☐Religion	☐Sexual Orientation
		☐Other (explain): _____

3. Indicate the type of relief you seek and/or the dollar amount, if any, of your claim(s) (i.e., the amount of damages you seek to recover). Note: Peer Review is limited to reinstatement or other "make whole" relief.
Description of relief sought: _____
_____

Dollar amount, if any, of claim(s): _____

I hereby authorize the Peer Review panel and the mediator or Arbitrator to review those portions of my personnel file which may be relevant to the proper investigation of my claim.

Date _____   Employee Signature _____

This Peer Review/Mediation/ Arbitration Request Form received on this date by _____

To be completed by the Dispute Resolution Facilitator and copy sent to employee.

Peer Review conducted on _____ and completed _____ . Result _____
Mediation conducted on _____ and completed _____ . Result _____
Arbitration conducted on _____ and completed _____ . Result _____

KEY DECISION

The following decision describes another effort by a national restaurant chain to establish a sort of employee dispute resolution program. The Hooters program, however, was designed, at least in the judgment of the court, not to honestly resolve internal employee disputes, but to place the company at an advantage in the event a suit was filed by employees alleging injury of any kind. The case is presented for two reasons: First, to contrast the Darden Program with one not created in good faith, and second, to provide the standards by which an internal program designed to avoid litigation will be measured.

HOOTERS OF AMERICA, INC. v. Annette R. PHILLIPS v. Hooters of Myrtle Beach, Incorporated; National Restaurant Association; Society of Professionals in Dispute Resolution; National Academy of Arbitrators; Equal Employment Opportunity Commission, Amici Curiae
1999 WL 194438 (1999)
United States Court of Appeals for the Fourth Circuit.

Annette R. Phillips worked as a bartender at a Hooters restaurant in Myrtle Beach, South Carolina. Phillips alleges that in June 1996, Gerald Brooks, a Hooters official and the brother of Hooters principal owner, sexually harassed her by grabbing and slapping her buttocks. After appealing to her manager for help and being told to "let it go," she quit her job. Phillips then contacted Hooters through an attorney claiming that the attack and the restaurant's failure to address it violated her Title VII rights. Hooters responded that she was required to submit her claims to arbitration according to a binding agreement to arbitrate between the parties.

This agreement arose in 1994 during the implementation of Hooters' alternative dispute resolution program. As part of that program, the company conditioned eligibility for raises, transfers, and promotions upon an employee signing an "Agreement to arbitrate employment-related disputes." The agreement provides that Hooters and the employee each agree to arbitrate all disputes arising out of employment, including "any claim of discrimination, sexual harassment, retaliation, or wrongful discharge, whether arising under federal or state law." The agreement further states that

> The employee and the company agree to resolve any claims pursuant to the company's rules and procedures for alternative resolution of employment-related disputes, as promulgated by the company from time to time ("the rules"). Company will make available or provide a copy of the rules upon written request of the employee.

The employees were initially given a copy of this agreement at an all-staff meeting.

Hooters general manager, Gene Fulcher, told the employees to review the agreement for five days and that they would then be asked to accept or reject the agreement. No employee, however, was given a copy of Hooters' arbitration rules and procedures. Phillips signed the agreement on November 25, 1994. When her personnel file was updated in April 1995, Phillips again signed the agreement. After Phillips quit her job in June 1996, Hooters sent to her attorney a copy of the Hooters rules then in effect. Phillips refused to arbitrate the dispute. Hooters filed suit in November 1996 to compel arbitration. Phillips defended on the grounds that the agreement to arbitrate was unenforceable. The district court denied Hooters' motion to compel arbitration. The court found that there was no meeting of the minds on all of the material terms of the agreement and even if there were, Hooters' promise to arbitrate was illusory. In addition, the court found that the arbitration agreement was unconscionable and void for reasons of public policy. Hooters filed this appeal.

The benefits of arbitration are widely recognized. Parties agree to arbitrate to secure streamlined proceedings and expeditious results that will best serve their needs. The arbitration of disputes enables parties to avoid the costs associated with pursuing a judicial resolution of their grievances. By one estimate, litigating a typical employment dispute costs at least $50,000 and takes two and one-half years to resolve. Further, the adversarial nature of litigation diminishes the possibility that the parties will be able to salvage their relationship. For these reasons parties agree to arbitrate and trade the procedures and opportunity for review of the courtroom for the simplicity, informality, and expedition of arbitration. In support of arbitration, Congress passed the Federal Arbitration Act. Its purpose was to reverse the longstanding judicial hostility to arbitration agreements that had existed at English common law and had been adopted by American courts, and to place arbitration agreements upon the same footing as other contracts. When a valid agreement to arbitrate exists between the parties and covers the matter in dispute, the Federal Arbitration Act commands the federal courts to stay any ongoing judicial proceedings and compel arbitration.

The threshold question is whether claims such as Phillips' are even arbitrable. The EEOC contends that employees cannot agree to arbitrate Title VII claims in predispute agreements. We disagree. The Supreme Court has made it plain that judicial protection of arbitral agreements extends to agreements to arbitrate statutory discrimination claims. In Gilmer v. Interstate/Johnson Lane, the Court noted that by agreeing to arbitrate a statutory claim, a party does not forgo the substantive rights afforded by the statute; it only submits to their resolution in an arbitral, rather than a judicial, forum. Thus, a party must be held to the terms of its bargain unless Congress intends to preclude waiver of a judicial forum for the statutory claims at issue.

Predispute agreements to arbitrate Title VII claims are thus valid and enforceable. The question remains whether a binding arbitration agreement between Phillips and Hooters exists and compels Phillips to submit her Title VII claims to arbitration. The Federal Arbitration Act provides that agreements "to settle by arbitration a controversy thereafter arising out of such contract or transaction ... shall be valid, irrevocable, and enforceable, save upon such grounds as exist at law or in equity for the revocation of any contract." Hooters argues that Phillips gave her assent to a bilateral agreement to arbitrate. That contract provided for the resolution by arbitration of all employment-related disputes, including claims arising under Title VII. Hooters claims the agreement to arbitrate is valid because Phillips twice signed it voluntarily. Thus, it argues the courts are bound to enforce it and compel arbitration.

We disagree. In this case, the challenge goes to the validity of the arbitration agreement itself. Hooters materially breached the arbitration agreement by promulgating rules so egregiously unfair as to constitute a complete default of its contractual obligation to draft arbitration rules and to do so in good faith. Hooters and Phillips agreed to settle any disputes between them not in a judicial forum, but in another neutral forum--arbitration. Their agreement provided that Hooters was responsible for setting up such a forum by promulgating arbitration rules and procedures. To this end, Hooters instituted a set of rules in July 1996. The Hooters rules when taken as a whole, however, are so one-sided that their only possible purpose is to undermine the neutrality of the proceeding. The rules require the employee to provide the company notice of her claim at the outset, including "the nature of the Claim" and "the specific act(s) or omissions(s) which are the basis of the Claim." Hooters, on the other hand, is not required to file any responsive pleadings or to notice its defenses. Additionally, at the time of filing this notice, the employee must provide the company with a list of all fact witnesses with a brief summary of the facts known to each. The company, however, is not required to reciprocate.

The Hooters rules also provide a mechanism for selecting a panel of three arbitrators that is crafted to ensure a biased decisionmaker. The employee and Hooters each select an arbitrator, and the two arbitrators in turn select a third. Good enough, except that the employee's arbitrator and the third arbitrator must be selected from a list of arbitrators created exclusively by Hooters. This gives Hooters control over the entire panel and places no limits whatsoever on whom Hooters can put on the list. Under the rules, Hooters is free to devise lists of partial arbitrators who have existing relationships, financial or familial, with Hooters and its management. In fact, the rules do not even prohibit Hooters from placing its managers themselves on the list. Further, nothing in the rules restricts Hooters from punishing arbitrators who rule against the company by removing them from the list. Given the unrestricted control that one party (Hooters) has over the panel, the selection of an impartial decision maker would be a surprising result.

Nor is fairness to be found once the proceedings are begun. Although Hooters may expand the scope of arbitration to any matter, "whether related or not to the Employee's Claim," the employee cannot raise "any matter not included in the Notice of Claim." Similarly, Hooters is permitted to move for summary dismissal of employee claims before a hearing is held whereas the employee is not permitted to seek summary judgment. Hooters, but not the employee, may record the arbitration hearing "by audio or videotaping or by verbatim transcription." The rules also grant

Hooters the right to bring suit in court to vacate or modify an arbitral award when it can show, by a preponderance of the evidence, that the panel exceeded its authority. No such right is granted to the employee.

In addition, the rules provide that upon 30 days notice Hooters, but not the employee, may cancel the agreement to arbitrate. Moreover, Hooters reserves the right to modify the rules, "in whole or in part," whenever it wishes and "without notice" to the employee. Nothing in the rules even prohibits Hooters from changing the rules in the middle of an arbitration proceeding.

If by odd chance the unfairness of these rules were not apparent on their face, leading arbitration experts have decried their one-sidedness. George Friedman, senior vice president of the American Arbitration Association (AAA), testified that the system established by the Hooters rules so deviated from minimum due process standards that the Association would refuse to arbitrate under those rules. George Nicolau, former president of both the National Academy of Arbitrators and the International Society of Professionals in Dispute Resolution, attested that the Hooters rules "are inconsistent with the concept of fair and impartial arbitration." He also testified that he was "certain that reputable designating agencies, such as the AAA and Jams/Endispute, would refuse to administer a program so unfair and one-sided as this one." Additionally, Dennis Nolan, professor of labor law at the University of South Carolina, declared that the Hooters rules "do not satisfy the minimum requirements of a fair arbitration system." He found that the "most serious flaw" was that the "mechanism [for selecting arbitrators] violates the most fundamental aspect of justice, namely an impartial decision maker." Finally, Lewis Maltby, member of the Board of Directors of the AAA, testified that "This is without a doubt the most unfair arbitration program I have ever encountered." In a similar vein, two major arbitration associations have filed amicus briefs with this court. The National Academy of Arbitrators stated that the Hooters rules "violate fundamental concepts of fairness ... and the integrity of the arbitration process." Likewise, the Society of Professionals in Dispute Resolution noted that "[i]t would be hard to imagine a more unfair method of selecting a panel of arbitrators." It characterized the Hooters arbitration system as "deficient to the point of illegitimacy" and "so one sided, it is hard to believe that it was even intended to be fair."

We hold that the promulgation of so many biased rules--especially the scheme whereby one party to the proceeding so controls the arbitral panel--breaches the contract entered into by the parties. The parties agreed to submit their claims to arbitration--a system whereby disputes are fairly resolved by an impartial third party. Hooters by contract took on the obligation of establishing such a system. By creating a sham system unworthy even of the name of arbitration, Hooters completely failed in performing its contractual duty. Given Hooters' breaches of the arbitration agreement and Phillips' desire not to be bound by it, we hold that rescission is the proper remedy. As we have explained, Hooters' breach is by no means insubstantial; its performance under the contract was so egregious that the result was hardly recognizable as arbitration at all. We therefore permit Phillips to cancel the agreement and thus Hooters' suit to compel arbitration must fail. By promulgating this system of warped rules, Hooters so skewed the process in its favor that Phillips has been denied arbitration in any meaningful sense of the word. To uphold the promulgation of this aberrational scheme under the heading of arbitration would undermine, not advance, the federal policy favoring alternative dispute resolution. This we refuse to do.

CHAPTER 5

DOLLAR GENERAL CORPORATION[1]

A comprehensive program in employee dispute resolution

DUE DILIGENCE[2]

Dollar General Corporation
104 Woodmont Boulevard
Suite 300
Nashville, Tennessee 37205
615.783.2000
www.dollargeneral.com

Cal Turner, Jr., Chairman/President/CEO
Brian M. Burr, Executive Vice President/CFO
Bob Carpenter, Executive Vice President/Chief Administrative Officer
Leigh Stelmach, Executive Vice President Operations
Earl Weissert, Executive Vice President Operations

Total assets exceeding $914 million
Net income of $144.6 million
Total liabilities of $330.9 million
Total equity of $583.8 million

COMPANY STORY

From its origin as a single store in Scottsville, Kentucky, Dollar General has grown into a billion dollar business. Dollar has cultivated an interesting corporate image, not as a retailer, but as a distributor of "customers' most basic needs." It focuses on providing "items that are used and used up," like toiletries and cleaning supplies. Because the company conceives of itself as a distributor rather than a retailer of the "basics," they do not advertise special sales or promotions. Furthermore, unlike large store retailers with a business model emphasizing assortment and low prices, the Dollar General small store niche promotes convenience and low prices. According to Dollar, its typical customer "is a female, rearing a family of three on a

---

[1] The author is deeply grateful to Janet Rasmussen, Dollar General ADR Program Manager, for her kind and invaluable cooperation in the preparation of this chapter.
[2] Year ended January 30, 1998.

household income of $25,000 or less," who aggressively seeks bargain level pricing. The Dollar General store she shops at is usually three to five miles from her home. Dollar believes in knowing what these typical customers want and maintaining ample stock of those items. It continually refines its merchandise assortment, adding over 700 new items in 1997 alone.

Dollar General's origins reach back to an era before the first large retail stores were introduced to Americans. In the late 1890's, J.L. Turner had to quit school to help support his family and began running a local general store. Later, he bought two stores of his own, both of which failed. A fellow merchant noted shortly thereafter that the depression was forcing near bankrupt retailers to sell complete inventories at a fraction of their original and actual value. Turner developed a successful new business strategy in that environment, consisting of taking out short-term bank loans to buy-out complete inventories from struggling merchants, and then selling the merchandise as quickly as possible to repay the bank, often within the same month.

In 1939, Turner formed his own company in Scottsville, Kentucky with his son; each invested $5,000 in the new venture. "J.L. Turner & Son" began work as wholesalers of basic dry goods. In 1945, the Turners switched from wholesale to retail and opened their first retail store in Albany, Kentucky. By 1955, J.L. Turner & Son owned and operated 35 self-service dry goods stores with annual sales reaching $2 million. The Turners' dollar store concept, no item above $1, was instituted on an experimental basis in 1956, and the first Dollar General Store opened in Springfield, Kentucky, in May of that year. The new concept was extremely successful, and in 10 years the company had grown to 255 stores with annual sales of $25.8 million. Cal Turner, Jr., the current CEO, joined the company in 1965 and became a director one year later.

The company changed its name to "Dollar General Corporation" and went public in 1968. By the end of 1976, retail sales reached $109 million, exceeding annual sales of $100 million for the first time in company history. In 1977, the company acquired United Dollar Stores, an Arkansas-based retail chain, and in 1983, it bought the entire 280-store P.N. Hirsch chain, a division of Interco, Inc. Two years later, the company substantially increased its presence in the Florida market by acquiring the complete 203-store Eagle Family Discount chain, also an Interco, Inc. property. In 1993, Dollar sales exceeded $1 billion for the first time, and in 1996, the company surpassed $2 billion in annual sales and $100 million in net income for the first time.

The company is headquartered in Nashville, Tennessee, and operates six massive distribution centers to stock over 3,100 stores in 24 states, each of which attracts as many as 200,000 customers annually. Collectively, the stores now generate more than $2.6 billion in annual sales. Dollar employs in excess of 40,000 people. Dollar plans to increase revenues in the range of 20 to 23 percent per year, while increasing earnings at a slightly greater rate. For the tenth consecutive year, in 1998, the company increased its total number of store units adding 435 units and ending the year with 3,169 stores. This increase in store units represents the largest number of annual new store openings in the company's history.

Dollar General corporate ideals support a commitment to healthy and reciprocal employee/employer relations; the extensive internal dispute resolution program it has developed is consistent with an supportive of that commitment. The Dollar General *Mission Statement* is a simple one: "Serving Others!" That brief statement is defined further by three themes the company strives to provide, the third of which is particularly germane to the company's dispute resolution efforts:

- A better life for our customers;
- A superior investment for our shareholders; and,
- A partnership in total development with our employees.

Dollar General corporate values are similarly straight-forward. Dollar seeks to build a company of people who:

- Have a living commitment to moral integrity;
- Have an enthusiastic sense of mission;
- Have a sense of humor and mature assessment of themselves;
- Model total development in their lives; and,
- Respect the creative potential of others.

Finally, Dollar General completes the definition of its corporate ideals by affirming that the company:

- Believes in leadership which results in team creativity and prompt decision-making close to the action;
- Believes in hard work; we also believe in the dignity of work and in the dignity of every person;
- Believes that productivity is attained by emphasizing strengths in a positive environment, not by dwelling on weaknesses in an environment of guilt or blame; and,
- Believes that any success is short-lived if it does not involve mutual gain.

ALTERNATIVE DISPUTE RESOLUTION PROGRAM

The Dollar General *Dispute Resolution Program* is similar to the Darden Restaurants program in several respects. It is, like the Darden program, a multi-step, multi-process program for the resolution of internal employee disputes. It offers, however, more steps and process options than does the Darden program, and represents the most comprehensive program for internal dispute resolution covered in this text. Dollar regards the program as a commitment to its employees that reflects the company's desire to equip all employees "with the tools [they] need to solve specific issues that interfere with [their] career[s] at Dollar General."

The objectives of the program include increasing employee involvement in the workplace, generating greater employee connectedness with the company, promoting prompt and fair resolution of employee disputes with another employee and/or the company, and preserving important workplace relationships. Dollar employee program materials describe the program as one "supporting an environment of mutual respect." They continue, "we think this program makes sense for our family of employees because it provides more ways to resolve conflict that are flexible, fair and confidential. You are our most valuable asset and this program has been created for you."

The start date of the Dollar General *Dispute Resolution Program* was August 1, 1997. The program covers all Dollar General employees and is the exclusive in-house means of resolving workplace disputes for both employees and the company. Despite this limitation, Dollar notes in its employee program materials, that the *Dispute Resolution Program* does not alter the company's at-will employment policy, nor does it alter other company employment policy statements or practices.

The program is administered by a full-time "Program Manager," who is assisted by a full-time, trained "Program Representative;" both are accessible via a toll-free telephone number from anywhere in the country. The Program Manager, who is not a member of the law department staff, has several functions. She **administers** the *Dispute Resolution Program* generally, and with respect to particular cases. She **educates** company personnel on the use and merits of the program. This education function is accomplished through scores of annual in-person presentations, careful development of descriptive program materials for company-wide dissemination, including a professionally developed videotape presentation, and a variety of other avenues including the company newsletter. Finally, she **evaluates** the program, again in terms that are both general and case specific. Careful case tracking forms have been created to generate and evaluate economic savings estimates resulting from use of the dispute resolution program.

The Dollar program provides recourse to employees for a wide variety of employment related matters including, but not limited to: demotion, termination, discrimination and sexual harassment. The program has seven chronologically ordered process options from which aggrieved employees may choose:

1. "Open Door Tradition" and flexible chain of command meetings;
2. Human resources support;
3. ADR Program Manager conferences;
4. Internal facilitation;
5. Internal mediation;
6. Peer review; and,
7. External mediation.

> **BRIEFING POINT 5.1**
> The general civil caseload in federal courts increased 125% from 1970 to 1989. Employment discrimination case filings increased by 2166% in the same period of time. "Tentative Recommendations for Public Comment" Federal Courts Study Committee (1989).

Option 1: Open Door Tradition and flexible chain of command.

Dollar General's *Open Door ·Tradition* is a voluntary process that encourages employees to resolve disputes at the lowest possible level. The *Open Door* process begins with remedial contact with an employee's immediate supervisor, either orally or in writing, unless the supervisor cannot resolve the issue or is part of the problem. When either of those conditions occurs, employees are encouraged next to move outside the 'chain of command' and contact a higher or different level of management, from the supervisor's supervisor, through and including the vice president of the employee's group or a human resources representative. Dollar commits all of its managers in the *Open Door* process to "listen to employee concerns, review the facts and work toward a prompt resolution."

The Dollar employee program materials describe the advantages of using the *Open Door* process:

- It helps you help yourself;
- It makes early and faster problem-solving more likely;
- It ensures management hears what you've got to say;
- You get your questions answered and learn about your options;
- There is no cost to the employee;
- It is flexible; and,
- Retaliation for use of the process is forbidden.

Option 2: Human Resources Support.

Human Resources Support is an extension of the *Open Door Tradition* and is reserved for highly sensitive issues, sexual harassment, for example, that need specialized attention not available from a direct supervisor or other management representative. *Human Resources Support* is also the most appropriate initial option for employees who have a sensitive dispute with an immediate supervisor, and who wish to step outside the management order altogether to seek satisfaction. Human Resources department personnel are described as employee "allies" in the *Human Resources Support* process and essentially function as ombudsmen, establishing essential facts, identifying important issues and informally seeking to resolve the dispute early and with minimal company involvement and cost.

Option 3: Conference.

A third extension of the *Open Door Tradition*, for disputes of an even greater level of sensitivity or complexity, makes the Dispute Resolution Program Manager available to *Conference* with employees should they wish to begin the process of fact-finding and resolution with her. Unlike the *Human Resources Support* option, in which the task of the Human Resources representative is to attempt resolution of the dispute, the Program Manager is chiefly involved during the *Conference* stage in evaluating the case for resolution through one of the more formal processes that are described below. While the *Conference* may lead to an employee deciding not to pursue other avenues, the principal tasks of the Manager in the *Conference* are to understand the nature of the particular problem, and to counsel the employee on the range of settlement and review processes available, as well as the strengths and weaknesses of each process. The Manager may also independently gather facts, and assist the employee in accessing high level management when it is appropriate to do so. The choices normally available to the employee following the *Conference* are to either "loop back through the chain of command" or pursue one of the formal processes described below. With certain rare exceptions, for example, legally imposed reporting obligations, the *Conference* is strictly confidential.

BRIEFING POINT 5.2

Fortune 500 executives report spending 20% of their time in litigation related activities. Rosenberg, S. (1998) www.resolutionworks.org/cost_calculator.htm. Likely this is due to the fact that "the median time between the date a lawsuit is filed and the commencement of a civil trial is 2.5 years." Bush, R., "The Conundrum: Conflict – The Solution: Designing Effective Conflict Management Systems," 16 Preventative L. Rep. Note 4 at 13 (1997).

Option 4: Internal Facilitation.

The goal of *Internal Facilitation* is to help employees resolve disputes "in a relaxed, informal setting with little time taken away from jobs and responsibilities." The process is conducted by a group of Dollar General employees trained thoroughly and specifically to serve as internal facilitators by an external professional ADR training provider. The internal facilitator is chosen by the employee from a list furnished by the Dispute Resolution Program Manager, who will also make the necessary arrangements to begin this relatively informal process. The internal facilitator acts as a "personal advisor" to the employee, and is required to handle the dispute in a "fair" and, to the extent possible, confidential manner. However, facilitators are never permitted to alter company policy to resolve a dispute.

The facilitator will listen to the details of the situation, ask appropriate questions and may even engage in independent fact-finding, which usually includes, at a minimum, talking to all other involved parties. Facilitation usually involves several short meetings with the aggrieved employee and perhaps others to resolve the dispute in a way that meets the needs of all of the parties involved, as well as the company. The internal facilitation meeting is conducted in a face-to-face setting whenever possible, although differences in geographic location may make it necessary for the facilitator to participate by phone.

Option 5: Internal Mediation.

Internal Mediation is a step beyond the *Internal Facilitation* process in terms of process formality. It is designed to be more comprehensive in scope, although the procedure in many ways parallels the *Internal Facilitation* process. As in the *Internal Facilitation* process, a group of employees is specially trained to resolve disputes, only through the more structured mediation process. The Program Manager will furnish a complete list of mediators from which the employee may select a neutral for a particular case. The Manager will also contact the mediator and instruct all parties on the mediation process generally.

Dollar General *Internal Mediation* is a process in which the parties involved discuss their dispute with an impartial person who assists them in resolving their differences by considering a variety of settlement options. The mediator may even suggest ways of resolving the dispute, but may not impose a settlement on the parties. More specifically, *Internal Mediation* is a six-step process at Dollar. After a party requests *Internal Mediation*, using the form included in the "Forms & Materials" section below, the mediator will, according to the Dollar General ADR Program guide:

1. Make the contact with all involved parties to secure agreement to mediate;
2. Arrange a meeting place and time convenient for the parties involved in the dispute;
3. Conduct private meetings with each party to collect and analyze facts;
4. "Coach" the parties through joint meetings with the goal of resolving the complaint;
5. Close the meeting with agreement from both parties on the resolution of the dispute, including any required plans for follow-up; and,
6. Furnish a written, signed agreement to both parties.

Dollar suggests several advantages of mediation in the materials it provides to employees describing the process:

- Mediation allows employees to explain fully opinions, beliefs or feelings bearing on the dispute;
- Mediation gives the employee the opportunity to have a less formal "day in court;"

- Mediation helps to reduce feelings of hostility and to separate emotional issues from factual issues;
- Mediation promotes discussion of creative solutions over which the parties retain control;
- Mediation ensures fairness, privacy and confidentiality while allowing employees to work things out themselves; and,
- Mediation is offered at no cost to employees.

Option 6: Peer Review.

"Dollar General believes that for even serious employee issues, employees themselves are the best decision-makers. We believe in you. We believe in your ability to make good decisions and to resolve issues fairly and to support our shared values of integrity, accountability and teamwork." So starts the section of the employee materials describing *Peer Review*, a process offered as an alternative to the facilitative dispute resolution approaches previously described. The *Peer Review* process is available to "distribution center and office employees only," presumably due to the cost involved in offering the process more widely. For those employees, the process provides an opportunity to present a complaint before a trained panel, including peers as well as management representatives.

The basic concept of *Peer Review* is simple, but powerful. Impartial managers and employees work together on a formal review panel to adjudicate employment related matters fairly and in a manner consistent with company employment policies, procedures and practices. The *Peer Review* panel considers a situation and fashions a solution, after listening to all the facts and deliberating among themselves. In a clever turn of phrase, the Dollar employee program materials offer that the *Peer Review* panel, "much like a jury would do ... determine[s] 'what's right' rather than 'who's right.'

The *Peer Review* process is considerably more formal than the facilitative approaches because it is an adjudicative process in which the panels are empowered to decide cases in a final and binding fashion and therefore owe the participants some level of due process. While the *Peer Review* panel' duty is to make certain that company policy is fairly applied; the panel cannot make or change company policy. To the maximum extent possible, confidentiality is maintained in the *Peer Review* process. The *Peer Review* process consists, generally, of four stages:

Step 1: *Peer Review* is initiated by the employee submitting a *Peer Review Request Form* (included below in the "Forms & Materials" section). On the form, the employee describes the work-related problem and any previous efforts made by the employee to resolve the situation.

Step 2: The Manager contacts the employee within 48 hours of receiving the formal complaint to provide detailed information on *Peer Review*; the Manager also will make arrangements to convene a *Peer Review* panel. The

Peer Review hearing itself normally will take place within 14 business days following panel selection by the employee, consistent with the guidelines provided below.

Step 3: As in most adjudicative processes, both the initiating party and the respondent provide live testimony and supporting evidence to the panel describing the problem; both parties are entitled to call witnesses to support their version of the facts. The standards for this presentation of evidence are very flexible and lean toward inclusion of anything the panel deems relevant and useful.

Step 4: The panel concludes the hearing by discussing the merits of the case, considering outcome options and casting a confidential ballot recommending a solution. The panel's decision must be reached by a majority vote and is communicated to the employee within five working days of the decision.

The volunteer, five-member *Peer Review* panel includes three peers and two management-level employees. All panelists must meet several threshold eligibility requirements including one year of service with the company, a "standard performer" rating, freedom from disciplinary action during the past six months and lack of participation in progressive counseling at the time of panel application. Each distribution center/office location maintains a minimum of ten volunteers who are eligible to serve on a *Peer Review* panel. The volunteer pool of ten is comprised of six hourly employees and four management-level employees. To ensure fairness, none of the panel members hearing a matter will work in the department of the aggrieved party, nor will any of the management-level panel members report to, or receive reports from, the manager involved in the issue. Volunteers who meet the eligibility requirements are placed on the panel list for that facility on rotating two-year terms to ensure an ongoing supply of experienced panel members to hear cases and to mentor new panelists.

The employee who requests the *Peer Review* selects the five panel members who will hear the case. The process for doing so involves choosing four names from the peer panelist list, three to serve on the panel and one to serve as an alternate. The employee selects the two management representatives by drawing three names at random from the management pool, two to serve on the panel and one to serve as an alternate. If two or more employees requesting *Peer Review* are involved in the same incident, one panel reviews both cases. In such instances, the employees select the panelists to review their cases together, but each case is heard separately. Employee panelists may not serve if they have a conflict of interest with the initiating party. In addition, a panelist may decline to serve on a panel without specifying a reason; in that event, the appropriate (hourly or management) alternate is impaneled. Hourly employees serving as panelists are eligible for compensation for panel meetings which are held outside normal working hours. The hourly employee who files a complaint is also eligible for compensation for time spent in the panel meeting, if it is held outside normal working hours, but is not compensated for time spent preparing for the review panel hearing.

The Program Manager is available to assist employees throughout the *Peer Review* process. The Manager may provide additional explanation of how the process works, how to prepare for a hearing, the roles and responsibilities of all participants, what happens during the *Peer Review* hearing and what "appropriate action(s)" might be taken following the panel's decision.

Option 7: External Mediation: "The STEPS Program."

Dollar General's *Dispute Resolution Program* emphasizes the use of trained employee mediators. Dollar has, however, contracted with an independent company to assist in cases that cannot be managed through internal mediation. That company provides facilitation, fact-finding and/or mediation in some disputes under a program called "STEPS." This program offers Dollar employees the opportunity to participate in these processes, but to have them conducted by a trained and experienced employment dispute resolution professional who is normally an attorney or former judge, and who is not a Dollar General employee.

When an employee is involved in a dispute that is not or cannot be resolved through the company's internal procedures, they may contact the Program Manager to determine whether the case is an appropriate one to be submitted to the STEPS program. In the event the case is appropriate for STEPS, the Dollar ADR Program Manager will arrange for the employee to speak directly with the STEPS national case manager who will further evaluate the case and take charge of administering it should it be accepted for STEPS intervention.

To proceed further, assuming the STEPS case manager advises doing so, the employee must complete a STEPS mediation request form and make a payment of $25.00 made to the STEPS provider. Dollar believes this nominal contribution demonstrates a commitment to the external mediation process, although Dollar pays the balance of the mediation costs, including the mediator's fee and employee travel and other miscellaneous expenses. Moreover, the mediator will not know who has paid the expenses, because Dollar General pays the provider, who in turn pays the mediator, so genuine neutrality is preserved. Should an employee desire the assistance of an attorney or expert, both of which are permitted by program rules, the employee is responsible for those additional expenses. In addition, employees are paid normal salary for time spent in the mediation conference, but not for time spent preparing for the mediation.

Dollar believes this final, external option provides several important benefits to employees considering litigation to resolve matters not resolved internally; these benefits are similar to those realized by Dollar *Internal Mediation*:

- **STEPS is confidential.** While judicial proceedings are open to the general public, STEPS maintains the privacy and confidentiality of parties involved in the dispute.
- **STEPS is fast.** Resolution of disputes is swift and timely, unlike court cases, which may take months of preparation and several years to be fully and finally resolved.
- **STEPS is fair.** The neutral and independent professionals retained JAMS/Endispute are not connected to either party. They are attorneys and former judges who are trained and experienced in employment dispute resolution and are sworn to impartiality.
- **STEPS is less expensive than court.** Other than certain costs associated with your participation in a mediation, most of the cost of using the STEPS program is paid by Dollar General.
- **STEPS is less adversarial than a lawsuit.** The program is intended to provide you with a less adversarial way to resolve disputes and the parties participating in the mediation remain responsible for control of the result.
- **STEPS is final.** Once the matter is resolved through mutual agreement, the outcome is final and binding on both the employee and the company.

ASSESSMENT

At considerable company expense, Dollar General has constructed a series of internal and external processes designed to resolve employee disputes. When one considers the willingness of the company to absorb all costs attendant to the various processes, excluding the nominal STEPS filing fee, there is little doubt about the serious commitment Dollar has made to its employees with its *Dispute Resolution Program*. The program has several unique advantages.

First, the *Internal Mediation* option improves on the Darden model by allowing the employee who is not distrustful of or alienated from the company to seek a non-adjudicative process delivered by peers, as opposed to the Darden model which uses external mediators under American Arbitration Association rules. Doing so enhances employee connectedness with and involvement in the program. Inasmuch as an external provider is available to manage cases for employees unwilling to use internal mechanisms, employees continue to have complete control over the disposition of their case, but with substantially enhanced options.

Second, the three-process initial level of intervention (*Open Door, Human Resources* and *Conference*) also improves somewhat on the Darden model by providing a variety of settings for early resolution from which the employee may choose based on the nature of the case. It is difficult to imagine why an employee would decline to use at least one of the three informal options at the outset of a case, though if they did not feel comfortable doing so, the STEPS option is also available.

The Dollar *Peer Review* model arguably is another improvement on the Darden peer review approach in some respects. For example, it enlarges the size of the review panel to the benefit of both parties. A five-member panel is one that no reasonable person could argue is biased, given the very employee-oriented selection method and the '3+2' composition of the panel. In addition, it is sequenced to <u>follow</u> the full range of facilitative processes. Placing the more adversarial *Peer Review* hearing after the facilitative processes provides the greatest possibility for both types of processes to work. Employees who have tried to negotiate and/or mediate and failed, understand their cases better as a result and are likely to present them more effectively in the *Peer Review* hearing. Employees seeking a non-adversarial approach are offered facilitative options before the adjudicative process poisons the working relationship often necessary for agreement in a facilitative setting.

The fact that the Program Manager position functions outside the legal department is also significant. Clearly, legal issues of considerable consequence are addressed through the program, and lawyers would likely participate occasionally. However, avoiding the appearance of the highly formal and adversarial litigation process by placing dispute resolution services under the aegis of a Program Manager, rather than general counsel is wise.

For these reasons, Dollar's Dispute Resolution Program is working very well overall. An analysis, for example, of forty-two 1997-1998 discrimination and sexual harassment cases settled through the program revealed savings of approximately $850,000. Those savings included attorney fees and litigation costs only, and did not account for potentially significant exposure for compensatory and punitive damages.

As with all of the programs covered in this text, there are concrete ways in which the Dollar General program could be improved. The cost of the program could be significant, perhaps overly so. The company's assumption of the salary costs of the participants as well as the process costs is generous and encourages participation, but may ultimately be excessively expensive. In addition, the program is not subject to precise accounting methods for cost savings realized as a result of settlement. Accordingly, the benefits of the program may be more difficult to articulate than the costs of the program, which are relatively easy to quantify.

These economic concerns highlight another difficulty with the program, the decision to limit *Peer Review* participation. The Dispute Resolution Program is truncated relative to some employees because the *Peer Review* option is not available to a substantial number of Dollar General employees. The consequence of constructing the program in this way may be to encourage external adjudication of cases not ripe for settlement, as no in-house adjudicative option exists for these employees. Perhaps by streamlining the *Peer Review* process, a broader application of the process could be achieved.

Fourth, no external adjudicative process, like arbitration, is provided when internal processes fail and mediation is not appropriate. This may have the effect of encouraging the use of litigation. While arbitration is not always preferable to litigation, it may reduce the time to resolution and thus should be an option explicitly described, if not prescribed in the Dollar General program.

Finally, a signed document of consent to program participation from all employees is advisable in light of the exclusive nature of the processes offered and the finality of the remedies achieved. The courts appear likely to enforce the obligation to participate in reasonable employee dispute resolution programs as a condition of employment. However, the safer approach is to fully explain the program to employees, including the rights afforded to and obligations imposed on them, and to seek their written agreement to participate or a simple statement that they have been advised of the key provisions of the program.

BRIEFING POINT 5.3

While national statistics are virtually impossible to gather, research suggests that somewhere between 18 and 30 million cases move through the civil justice system each year representing huge costs to, among others, business litigants. Consider the statistics in just one state court county courthouse for one year (10/1/96 to 9/30/97): The average jury award in all civil cases was $1.22 million and plaintiffs won over 46% of the cases tried.

DOLLAR GENERAL FORMS & MATERIALS

The following sample letters will assist counsel or management in identifying the full range of potential dispute resolution program users and in creating correspondence targeted to each constituency.

To: **Vice Presidents, Region Managers, District Managers, Certified Training Managers, Store Managers, DC Managers, Office Department Heads**
From: **Cal Turner, Jr.**
Re: **Dispute Resolution Program Announcement**

On August 1, Dollar General will introduce a new benefit called The Dispute Resolution Program, which offers new options for early resolution of employment-related conflict.

The goal for this new approach is to resolve disputes at the lowest possible level, in a "user-friendly" way which ensures fairness and reduces stress. Over the coming months we will begin an education process to equip every employee with the tools needed for problem solving in the workplace --- tools valuable in every aspect of a person's life.

Offering a menu of options, The Dispute Resolution Program will enable everyone to seek help for specific problems using the method most appealing and appropriate for his or her need. The program's 1-800 hotline number will be convenient and confidential.

We feel that an employee ready to use the program will likely call the hotline as a first step but please take a moment to read the attached information so you'll be more fully informed and ready to answer any questions that may come your way.

Attachment: Brochure

Dear Fellow Employee:

Our goal is to value, respect and develop every employee, and, as our employee numbers have grown over the years, we have attempted to provide the best work environment possible.

Even in the best workplaces, just as in good families, problems and disputes happen and we need to work together to resolve them. We have been working to develop a more effective way to resolve workplace disputes, and believe we have developed a new program that will enhance our current open door tradition and further open lines of communication.

Dollar General wants its employees to talk about the issues that concern them. We want to listen and have always been committed to answering any work related questions, problems or complaints.

We're asking everyone to begin using The Dispute Resolution Program on August 1, 1997, when there is a need --- and we will maintain the highest level of support for each of our valued employees.

Sincerely yours,

Cal Turner, Jr.
Chairman & CEO

Dear New Employee:

Welcome to Dollar General. I hope you had an opportunity to review your New Hire Packet and meet with your supervisor or manager to discuss the company policies and benefits. You have probably seen or heard about our mission statement and know the value and respect we have for every employee and our interest in their development. And, as a company of over 25,000 employees, we are fortunate to have a good workplace and few disputes that are not quickly and fairly resolved by employees and their supervisors.

But even in good workplaces problems and disputes happen and we need to work together to resolve them. We have an effective way to do that, one that opens the line of communication, reduces the delay and difficulty in problem solving and promotes "win-win" situations. This benefit is called our Dispute Resolution Program and is available to every employee. The Program's brochure was included in your new hire information packet.

If you have any questions or need a copy of the Program brochure, please talk with your supervisor or call the Program Manager at 1-800-297-5527, and again, welcome to Dollar General.

Sincerely,

Vice President, Human Relations

Dollar General uses the following form to track initial contacts with potential dispute resolution program clients.

Dollar General Corporation Dispute Resolution Program
Contact Form

Case No. _____
(To be filled in by Manager)

Caller Name _____ Date _____

Caller Social Security Number _____

Your Name _____

Your Role ☐DRP Staff ☐Facilitator ☐In-house mediator ☐HR Staff ☐Legal ☐Other

Demographic: (Initial Contact Only)

☐Store   Store No. _____   Region _____

☐Office ☐dc   Where: ☐Scottsville ☐Homerville ☐Ardmore
                                     ☐South Boston   ☐Nashville

☐Field

CASE NOTES: (incident dates, persons involved, concerns, key facts, previous attempts to resolve)

RESOLUTION: (apologies, restitution, future plans, etc. – **who** will do **what** by **when**?)

Prior Contact (if applicable):   Time spent on this contact: _____

☐DRP ☐HR ☐Legal

☐Facilitator ☐Other   Resolved: ☐Yes ☐No

☐In-house mediator   Expenses: _____

white sheet to dispute resolution   *yellow sheet for your reference*

Dollar General uses the following form for initial requests from potential dispute
resolution program clients for internal facilitation.

Dollar General Corporation Dispute Resolution Program
Request for Internal Facilitation

Employee Name _____

Employee Social Security Number _____

Work Location: (please fill in and check appropriate boxes)

☐ Store   Store No. _____   Region _____

☐ Office ☐ dc   Where: ☐ Scottsville   ☐ Homerville   ☐ Ardmore
                               ☐ South Boston   ☐ Nashville

☐ Field

Work Address: _____

_____

Work Phone: (   ) _____

Home Address: _____

_____

Home Phone: (   ) _____

****

I request that the Dispute Resolution Manager schedule a date and time, agreeable to the persons involved
in the dispute, for internal facilitation of the following issue(s):

_____   _____
Employee Signature   Date

Send to:
The Dispute Resolution Program Manager   Phone: 1-800-297-5527
Dollar General Corporation   or
104 Woodmont Boulevard, Suite 300   (615) 783-2133
Nashville, TN 37205   Fax to: (615) 783-2051

Dollar General uses the following form for initial requests from potential dispute resolution program clients for internal peer review.

Dollar General Corporation Dispute Resolution Program
Request for Peer Review

Employee Name _____

Employee Social Security Number _____

Work Location: (please fill in and check appropriate boxes)

☐Store   Store No. _____   Region _____

☐Office ☐dc   Where: ☐Scottsville ☐Homerville ☐Ardmore
                                                      ☐South Boston   ☐Nashville
☐Field

Work Address: _____

_____

Work Phone: (   ) _____

Home Address: _____

_____

Home Phone: (   ) _____

****

1. Describe your work-related problem. You may attach additional pages and any relevant supporting documents.

2. Indicate and previous efforts you have made to resolve your problem and the reasons you are dissatisfied with the results.

_____   _____
Employee Signature   Date

Send to:
The Dispute Resolution Program Manager   Phone: 1-800-297-5527
Dollar General Corporation   or
104 Woodmont Boulevard, Suite 300   (615) 783-2133
Nashville, TN 37205   Fax to: (615) 783-2051

KEY DECISION

The peer review panel is a dispute resolution process that remains largely untested in the state and federal courts. As a result, some level of uncertainty exists relative to the due process obligations owed to the participants in such proceedings and the enforceability of the panel judgments. This decision considers the scope of authority possessed by employee peer review panels. The decision, while drawn from a collective bargaining setting, strongly suggests that panel authority is created by and subject to the document describing the peer review process. Such a holding counsels considerable care in crafting such program documents as they are likely to enforced, albeit after a fairly strict construction.

GRAPHIC COMMUNICATIONS INTERNATIONAL UNION, LOCAL 735-S v. NORTH AMERICAN DIRECTORY CORPORATION II
1996 WL 652683 (1996)
United States District Court, M.D. Pennsylvania.

At issue in this case is whether a dispute concerning a company-provided health care plan may be submitted to a "peer review panel" established under the parties' collective bargaining agreement ("CBA") as the final arbiter of certain employee grievances. Plaintiff Graphic Communications International Union, Local 735-S contends that the dispute, which concerns what the parties intended when they agreed to health care benefits falls within the prerogative of the peer review panel to interpret the CBA. Defendant North American Directory Corporation II opposes submission of the parties' dispute to the peer review panel, arguing that it is outside the authority of that dispute resolution body.

NADCO produces telephone directories from its printing plant located in Hazleton, Pennsylvania. The Union is the collective bargaining representative of production and maintenance employees working at the NADCO plant. During the fall of 1992, the parties engaged in negotiations that culminated in a written collective bargaining agreement. During the course of the negotiations, NADCO proposed establishment of a peer review panel as a final dispute resolution body with respect to employee grievances. The Union acceded to the peer review proposal.

Article 26 of the CBA sets forth the agreed upon three-step grievance procedure. Step 1 requires that a grievance, which is "defined and restricted to an allegation that the employer has violated a specific provision of the collective bargaining agreement," be presented to the grievant's supervisor within five working days of the act or omission being grieved. If the matter is not resolved at that level, the grievant may then "file a written grievance with his/her department head (or designated Company representative)." The written grievance is to state: The exact nature of the grievance; when it occurred; the identity of the employee or employees who claimed to be aggrieved; the provisions of the Agreement that the employee or employees claim the Employer violated; and the remedies sought. If the grievance is not resolved at this step, the grievant has three (3) working days from receipt of the company representative's answer in which to appeal the second step decision in writing by submitting the grievance either to a peer review panel or the Plant Manager. The decision at this third step is to "be final and binding on the grievant, management and the Union."

The peer review panel's scope of authority, however, was circumscribed. The CBA provided that the peer review panel did not "have the authority to render a decision which will add to, subtract from, or change the meaning of specific provisions of this contract; nor shall the Panel have any authority to change Company or plant policy, pay rates, benefits, work rules or to determine future contract terms." Article 26 of the CBA left "[s]pecific details of the Peer Review Procedure [to] be developed by a joint committee of Union members and management within thirty (30) days of ratification." Such details were to be incorporated as an addendum to the CBA. This "addendum," signed by the parties on February 16, 1993, in pertinent part, states:

INTRODUCTION:
The company and the union recognize that from time to time an associate may encounter a problem, question or complaint that, if left unresolved, could affect job satisfaction and work performance ....

As always, associates are encouraged to speak up when they have a concern or complaint about how the application of a union contract provision has affected them. The Open Door Policy provides access to any member of management with whom an associate wishes to express a concern. This can be a very effective way to solve problems.

However, when an associate is faced with a situation that has not been satisfactorily resolved by traditional means, the PEER REVIEW procedure may be used. Peer Review is a formal problem solving system designed to ensure that each associate's concerns are given careful consideration and conflicts are resolved quickly and fairly.

SCOPE OF AUTHORITY:
A Peer Review Panel will hear grievances that have not been resolved at an earlier step of the Grievance Procedure. In other words, peer panels may review management's actions to ensure that the application of the contract was followed correctly and fairly. If they find otherwise, they have the authority to rectify the situation consistent with contract provisions, company practices and/or policies.

The Peer Review Panel can not change contract provisions, company policy, work rules, wage scales, or benefits....

The Addendum goes on to describe the process for selecting two management panelists and three employee panelists. In addition, the addendum specifies the procedure to be followed at the peer review meeting, culminating with a vote by secret ballot to grant, modify or deny the grievance's proposed remedy. Votes are counted only until three like votes are found and each panelist is obligated to sign the final decision form, regardless of his or her vote on the matter.

Article 17.1 of the CBA, in pertinent part, states that "NADCO will provide Health Insurance Benefits, including dental, as described 12/22/92, subject to employee copay of 10% of prevailing premium rate." No other details pertaining to health care insurance benefits are expressed in the CBA. Moreover, there is no attachment to the CBA that sets forth what specific health care insurance benefits were described on December 22, 1992. While the parties disagree as to what changes in existing health care benefits were made by the CBA, they are in agreement that changes to existing coverage were to go into effect on February 1, 1993. Complaints by Union members concerning the changes in insurance coverage culminated in August of 1993 with the filing of a Step 2 written grievance by the Union's Chief Shop Steward. NADCO denied the Step 2 grievance by way of a written memorandum dated August 20, 1993. Contending that it is entitled to have the parties' dispute resolved by a peer review panel, the Union commenced this action on December 22, 1993. The Union requests an Order compelling submission of its grievance to the peer review panel, and has not sought a judicial determination of its underlying claim that the level of benefits provided was inconsistent with the terms agreed to in the CBA.

In this case, NADCO agreed to an employee-dominated peer review panel for the final adjustment of employee grievances. It is this agreement of the parties that federal labor policy seeks to protect. In this case, therefore, the principles developed in the context of labor-management arbitration agreements should apply with equal force to the dispute resolution mechanism to which NADCO had not only assented, but which it had also proposed. In this regard, it is not to be presumed that the composition of the peer review panel guarantees a result favorable to the grievant. Like arbitrators, it is expected that members of such a panel will "decide each case honestly and conscientiously on its merits."

"In applying these principles to a particular collective bargaining agreement, the 'courts must carefully analyze the contractual language to determine whether a particular dispute is arbitrable.'" Trap Rock Industries, 982 F.2d at 888. As noted above, the grievance mechanism in this case extends to any "allegation that the employer has violated a specific provision of the collective bargaining agreement." Because the grievance in question effectively alleges a violation of Article 17.1 of the CBA, it clearly falls within the CBA's definition of the term "grievance." The dispositive issue, therefore, is whether, "because of express exclusion or other forceful evidence," AT&T Technologies, 475 U.S. at 652, the dispute concerning the healthcare package falls outside the jurisdiction of the peer review panel.

In contending that the peer review panel cannot decide the dispute in question, NADCO relies on the express CBA provision that prohibits a peer review panel from changing Company "benefits." The Union's grievance undeniably concerns "benefits," and the remedy sought by the Union is to change benefits provided by the Company under the terms of the CBA that went into effect on December 1, 1992. Thus, on its face, the exclusion from the peer review panel's authority is applicable.

The Union contends that the CBA's limitation on the authority of the peer review panel presents a contract interpretation issue that itself must be submitted to a peer review panel. The CBA, however, does not "clearly and unmistakably" provide that the scope of a peer review panel's authority is to be determined by the panel itself. See AT&T Technologies, 475 U.S. at 649. As recognized in AT&T Technologies, "long standing federal policy of promoting industrial harmony through the use of collective- bargaining agreements" would be undermined if a presumption of arbitrability extended to the question of whether a particular dispute fell within the arbitration clause. Id. at 650-51. The Court explained: The willingness of parties to enter into agreements that provide for arbitration of specified disputes would be "drastically reduced" ... if a labor arbitrator had the "power to determine his own jurisdiction .... Were this the applicable rule, an arbitrator would not be constrained to resolve only those disputes that the parties have agreed in advance to settle by arbitration, but, instead, would be empowered 'to impose obligations outside the contract limited only by his understanding and conscious.'" This concern applies with equal force here. Accordingly, contrary to the Union's assertion, the question of what disputes the parties intended to be submitted to a peer review panel is a question to be decided by the court, and not by a peer review panel.

The Union contends that the language in question merely "prevents the Peer Review from altering the terms of the agreement, not from interpreting the agreement." The Union further asserts that the limitation on the peer review panel's authority was intended to prevent the Panel from becoming "an interest arbiter," and thus unable to determine "the proper amount of benefits," as opposed to interpreting what benefits the parties intended in the CBA.

Had Article 26.1 of the CBA merely provided that "[t]he Panel will not have the authority to render a decision which will add to, subtract from, or change the meaning of specific provisions of this contract," the Union's argument would have great force. As recognized by our Court of Appeals, such language signifies an intent to preclude "interest arbitration." In this case, however, the language in question not only prohibits interest arbitration, but also removes from the peer review panel's authority any power to "change Company or plant policy, pay rates, benefits, [or] work rules ...." This language is expressed as an addition to the prohibition against adding to, subtracting from, or changing the meaning of specific provisions of the contract. Had the parties intended to simply prohibit "interest arbitration" by a peer review panel, there would have been no need to express the additional limitation on authority "to change Company ... benefits ...."

This limitation on a peer review panel's authority concerning changes in Company benefits is not restricted to those disputes that fall outside the CBA's provisions. The limitation is expansive and unambiguous -- a peer review panel cannot reach a decision that requires the Company to provide benefits different than those benefits which the Company believes it is obligated to pay under the CBA.

The fact that NADCO offered to submit the matter to the Plant Manager does not warrant a conclusion that NADCO waived its right to object to having the matter decided by a peer review panel. The CBA does not disqualify the Plant Manager from deciding the issue. It is also noteworthy that NADCO concedes that matters outside a peer review panel's authority may be pursued as breach of contract claims under 29 U.S.C. §185(a). Thus, the Union is not limited to having a management representative decide disputes outside a peer review panel's jurisdiction.

The Union implies that, having agreed to a dispute resolution mechanism in lieu of arbitration, NADCO is obligated to submit any dispute arising under the CBA to a peer review panel. But "[n]o obligation to arbitrate a labor dispute arises solely by operation of law. The law compels a party to submit his grievance to arbitration only if he has contracted to do so." Accordingly, where, as here, the language of the parties' agreement expressly exempts certain disputes from the dispute resolution mechanism, that limitation has been enforced.

The Union asserts that if the dispute in question does not fall within the peer review panel's jurisdiction, "labor strife will persist." The fact that this issue cannot be submitted to a peer review panel, however, does not mean that the Union was without recourse in pursuing its breach of contract claim. The Union plainly had the option of bringing an action in federal court for violation of the CBA under 29 U.S.C. § 185(a). Having expressly limited this case to whether the dispute in question should be submitted to a peer review panel, the Union cannot now be heard to complain that the dispute will remain unresolved because the sole claim presented in this case has been decided in favor of NADCO.

In this case, I find, with "positive assurance," that the CBA is not susceptible of a reasonable interpretation that grievances seeking to change employee benefits may be resolved by a peer review panel.

CHAPTER 6

AIR PRODUCTS & CHEMICALS, INC.[1]

Planning for and Initiating ADR in Complex Business Disputes

DUE DILIGENCE[2]

Air Products & Chemicals, Inc.
7201 Hamilton Boulevard
Allentown, PA 18195-1501
www.airproducts.com

Harold A. Wagner, Chairman/CEO
John P. Jones III, President/COO
Joseph J. Kaminski, Corporate Executive Vice President

Total assets exceeding $ 7.48 billion
Revenues exceeding $ 4.9 billion
Net Income of $ 547 million
Total liabilities of $ 4.82 billion

COMPANY STORY

Air Products and Chemicals, Inc. ("APC") is an international supplier of industrial gases and related equipment, intermediate chemicals and environmental and energy systems. These products are sold to a diverse base of customers in the manufacturing, process, and service industries. APC employs approximately 17,000 people at operations in over 30 countries. The company is headquartered in Pennsylvania's Lehigh Valley and has sales of nearly $5 billion to more than 100 countries around the world. Since its creation, the company has expanded its business through internal development and acquisitions. Air Products ranked 319th in sales and 264th in total assets among *FORTUNE* magazine's April, 1996 list of the 500 largest corporations in the U.S.

APC was founded by Leonard Pool in 1940, in Detroit, Michigan. The company was created to develop a relatively simple, but new idea: on-site production of industrial gases, primarily oxygen. At the time APC was founded, most oxygen

---

[1] The author is deeply grateful to R. Bruce Whitney, Air Products Assistant General Counsel, for his kind and invaluable cooperation in the preparation of this chapter.
[2] Year ended December 31, 1998.

was sold as a highly compressed gas in cylinders that weighed considerably more than the gas product. Air Products proposed building oxygen gas generating facilities adjacent to large-volume gas users, thereby reducing distribution costs. The concept of piping the gas directly from the generator to the point of use proved sound and technically feasible.

APC's mission statement is very thoughtfully crafted. The company objectives, for example, are straightforward, but ambitious:

- Be the first choice of our employees and customers;
- Be an industry leader in safety, health, and the preservation of the environment;
- Build leadership positions relying on our strengths and flawless execution;
- Globalize our business with more than 50 percent of our total corporate sales generated outside the United States; and,
- Achieve consistent, superior financial performance.

The company is also "committed to building lasting commercial relationships based on understanding our customers' businesses. And through this understanding, we continually find ways to help them win in their markets around the world—while maintaining our focus on being an industry leader in safety, health, and preservation of the environment."

A lengthy list of corporate beliefs is also part of the APC mission language. Several portions of the "beliefs" document suggest, at least indirectly, a commitment to ADR in resolving disputes. For example, the company commitment to integrity and ethical conduct describes a philosophy of going beyond simple compliance with the law and of placing honesty with customers and employees in a position of significance.

We demonstrate integrity and ethical conduct in our business and professional relationships.

We value integrity. Our commitment to integrity is the warranty we offer in all we do. A difficult standard? Yes, but a condition of employment. How do we exhibit integrity and ethical conduct in our everyday business lives?

- We strive to be honest at all times, to tell the truth, even when the truth may be uncomfortable.
- We try to live up to our promises. And never promise what we can't deliver. This means we follow through on commitments, we meet deadlines, and we get back to people when we say we will.

- We handle information and data with care, and when appropriate, with confidentiality. This includes budgets, expense reports, promotions, compensation, product specifications, research data, and all other company matters.
- We obey the law, and we don't knowingly do business with those who don't.
- We acknowledge courageous employees who have demonstrated high ethical standards through their behavior.
- And when we make a mistake, we acknowledge it, correct it, learn from it, and then we move on.

We measure our honesty by how others react to us. We want others to trust us, and we work hard to earn and keep that trust: When we work together; when we communicate; when we hire, evaluate, and promote. In everything we do, everywhere we do it. Integrity and ethical conduct. At Air Products, that's the right choice.

Consistent with this value, APC is often the first to suggest the use of ADR in complex litigation settings. It does so by many means, including the letters, clauses and agreements provided in the "Forms & Materials" section of this chapter.

ALTERNATIVE DISPUTE RESOLUTION PROGRAM

APC advocates the use of ADR principally in complex civil litigation matters, though the company is not averse to using it in less significant cases as well. In many ways, this turns on its head the conventional, though arguably misguided, wisdom regarding ADR. Companies often regard the use of ADR as a way to clear away smaller matters, so litigators can focus their attention and energy on the larger and more complex matters, pursuing them in the courtroom through full-blown litigation. APC takes the position that the economic savings potentially realized by ADR are maximized in complex cases in which litigation is normally lengthy, costly and risky. This logic is difficult to rebut.

APC's ADR program has several important innovations. After addressing the APC preference for mediation, we will cover the APC team approach to dispute resolution and litigation management, an ADR oriented method of structuring outside counsel fees, the APC *Mediation Resource Center* and the thoughtful sequence of dispute resolution procedures employed by APC under contract. Following this ADR program overview, two cases in which APC used ADR successfully are described briefly. Finally, APC offers a wealth of very effectively drafted contract clauses and related documents, some of which are included in the "Forms & Materials" section of this chapter.

Preference for Mediation. APC counsel prefer mediation to other forms of ADR and to litigation for many of the same reasons as other companies profiled in this text. First, mediation represents for APC an opportunity to preserve a business relationship that may have future profit potential. Second, mediation can be conducted earlier in the life of a dispute than can a trial, so less costly resolutions are possible. Third, mediation preserves party control over the outcome of a matter. Because many APC cases present highly complex technical issues about which juries likely know very little, it is a significant procedural strength that those who are best able to understand the merits of the case, are the ones who actually decide it. Fourth, mediation is the only formal dispute resolution process in which clients are encouraged to participate directly and substantially throughout the process. Indeed, Bruce Whitney, Air Products Assistant General Counsel, favors strongly the "total involvement of the client in shaping the mediation process and, sometimes, actually presenting portions of the mediation."

Whitney believes that "nothing captures the attention of corporate executives more than letting them know one of them is making all or a major part of the opening statement at the first joint [mediation] session." Involving the client accomplishes two important objectives according to Whitney. First, the opposing party is made aware of the seriousness with which your client views the case. When the executive actually participates, he or she can argue the case in a way a representative cannot. Second, participation "rivets the client's attention on the case and causes a better appreciation not only of your position and its strengths, but of its weaknesses." In fact, when a client declines the invitation to participate directly in a mediation conference, Whitney believes the client can achieve a full understanding of the difficulties of trial practice. Whitney is quick to point out that not every client is an effective advocate, and thus, not every executive should be encouraged to negotiate in mediation. However, when the executive possesses an ability to express company positions clearly and rationally, it is highly advantageous to have the executive present for and involved in the mediation session.

BRIEFING POINT 6.1

"As to when an executive participates, timing is critical. Executive participation at Air Products is normally after the ADR ground rules have been established by lawyers. Thereafter, I completely favor total involvement of the client in ADR processes." **Bruce Whitney, Assistant General Counsel, Air Products and Chemicals, Inc.**

Finally, APC's preference for mediation is reflected in its choice of the cases selected for mediation. While it may seem "counter-intuitive to suggest that a proliferation of issues is" an indicator of a case suitable for mediation, Whitney takes precisely that view. Indeed, he believes the "the judicial approach of narrowing the issues for resolution" often leaves parties frustrated with the outcomes achieved in the courtroom. "Proliferation of issues expands the size of the pie to be divided," says Whitney, and "only mediation allows a complete analysis of the party's overall interests, not just those which are the center of the dispute." While he recognizes that there are settings where ADR might be inappropriate, mediation is Whitney's preferred dispute resolution process.

Trial and ADR Teams. A first specific innovative ADR practice at APC is the creation of separate trial and ADR teams to review and manage a case from its inception. The APC experience is that the major cost savings realized in ADR come from early resolution of complex matters. The company also applies ADR to select tort cases, but focuses its attention primarily on the potential for major complex commercial litigation cost savings through ADR. To maximize cost savings in this setting, APC immediately creates separate ADR and trial teams to manage the matter simultaneously, but from two distinct perspectives. The ADR team is responsible for a complete analysis of the settlement potential of the matter while the trial team begins the process of reviewing the case for effective litigation strategies. The teams consist of different members, because they have completely different missions, and the ADR team <u>always</u> has business representatives.

The teams do not, however, work completely independently of one another. Opposing counsel may have carefully orchestrated contact with each team, so that a message of willingness to settle is delivered from a position of legal strength. "In my view, the trial team gives the ADR team its standing to initiate some form of ADR procedure," says Whitney. Moreover, the trial team may convey to the ADR team deficiencies in the legal case that suggest a concerted effort to settle.

The team approach has several more advantages. First, it coordinates the efforts of experts while allowing them to focus their energies in the areas of their expertise. The team approach allows for settlement to be pursued by businesspeople making bottom-line dollar decisions from a management perspective, while the legal team is free to develop the most effective litigation strategy possible – even if it is a 'scorched-earth' approach that would make settlement offers from the lawyers more difficult. Second, the approach allows each group to work single-mindedly. The ADR team is liberated from trial concerns, while the attorneys on the trial team are not required to attend to settlement at the same time they are aggressively litigating the case. Third, the allocation of this level of resources to a matter conveys clearly to the opposing party that APC takes the case very seriously and intends to pursue all avenues for resolution of the case.

Fee Structuring for ADR. A second noteworthy and innovative feature of the APC ADR program is the fee structure paid to outside counsel on the trial team. APC negotiates with outside counsel to receive a meaningful discount from the firm's standard hourly rates. The firm is then able to earn back the difference between their regular hourly rate and the discounted level. Indeed, APC will pay the hourly rate difference and, in some cases, an additional bonus, if the case is brought to a satisfactory conclusion prior to trial <u>via ADR</u>. The two variables used to calculate the amount of any bonus are time and recovery value if APC is a plaintiff, or time and a reduction from an agreed upon case value if APC is a defendant. When the trial team employs ADR procedures and achieves a favorable ADR settlement early in the case, it receives the deferred fees and, in some particularly favorable cases, an additional bonus. "If, on the other hand, they have not created the ADR opportunity and the case goes into the final pretrial mode and actually commences trial, the deferred fees are gone, no bonus" says Whitney.

This fee system clearly has the effect of motivating outside counsel in a tangible and highly efficient way to use ADR consistent with the client's interest. This is particularly important as outside defense counsel, paid by the hour in most cases, do not share the company's interest in early settlement, unless there is some meaningful fee-related mechanism for rewarding it.   Even outside counsel representing APC as a plaintiff may not gravitate toward the early use of ADR without an economic incentive, because it is simply not the conventional approach to case management.

Mediation Resource Center. Whitney sees his in-house Law Department mission as "making the concept of mediation more user-friendly." Thus, a third 'best practice' in the ADR area: Whitney has created a *Mediation Resource Center* consisting of a substantial collection of files containing ADR-related materials.   Given the APC preference for mediation, the files are largely devoted to that process.   Beyond answering a variety of questions on the use of mediation for in-house counsel, the files function to eliminate the initial objections often raised to the use of mediation in a given matter.   The *Center* also provides resources on locating and selecting a mediator, including appropriate and important questions to be used to conduct an interview of the potential mediator.   In addition, materials on the mediation process and mediation advocacy, representing a client in mediation, are provided.   Finally, materials on ADR contract clause selection and draftsmanship are available for all in-house attorneys.

Structured Negotiation.   While many companies place ADR provisions in their contracts, those clauses often fail to describe the preliminary process of negotiation that ought to precede the use of more formal ADR processes.   APC has crafted a range of contract clauses that address this matter very artfully.   In each, the participants and time frame for the negotiation effort are specifically described, so that the threshold negotiations will have structure and time limitations, failing which a formal ADR process, also specified in the clauses, will be commenced.

In addition to identifying participants, the clauses describe the nature of the information the parties will exchange to support the negotiation.   Without such highly desirable agreements, parties may decline to provide any information without legal requirements to do so, perhaps a discovery request.   As a result, negotiations are doomed before they start, because there is inadequate information to evaluate liability and case value, and therefore, upon which to establish a settlement offer. APC clauses provide the groundwork for a meaningful attempt to negotiate an agreement before any real legal involvement takes place.

Finally, the negotiation clauses have been drafted to lead into a range of other ADR procedures, including mediation, arbitration and the mini-trial, as well as litigation. As a result, parties are aware from the outset of the consequences of failure to successfully negotiate an agreement. Accordingly, the negotiations can be pursued to the extent, and with the effort, each party deems appropriate in light of the process that follows.

ADR Case Successes. Whitney uses two APC cases as examples of the benefits of ADR use in complex litigation. The first involves an engineering company that supplies a range of products through a variety of affiliates. One of the affiliates, an industrial maintenance company, was sued by a consortium of oil companies who alleged that the maintenance company's service was negligent, resulting in an accident at a refinery jointly-owned by the oil companies. The accident caused the refinery to explode catastrophically. The refinery was, as a result, off-line for over 100 days and the property and business interruption damages were initially estimated to be in the $1 billion range.

A trial of the case would have taken weeks, been preceded by years of costly discovery and could have yielded a sizable judgment. In an ADR process, it became clear quickly that the refinery, if cleverly rebuilt, could have significantly increased capacity, something very desirable to the plaintiff oil companies. It was also clear that the refinery needed specialized equipment that the parent of the defendant engineering company was uniquely situated to provide. This equipment could be supplied by the defendant, at a cost much lower than that perceived by the oil companies, which valued the equipment higher than its actual base cost. An agreement reached early on in the dispute, through ADR, and without litigation, leveraged both the promise of increased refinery capacity and the provision of the specialized equipment as the basis for settlement. The oil company plaintiffs received two items of considerable long-term value in the increased capacity and custom equipment. The defendant avoided a trial and the attendant risks, and provided two benefits that represented a much lower out-of-pocket expense than would a conventional money settlement or judgment. Moreover, the provision of the equipment and its long-term maintenance preserves the commercial relationship of the parties to the dispute.

A second noteworthy case resolved through ADR involved a disruption of natural gas flow and the allegation of resulting business interruption damages. An early analysis of the defendants' affiliate companies revealed that several non-party affiliates needed chemicals produced and sold by non-party affiliates of the plaintiffs. A settlement based on favorable long-term sale agreements between the subsidiaries to provide those chemicals was reached. The agreement, according to Whitney, "represented a way that value could be transferred, other than fighting over the dollars that the absence of natural gas may have caused the plaintiff. Further, the parties [could] pick new indices upon which future prices may rise or fall, thereby allowing each party to predict future victory based on different index projections."

ASSESSMENT

APC has successfully used ADR in the most complex of civil cases and achieved highly favorable financial and intangible results by doing so. In addition, it has innovated in areas that are traditionally problematic relative to ADR: outside counsel resistance to its use and in-house counsel ignorance of its value among others. Finally, it has standardized its practice by producing a range of carefully crafted, pre-dispute contract clauses as well as post-dispute agreements and letters promoting ADR use.

Two minor areas for improvement are evident. First, while the two-team approach has considerable merit, it could lead an opponent to wonder who has final authority and which team has precedence over the other. Very careful supervision of the teams would avoid that appearance, as could an initial letter to opposing counsel and client explaining the two-team approach and the APC goals driving it. Indeed, many of the benefits of the approach would be enhanced by providing opposing counsel and client with a standard form document describing the teams and providing instructions for communication with a single contact at APC who would filter information back to the respective teams in an appropriate and timely fashion.

In addition, the *Mediation Resource Center* could be enhanced. A first improvement would be the provision of formal training and continuing legal education in ADR for the in-house legal staff. While access to the materials in the *Center* is useful, it becomes much more effective in the context of a concerted education effort utilizing outside professionals to establish a foundation upon which the resource materials build. Second, to the extent that the materials in the *Center* are oriented toward lawyers, materials and training for non-legal staff is critical. This is particularly true given the expectation that APC executives will participate in the ADR processes in which APC is a party. An executive well-educated in ADR is far more likely to participate enthusiastically <u>and</u> effectively, than one relying on legal department guidance to support business decision-making and negotiations.

AIR PRODUCTS FORMS & MATERIALS

APC has created a range of very useful pre-dispute ADR contract clauses. They are provided below, along with this piece of advice from Bruce Whitney: develop ADR forms and clauses as a joint project involving business and legal participation, "rather than having the business-crafted clause be read for the first time by the litigation lawyers after a dispute has arisen."

ADR CONTRACT CLAUSES:

Art. 24 Negotiation via Neutral Executives - Mediation

24.1   The parties shall attempt in good faith to resolve any disputes arising out of or relating to this Agreement promptly by negotiation between executives who have authority to settle the controversy and who are at a higher level of management than the persons with direct responsibility for administration of this contract. Such higher level executive shall be a Vice President ...[Or other-named title]... and shall not have had any material involvement in the negotiation or performance of this agreement.

24.2   Any party may give the other party written notice of any dispute not resolved in the normal course of business. Within 15 days after delivery of the notice, the receiving party shall submit to the other a written response. The notice and the response shall include a statement, of each party's position and the name and title of the executive who will represent that party and of any other person who will accompany- the executive. Within 30 days after delivery of the disputing party's notice, the executives of both parties shall meet at a mutually acceptable time and place, and thereafter as often as they reasonably deem necessary, to attempt to resolve the dispute. All reasonable requests for information made by one party to the other will be honored.

24.3   If the matter has not been resolved within 60 days of the disputing party's notice, or if the pal-ties fail to met within 30 days, either party may initiate mediation of the controversy or claim as provided hereunder. Both parties may agree to extend the 60 day time limit if progress is being made, otherwise the dispute shall proceed to mediation.

Art. 24   Negotiation via Neutral Executives - Arbitration

24.1   In the event there exists any dispute, controversy or claim arising out of or relating to this Agreement or the breach, termination or validity thereof, the parties to such dispute will attempt to resolve it within ninety (90) days through the mechanism of discussions between one member of each of their respective management teams who did not personally and substantially participate in the events pertaining to the dispute, i.e., neutral executive. The neutral executive shall be a Vice President ...[Or other named title]...and have authority to settle the dispute.

24.2   Written notice to any party shall initiate this procedure. Such notice shall outline the issues in dispute, the identity of the neutral executive and the requested relief. The party receiving the notice shall respond within 15 days with identical information, from its perspective.

24.3   If such dispute cannot be resolved by the parties respective neutral executives within forty-five (45) days of their first meeting, or they fail to meet within forty-five (45) days of the last notice sent by the last responding party, then such dispute shall be finally settled by arbitration between the Parties in accordance with the rules of the American Arbitration Association ("AAA") then in force.

Art. 24   Negotiation via Contract Administrators/Neutral Executives - Then Litigation/Mediation or Arbitration

24.1   The parties will attempt in good faith to resolve any dispute or claim arising out of or relating to this agreement, or breach thereof, promptly via negotiations between representatives of the parties.

24.2   If a dispute or claim should arise, the contract administrator for both parties shall meet at least once and will attempt to resolve the matter. Either contract administrator may request the other to meet within thirty (30) days at a mutually agreed time and place.

24.3   If the matter has not been re solved within thirty (30) days of their first meeting, or if the parties fail to meet within thirty (30) days, the contract administrators shall refer the matter to higher level managers who have authority to settle the controversy and who were not materially involved in the negotiation or performance of this agreement, the "neutral executives". Thereupon, the contract administrators shall promptly prepare and exchange memoranda stating the issues in dispute and their positions, summarizing the negotiations which have taken place and attaching relevant documents. The neutral executives shall meet for negotiations within thirty (30) days of the end of the thirty (30) day period referred to in Art. 24.2, at a mutually agreed time and place.

24.4   If no agreement is reached by the neutral executives within 45 days or the neutral executives fail to meet within 30 days after the end of the 30 day period in Art. 24.2, then ...[litigate, mediate or arbitrate]...

Art. 24   Negotiation Before Litigation

24.1   The parties shall attempt in good faith to resolve any controversy or dispute arising out of or relating to this agreement promptly by negotiations between executives who have authority to settle the controversy. No party shall bring a civil action until the negotiation and mediation provisions of this Agreement have been exhausted.

24.2   Any party may give the other party written notice of any dispute not resolved in the normal course of business. Within fifteen (15) days the receiving party shall submit to the other a written response. The notice and the response shall include (a) a statement of each party's position, and (b) the name and title of the executive who will represent that party and of any other person who will accompany the executive.

24.3   Within thirty (30) days after delivery of the disputing party's notice, the executives of both parties shall meet at a mutually acceptable time and place, and thereafter as often as they reasonably deem necessary, to attempt to resolve the dispute. All reasonable requests for information made by one party to the other will be honored.

24.4   If the matter has not been resolved within sixty (60) days of the disputing party's notice or if the parties fail to meet within thirty (30) days, either party may initiate mediation of the controversy or claim as provided hereinafter.

Art. 24   Dispute Resolution

24.1   Negotiations Between Executives - Mediation then Arbitration

24.1.1   The parties shall attempt in good faith to resolve any disputes arising out of or relating to this Agreement promptly by negotiation between executives who have authority to settle the controversy and who are at a higher level of management than the persons with direct responsibility for administration of this Agreement.

24.1.2   Any party may give the other party written notice of any dispute not resolved in the normal course of business. Within fifteen (15) days after delivery of the disputing party's notice, the receiving party shall submit to the other a written response. The notice and the response shall include (a) a statement of each party's position and a summary of arguments supporting that position, and (b) the name and title of the executive who will represent that party, as well as the name of any other person who will accompany the executive. Within thirty (30) days after delivery of the disputing party's notice, the executives of both parties shall meet at a mutually acceptable time and place, and thereafter as often as they reasonably deem necessary, to attempt to resolve the dispute. All reasonable requests for information made by one party to the other will be honored.

Mediation

If the dispute has not been resolved by negotiation within forty-five (45) days of the giving of the disputing party's notice as set forth in sub-section 24.1.2 hereof, or if the parties have failed to meet within thirty (30) days of the giving of such notice, the parties shall endeavor to settle the dispute by mediation administered by the American Arbitration Association under its Commercial Mediation Rules, before resorting to arbitration.

Arbitration

24.3.1   Any dispute arising out of or relating to this Agreement or the breach, termination or validity thereof, that has not been resolved in the manner set forth in sections 24.1 or 24.2 hereof within ninety (90) days of the giving; of the disputing party's notice as set forth in subsection 24.1.2 hereof, shall be settled by arbitration administered by the American Arbitration Association in accordance with its Commercial Arbitration Rules, as part of its Large, Complex Case Dispute Resolution Program.

24.3.2   Any arbitration shall be conducted in Philadelphia, Pennsylvania, by a panel of three (3) arbitrators, each of whom shall be an attorney with not less than ten (10) years of experience in business or commercial matters.

24.3.3   Any award of the arbitrators shall be accompanied by a statement of the reasons upon which such award is based.

24.3.4   Judgment on any award rendered by the arbitrators may be entered in any court having jurisdiction.

24.3.5   The statutes of limitation of the Commonwealth of Pennsylvania applicable to the commencement of lawsuits shall apply to the commencement of an arbitration hereunder, except that no defense shall be available based upon the passage of time during from the giving of the disputing party's notice under section 24.1.2 hereof or during and negotiation or mediation called for by the terms of sections 24.1 and 24.2 hereof.

In addition to the ADR contract clauses provided, samples of three post-dispute documents used by APC are provided.   The first is a letter to opposing counsel outlining an agreed approach to case settlement efforts.   It is followed by a formal *Agreement to Mediate* and then by a Formal *Confidentiality Agreement*.

Dear :

Outlined below, please find the alternative procedure which _____ and I discussed with you by phone and which you and I have discussed several times since.   As we discussed, I believe this resolution procedure will facilitate our ongoing working relationship, while at the same time it minimizes costs, minimizes the involvement of the various attorneys, and keeps the matter private.

The recommended procedure is as follows:

1. Counsel for the insurance companies have agreed, in principle, to withdraw the suit without prejudice if we can agree with you and the insurance companies on the following terms.

2. The discovery and mediation terms below are compulsory. If the procedures are not followed on the schedule set, the suit may be refiled.

3. _____ agrees to suspend all limitation periods and waive any argument based on the delay caused by this alternative dispute resolution procedure. _____ further agrees not to file any form of lawsuit related to this subject matter while this procedure is being followed.

4. _____ will pay 50% of the mediation costs.

5. _____ and the insurer's counsel will pick a mediator by [date]. If _____ and the insurance companies cannot agree on a mediator, then each party agrees that the Center for Public Resources will select a mediator. The lawsuit will not be withdrawn until a mediator is picked.

6. Once a mediator has been appointed, a mediation protocol conference will be held with the mediator. At the conference, the facts, expert opinion and legal argument which need to be exchanged by the parties will be discussed and itemized. This conference will include businessmen as well as lawyers.

7. Each party agrees that all the facts, expert opinion, depositions (if necessary) will be completed and exchanged within 60 days of the mediation protocol being sent to each party by the mediator.

8. Within 30 days of the end of discovery, a two (consecutive) day mediation will be held, again, including businessman and lawyers. If no agreement can the reached during the two day mediation, both parties agree the mediator will render an award which shall be treated as an arbitration award under California procedure in order to finally resolve the disagreement between _____ and the insurance companies.

9. The subject matter of this procedure shall be limited to contractual property damage claims a approximately _____. Pursuant to the *Rebuild Agreement*, those costs were previously split between the parties. Upon award or settlement under this procedure, the parties will waive the right to bring any other claims related to this incident.

I hope this procedure fits your needs. We are working to persuade the insurance companies that it fits theirs. If you are in agreement, please sign below and return by fax.

Very truly yours,

agreed:_____ date: _____

Mediation Agreement

This Mediation Agreement, dated as of _____, 1998, by and between ("Plaintiffs") and Air Products and Chemicals, Inc.,   (the "Defendants"), and all collectively referred to herein as (the "Litigants").

WHEREAS, the Litigants are involved in a lawsuit captioned _____ et. al. v. Air Products and Chemicals, Inc., et al, pending in the Court of Common Pleas of _____ , Civil Division-Las, No. _____ (the "Lawsuit"); and,

WHEREAS, the Litigants desire to resolve the Lawsuit through the following Alternate Dispute Resolution process, and,

NOW THEREFORE, in consideration of these presents, and intending to be legally bound hereby, the Litigants agree as follows:

Mediation

The Litigants shall within thirty (30) days after the date of this Agreement enter into informal, non-binding mediation, using a third-party mediator, who is mutually acceptable to all Litigants, to mediate the Lawsuit (the "Mediator").

The Mediator

(a) The Litigants agree that the Mediator must have mediation and dispute resolution experience and may have, in addition, one or more of the following qualifications:

- Chemical Engineer with experience in wastewater treatment plant construction and operation;
- Senior Judge with experience and background in construction litigation matters;
- Attorney who specializes in alternate dispute resolution matters and has experience in mediating construction litigation; or

- An Environmental Engineer with experience in wastewater treatment plant construction and operation.

All parties agree, however, that it is important to commence this process and the choice of the mediator should be promptly and flexibly addressed. If no agreement on the mediator can be reached within ten (10) days of the execution of this agreement, the parties agree that a professional mediation service, a company called _____ will select and provide the mediator with the aforementioned qualifications in mind.

The Mediation Process

The following rules shall be followed in the mediation process:

(a)   The Mediator shall fix the date, time and duration of the first mediation session.

(b)   The mediation sessions shall take place at a neutral location agreeable to the Mediator and the Litigants.

(c)   Ten (10) days prior to the first scheduled mediation session, each Litigant shall provide the Mediator and the other Litigants with a brief and concise memorandum setting forth their respective positions with regard to the issues to be resolved.

(d)   The first mediation session shall be a joint session.

(e)   All mediation sessions shall be private.

(f)   The laws, statutes and rules of evidence of the Commonwealth of Pennsylvania shall apply to any mediation conducted hereunder.

(g)   The Mediator shall not be compelled to divulge confidential materials or to testify about the mediation in any adversary proceeding or judicial forum.

(h)   The above shall apply to anything said, done or occurring in the course of the mediation, including any private caucus or discussions between the mediator and any party or counsel before or after the joint mediation session. There shall be no stenographic record of the mediation process, except to memorialize a settlement record.

(i)   The mediation process is to be considered the same as settlement negotiations for the purpose of all state and federal rules protecting disclosures made during such conferences from later discovery or use in evidence. All conduct, statements, promises, offers, views, work product, draft expert reports prepared for the mediation, and opinions, oral or written, made during the mediation by any party or a party's agent, employee, or attorney are confidential and, where appropriate, are to be considered work product and privileged. Such conduct, statements, promises, offers, views, work product, draft expert reports, and opinions shall not be subject to discovery or admissible for any purpose, including impeachment, in any litigation or other proceeding involving the parties.

Provided, however, that evidence otherwise produced during discovery or admissible in evidence is not excluded from discovery or admission in evidence simply as a result of it having been used in connection with this settlement process.

(j)   Each Litigant shall appear at the mediation through counsel and a principal from each party Litigant, who has authority to settle on behalf of that Litigant.

(k)   Experts may be called by the Mediator to explain or clarify an expert's report, at the expense of the Litigant, if the Mediator deems it necessary.

(l)   There shall be no ex parte communication with the Mediator prior to the commencement of the mediation.

Authority of the Mediator

(a)   The Mediator does not have the authority to impose a settlement on the Litigants, but will attempt to help them reach a satisfactory resolution of the Lawsuit. The Mediator is authorized to conduct joint and separate meetings with the Litigants and to make oral and written recommendations for settlement.

(b)   The Mediator shall determine the duration of the meetings, whether they will be joint meetings or whether they will be meetings with one or more Litigants in private, and how long and for what duration the mediation process shall extend with regard to the initial session and any other sessions thereafter.

(c)   The Mediator is authorized to end the mediation whenever, in the judgement of the mediator, further efforts of the mediation would not contribute to a resolution of the Lawsuit between the Litigants. Otherwise, the mediation shall terminate: a) by the execution of a settlement agreement by the parties; b) a written declaration of the mediator to the effect that further efforts at mediation are no longer worthwhile; or, c) by a written declaration of all Litigants that the mediation proceedings are terminated.

(d)   The Mediator shall not be liable to any Litigant for any act or omission in connection with the subject mediation conducted hereunder.

Expenses of the Mediation

The expenses of the mediation shall be shared equally by all Litigants, unless agreed otherwise.

IN WITNESS WHEREOF, the parties hereto have executed this Agreement as of the day and year first above written.

Confidentiality Agreement

This confidentiality agreement is made and entered into this 1st day of October 1997 by and between _____ and Air Products and Chemicals, Inc. ("Air Products"). (Collectively the "Plaintiffs") and (collectively the Defendants").

The parties, acting on behalf of their officers, directors and employees, by and through their undersigned counsel, having agreed to mediation, and intending to be legally bound hereby, agree as follows:

1. At the suggestion of the Court, the parties have agreed to submit their dispute to mediation. To the extent not inconsistent with the provisions herein, the entire mediation process shall be governed by Rule 408 of the Federal Rules of Evidence.

2. All counsel and parties shall treat as privileged and confidential all "mediation communications" and "mediation documents." A "mediation communication" is any communication, verbal or nonverbal, oral or written, made by, between or among a party, its counsel, the mediator or any other person when the communication occurs in preparation for mediation., during a mediation session or outside a mediation session when made to or by the mediator. A "mediation document" is any written material, including copies, prepared or produced for the purpose of, in the course of or pursuant to mediation. The term includes, but is not limited to, memoranda, notes , files, records, financial models and work product of a party, its counsel, its consultants, and the mediator, except that any document which exists independent of the mediation process and which would be subject to discovery shall not be a mediation document.

3. To further the mediation process the parties will exchange certain documents that may be protected by the work product doctrine. Such documents shall be marked "Mediation Document" or "Mediation Communication" and shall be treated as "Highly confidential" pursuant to the terms of the Stipulated Protective Order entered by   on April 4, 1996. Neither party will assert that the production of a Mediation Document constitutes a waiver by the producing party of work product protection, nor will either party assert that this agreement constitutes a concession that any such work product protection is applicable. Among the Mediation Documents to be exchanged is Plaintiffs' damages financial model, which Defendants acknowledge is preliminary and subject to change.

4. At the request of Defendants, and to further the mediation process, representatives of Plaintiffs will meet with counsel for Defendants to provide information concerning Plaintiffs' calculation of lost profits. A transcript of the

meeting may be made, but the participants shall not be under oath. The parties agree that the entire meeting shall be a mediation communication as defined herein and treated as such.

5. Disclosure of mediation communications and mediation documents may not be required or compelled through discovery or any other process. In the event a third party seeks to compel the disclosure of mediation communications or mediation documents pursuant to lawful subpoena, demand by governmental authority, or other legal process, the party being compelled to disclose such materials shall promptly notify all parties to this agreement and resist the production of such materials through all lawful means, including the assertion of a claim of privilege pursuant to 42 Pa. Cons. Stat. Ann 5949.

6. Mediation communications and mediation documents shall not be admissible for any purpose (including impeachment) in any action or proceeding, including, but not limited to, any judicial, administrative or arbitration action or proceeding, except that a settlement document may be introduced in an action or proceeding to enforce the settlement agreement expressed in the document.

KEY DECISION

The following case addresses the critical question of when an agreement reached in a mediation conference is enforceable. While the court rendering the decision indicates that it "clearly possesses the power to enforce a settlement between the parties," it concludes that an enforceable agreement was not reached between the parties because the terms of the purported agreement were not sufficiently definite. The case suggests that companies pursuing mediated agreements should do so carefully and should memorialize in contract language any agreement reached.

THE THERMOS COMPANY v. STARBUCKS CORPORATION
1998 WL 299469 (1998)
United States District Court, N.D. Illinois.

Plaintiffs *The Thermos Company* and *Nippon Sanso Corporation* originally filed this action against Defendants Starbucks Corporation and Pacific Market, Inc. asserting eight separate causes of action. Seven of these eight counts alleged claims for trade dress infringement, unfair competition, false advertising, and other deceptive practices relating to the design and appearance of a stainless steel, vacuum-insulated travel tumbler then distributed by PMI and resold by Starbucks. The remaining count asserts a claim for infringement of Plaintiffs' '977 patent relating to the method used to manufacture Defendants' travel tumblers and other vacuumware products.

In an attempt to reach a voluntary settlement of this case, the parties agreed to conduct a mediation session with a retired federal district court judge-- Judge Nicholas Bua--from this District. This full-day mediation hearing was attended by counsel for all parties and their principals. The dispute presented on this motion centers on whether an enforceable settlement agreement was reached at the mediation session.

Plaintiffs contend that an oral settlement agreement was reached at the mediation. Defendants dispute that any agreement was ever reached at the mediation, let alone a binding oral settlement agreement. The sticking point, apparently then and now, was the parties' alleged agreement to identify a commercially acceptable method to manufacture tumblers for Defendants to use which would not infringe the '977 patent. On this point, the parties apparently decided to "let the Asians work it out"-- referring to PMI's Korean supplier, Seo Hung, and the Japanese headquarters of Nippon Sanso. Defendants' understanding as to what transpired at the mediation session was summarized in a letter from Defendants' counsel, Stuart Dunwoody, to Plaintiffs' counsel Michael Brody. In this letter, Dunwoody stated that "[m]y clients and I are pleased that we were able to reach agreement on all but one point, and are hopeful that the remaining point can be resolved soon." This letter also confirmed the parties agreement to a moratorium on further activity in the litigation to allow for consideration of the prospective "design around" of the tumbler manufacturing process.

Two weeks after the mediation session the parties appeared before the Court on a status hearing to report on their settlement discussions. Brody, appearing on behalf of Plaintiffs, informed the Court as follows: "We've agreed in principle to all the terms of a settlement. We've agreed to a 30-day moratorium in the lawsuit while we work around issues--work out issues on the process and design modifications that the defendants are going to make...." Brody did not recite to the Court any of the terms or conditions of the alleged settlement. Gordon Nash, appearing as Starbucks' local counsel at the status hearing, did not dispute anything that Brody said at the hearing.

Within days of the mediation session, the parties had apparently begun efforts to resolve the remaining "design around" issue. Sometime in early April, Thermos' counsel allegedly proposed two prior art methods--known as the "pinched tube" method and the "coin" method--to which they were prepared to concede would not infringe the '977 patent. Defendants rejected both of these alternatives, however, allegedly claiming that these methods would not produce products of acceptable quality and appearance. Defendants contend that their Korean supplier, Seo Hung, preferred not to use the coin or tube methods because these methods required a higher temperature which led to problems with maintaining the temper of the metal.

Defendants, through the efforts of Seo Hung, were also attempting to come up with a feasible design alternative. These efforts were focused, unlike Plaintiffs', on developing a modification to the "plug" method which would avoid infringement of the '977 patent. Dunwoody (Defendants' counsel) sent Plaintiffs' counsel a letter describing a new, but untested, method--the "plug and washer" method--and asking Plaintiffs whether they would be willing to covenant not to sue on this new method.

Subsequent trials of the plug and washer method, however, proved unsuccessful, and Seo Hung then commenced with experimentation for another alternative process--the "tilted plug" method. Dunwoody provided Plaintiffs' counsel with a settlement proposal and a description of the "tilted plug" method. Over the next several weeks, the parties continued to negotiate regarding the proposed alternative method but were unable to reach common ground.

Prior to a status hearing before the Court, Plaintiffs' counsel suggested to Defendants' counsel that, in view of the difficulty the parties were having in resolving the "design around" issue, it might make sense to sever that issue out and proceed to final settlement on the other issues. Brody informed the Court of the parties' inability to reach an agreement the next day, stating:

> Well, we are still struggling to work out the settlement. We have not gotten there.... We are going to continue working. We think we are probably going to be able to split off the design issues and settle those, but we may have a dispute as to the process issues.... I think we told you last time, we had gotten back some very promising results of the design--or on the method. It turned out that the method they were using to get those results was different from the method we had understood. We have a problem with that method. So, we are back at the discussion table, so to speak. The design issues, I think, are pretty much agreed to....

Upon hearing this presentation that the "design around" issue was seemingly not headed towards resolution, the Court established a discovery cut-off date for the case.

The parties went ahead with their idea to sever out the "design around" issue and proceed to settlement with the remainder of the case. Two written and executed Settlement Agreements were entered into. This settlement disposed of all of the design claims (on the terms allegedly reached at the original mediation), and provided for payment to Plaintiffs of $750,000 (one-half the original settlement amount allegedly agreed to at the mediation). The Settlement Agreement expressly stated that it constituted the "entire agreement" between the parties, and contained an attachment specifically providing that "[c]laims in the pending lawsuit for infringement of [Plaintiffs'] process patent remain unresolved and disputed."

The parties then resumed discovery with regards to the remaining process claim. In response to an interrogatory served by Thermos, Defendants' counsel notified Thermos of the following:

> With respect to the processes at issue, our client advises that since the summer of 1997 the vacuumware products supplied to PMI have been made using methods that Plaintiffs have admitted are prior art to the patent-in-suit. More specifically, the vacuumware products supplied to PMI since the summer of 1997 were made using "pinched" tube methods, which have been used since at least the 1970's, or a "com" method like that taught

in JP 60-36766 (Kokoku). PMI believes that once Plaintiffs come to appreciate that the vacuumware supplied to PMI since the summer of 1997 are made using methods that are without question prior art to the patent-in-suit, this case will be in condition for settlement on a reasonable basis.

This revelation that Defendants' had been using the "pinched tube" and "coin" methods--methods which Plaintiffs had previously proposed as commercially acceptable non-infringing alternatives to the infringing process--resulted in Plaintiffs filing the instant motion. Plaintiffs contend that Defendants use of these methods is a tacit admission as to their commercial acceptability, and that therefore the remaining "design around" issue had been effectively resolved to complete the settlement agreement between the parties. Thus, Plaintiffs' have filed this motion to enforce the oral settlement agreement, seeking payment of the $750,000 that remains unpaid from that alleged agreement. Defendants dispute whether any oral settlement agreement was ever reached at the mediation session.

The issue on this motion is whether the parties reached an enforceable settlement agreement at their March 18, 1997 mediation session. A court reporter was not present at the mediation session, and thus there is no formal record of what transpired at this session. In addition, the parties never prepared or executed a written summary of their alleged agreement at the mediation. Thus, if there is any agreement to be enforced in this case at all, it must necessarily have been an oral agreement between the parties.

Plaintiffs point out that it has long been recognized that oral settlement agreements reached during a mediation or pretrial conference are fully enforceable by the court presiding over the underlying litigation. This Court has previously explained that "a contract can be formed before there is an official document memorializing the deal." Furthermore, the fact that a settlement agreement calls for the parties to reach another agreement in the future--in other words, an "agreement to agree"-- will not prevent the settlement from being enforced. In fact, a party cannot avoid its performance of such an agreement to agree by withholding its consent, in bad faith, to the unresolved term.

In this case, Plaintiffs argue that a binding oral settlement agreement was reached at the mediation session. As evidence of this resolution, Plaintiffs note the parties' status report to the Court that they had "agreed in principle to all of the terms of a settlement." As to remaining "design around" issue, according to Plaintiffs, the parties had agreed to agree on a commercially acceptable, noninfringing manufacturing process for Defendants future use. Defendants refused to approve Plaintiffs' suggestions--the prior art "coin" or "pinched tube" methods--for the alternative process, allegedly claiming that they were not commercially acceptable. Plaintiffs argues that Defendants' subsequent adoption of these methods only months later, implying their "approval" of their commercial use, indicates that their prior refusals were in bad faith. Thus, since the law prohibits parties from avoiding their settlement obligations in bad faith, Plaintiffs now seek to enforce the balance of their alleged oral settlement agreement with Defendants.

Though acknowledging this Court's power to enforce any settlement agreement which was reached between the parties, Defendants vehemently dispute that any such agreement was ever reached at the March 18, 1997 mediation session or at any time thereafter. It is axiomatic that a district court does not have the power to impose a settlement agreement when there was never a meeting of the minds. Defendants argue that there was never a meeting of the minds as to the terms of any settlement agreement, and that there is no evidence that they ever communicated or indicated that they thought otherwise. As for all of the cases cited by Plaintiffs in which oral settlement agreements were enforced, Defendants contend that they are all distinguishable in that they involved parties either agreeing to the settlement in writing or stating on the record the terms of the settlement agreement. In this case, Defendants assert, no formal or written record of the settlement terms was ever created.

Defendants further insist that any "agreement to agree" on an acceptable noninfringing process was never resolved with sufficient definiteness to permit the consummation of a contract. As far as the "design around" issue was concerned, Defendants apparently believed that the alternative process would be some modification of the original "plug" method which was alleged to be violative of the '977 patent. On the other hand, Plaintiffs' understanding of the agreement was that any "commercially acceptable" process would satisfy the remaining condition. Thus, Defendants contend that their use of the "coin" and "pinched tube" methods, after they had been suggested as alternatives by Plaintiffs, was neither an acceptance of their viability nor a tacit admission that their prior rejection of these methods had been in bad faith. Defendants therefore assert that, since there never was a meeting of the minds with respect to the "design around" issue (at the very least), this Court cannot enforce the putative settlement agreement between the parties.

This Court clearly possesses the power to enforce a settlement between the parties in this case, but we must make sure that such a settlement was in fact reached before we do so. The parties both admitted before the Court that the mediation produced "an agreement in principle to all of the terms of a settlement," and expressly indicated a willingness to work out the particulars on the remaining issues. This Court must note, however, that it has seen many "agreements in principle" come apart at the seams, and thus this representation is not determinative of a binding settlement. In addition, the Court must admit that Defendants' conduct following the mediation session raises some suspicion that they have backpedaled from the positions they may have taken at the mediation. But, these matters are only tangential to the dispositive question of whether there is enough evidence to find, as a matter of law, that an enforceable oral settlement agreement was reached at the mediation session. In this Court's view, the present record does not sufficiently demonstrate that an enforceable settlement was reached between the parties.

Even if the parties did reach some sort of settlement in principle, this Court believes that their minds never met as to how the remaining "design around" issue would be resolved. In that regard, this case is very similar to the case of United

States v. Orr Constr. Co., 560 F.2d 765 (7 th Cir.1977), in which the Seventh Circuit reversed a district court's enforcement of a settlement agreement because it was evident that the parties had never had a meeting of the minds as to the proper construction to be given the term "proper legal releases" in their agreement. Though recognizing that "a contract is not invalid simply because it calls for the parties to reach another agreement in the future," the court refused to enforce this "agreement to agree" because (1) the parties' agreement to enter into "proper legal releases" as part of the settlement was too indefinite to be enforced, and (2) the subsequent conduct of the parties proved that they had different interpretations of what constituted "proper legal releases." The court found that the term "proper legal releases" did not have a fixed meaning, either based on linguistic interpretation or an industry practice, nor did the evidence reflect that the parties had subjectively reached a meeting of the minds as to the proper meaning of the term. Thus, the court held that "although the parties thought they had reached a meeting of the minds [to form an enforceable settlement agreement], they in fact had not done so."

Orr definitively teaches why an enforceable agreement cannot be found in this case. Assuming that the parties agreed to agree on a "commercially acceptable noninfringing process" for Defendants to use, such a term lacks sufficient definiteness to form a binding agreement. Plaintiffs have offered no evidence as to how this term is defined in the industry, and this Court is unaware of any formal definition that could be strictly applied in this context. Furthermore, the parties subsequent negotiations in search of an alternative process indicate that they each understood the alleged agreement to be something different. All of Defendants' efforts were geared towards conceiving a modification of the "plug" method which would not infringe the '977 patent, while Plaintiffs apparently felt that the prior art "coin" and "pinched tube" methods were acceptable. Clearly, the parties had diverging views as to what they deemed to be an acceptable alternative process, and this Court does not believe that Defendants later adoption of the prior art methods can be considered an admission that Plaintiffs' proposals satisfied the "design around" issue of their alleged agreement. Thus, under Orr, the Court finds the evidence insufficient to establish an enforceable agreement in this case.

CHAPTER 7

BP AMOCO PLC[1]

Settlement through Private Mediation for Bottom Line Results

DUE DILIGENCE[2]

BP Amoco PLC
200 E. Randolph Drive
Chicago, IL 60601-7125
312.856.6111
www.bpamoco.com

Sir John Browne, Group Chief Executive
Rodney F. Chase, Deputy Group Chief Executive and President, Exploration, Production, Refining, and Marketing
H. Larry Fuller, Co-Chairman
Peter D. Sutherland, Co-Chairman
Sir Ian Prosser, Deputy Chairman

Total assets exceeding $143 billion
Revenues exceeding $108 billion
Net income of $6.4 billion
Capital budget of $53 billion in 1998
Total liabilities of $16.03 billion

COMPANY STORY

BP Amoco, the third largest publicly traded producer of crude oil and natural gas in the world, is a worldwide, integrated petroleum and chemical company. The company finds and develops petroleum resources and provides petroleum-based products and services for a wide range of customers. BP Amoco believes that its business should be both competitively successful and a force for good. The company seeks to conduct its business in a manner that is distinctive, responsible and forward-looking. BP Amoco's business policy goals are:

---

[1] The author is deeply grateful to Messrs. Robert Agdern and Mark Holstein for their kind and invaluable cooperation in the preparation of this chapter.
[2] Year ended December 31, 1997.

1. Deliver excellent and ethical business performance;
2. Provide a benefit to the wider community - individuals and society - through our business performance; and,
3. Avoid accidents in our operations and do no harm to people and no damage to the environment.

To achieve these demanding goals, BP Amoco sets measurable targets, submits the results to external verification and publishes reports of its progress.

BP Amoco employs approximately 100,000 workers worldwide in 100 countries on six continents. It actively explores for product in 24 countries and engages in production activities in 18 countries. Eighteen refineries process a total of about 2.8 million barrels of crude oil daily. The company owns or operates about 23,000 miles of pipelines for transporting crude oil, refined products, natural gas, natural gas liquids and carbon dioxide. Its 1997 worldwide net production averaged 1.9 million barrels of crude oil and natural gas liquids per day and more than 5.7 billion cubic feet of natural gas per day. The company has proven reserves of 14.8 billion barrels of oil and gas equivalent (58% oil, 42% gas).

BP Amoco is the top North American private natural gas producer and the second most significant reserve holder. The company is a leading worldwide marketer of retail gasoline products with 15,500 service stations in the U.S. and 11,500 in the rest of the world. BP Amoco was ranked by consumers, in a national survey, as the highest quality unleaded gasoline brand. BP Amoco is also the world's largest producer of purified terephthalic acid (PTA), which is used to make polyester fabric, cassette tapes, microfilm, tire cord and many types of plastic containers. In addition, they are the world's largest producer of paraxylene, which is used in making PTA. They are the world's largest producer of polybutene, used in cable insulation, fuel additives, and adhesives. The total capacity of their chemical plants is 23 million tons of product a year. Total chemical revenues are $13 billion a year. Finally, BP Amoco is a leading producer of solar energy technology, with solar revenues of $144 million a year.

BP Amoco has a long and interesting corporate history. In 1889, John D. Rockefeller's Standard Oil trust founded the Standard Oil Company. Standard Oil quickly acquired control of nearly all oil related industries in the United States, including drilling, production, refining, marketing, and transporting. In 1911, the United States government filed suit against Standard Oil under the Sherman Anti-Trust Act. The lawsuit reached the Supreme Court, which held that Standard posed an unreasonable and undue restraint of trade in petroleum and its products moving in interstate commerce. The court then set forth the manner in which the Standard Oil Company was to be dissolved, generally on a state by state basis. From the Standard Oil break-up, the major American oil companies of today, including Amoco, were created. Many of these companies merged into new companies and renamed themselves. Ironically, many of BP Amoco's chief current competitors, including Chevron, Exxon and Pennzoil emerged from the break-up. Amoco originated from Standard Oil of Indiana. Shortly after World War I, Standard Oil of Indiana bought the rights to oil-rich land in Kansas, Arkansas, Wyoming, Oklahoma, and Louisiana. In 1925, it spread to Mexico and Venezuela, and in 1939, it bought Standard Oil of Nebraska. Standard Oil of Kansas was purchased in 1948, and in 1954, the American Oil Company was purchased. During this period Amoco expanded into the Gulf of Suez, Trinidad, and the North Sea. In 1985, Standard Oil Company of Indiana renamed itself Amoco Corporation and established its headquarters in Chicago, Illinois.

British Petroleum was founded by William Knox D'Arcy who, shortly after the turn of the century, invested time, money and labor in the belief that worthwhile deposits of oil could be found in Persia (now known as Iran). In the company's first six decades, its prime focus lay in the Middle East. But from the late 1960s the center of gravity shifted westwards, towards the USA and Britain itself. In 1998, British Petroleum and Amoco Corporation merged to form the company described above. In addition, BP Amoco announced in April, 1999, its intention to acquire Arco, a Los Angeles based energy company. This acquisition is, as of this writing, subject to regulatory approval. The ADR program described here was developed by the Amoco Law Department, and has been adopted by the BP Amoco Law Department.

ALTERNATIVE DISPUTE RESOLUTION PROGRAM

The BP Amoco PLC ("BP Amoco") ADR program focuses primarily, but not exclusively, on the use of private facilitative mediation to resolve external legal disputes. The program, launched in June 1998, represents an attempt by senior management to create a new "mindset" regarding dispute resolution. Indeed, inside counsel at BP Amoco are now charged with the duty of asking of each case they handle, 'why not use ADR?' rather than asking occasionally 'is this case appropriate for ADR?' While "pockets of excellence" with respect to the use of ADR have long-existed in the BP Amoco law department, the present ADR program seeks to create broad in-house expertise in ADR and case management.

The program BP Amoco uses for external disputes was created in response to the very substantial expenses it incurs from litigation related fees and expenses. According to the BP Amoco Guide to Alternative Dispute Resolution, 1997 Law Department expenditures on outside counsel fees and expenses related to litigation were $42 million. This sum amounted to 90% of all outside counsel expenditures for the year and over half the entire Law Department budget. In short, ADR presents BP Amoco with a "value proposition" to the extent that it can reduce overall expenditures on law related matters. Beyond cost savings though, BP Amoco counsel are aware of and endeavor to leverage the value of business relationships. Indeed, even where ADR approaches do not offer easily quantifiable cost savings, BP Amoco counsel may pursue such avenues to assure a continued productive business relationship.

Extensive training and resource material has been created to support the efforts made by BP Amoco counsel to use mediation and other ADR mechanisms successfully. Central to the BP Amoco strategy is effective early case evaluation to address the reality of exponentially increasing fees and expenses as the litigation process progresses. The ADR program specifically accounts for the fact that the vast majority of all civil cases settle before a trial, and encourages vigorous efforts by counsel to "use ADR generally, and voluntary mediation specifically," to solve business disputes early and far less expensively. BP Amoco has determined that the cost of litigating rises exponentially as the lawsuit progresses; early evaluation and prompt mediation address this crucial cost issue. The following chart represents a typical 'mid-level' civil case.

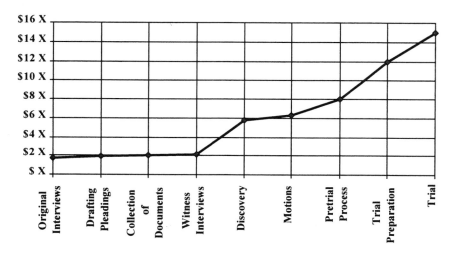

In addition to training and case evaluation guidance, BP Amoco has endeavored to address the inevitability of business disputes preemptively. Pre-dispute ADR agreements have been created to assist counsel in shepherding matters into ADR settings quickly when they arise.

When it is described to both BP Amoco and outside counsel, the BP Amoco dispute resolution program is guided by ten general principles:

1. Analyze the dispute in the context of overall business strategy.
2. Systematically assess financial and reputational exposures.
3. Communicate about litigation risks.
4. Look for leverage points, including relationships and business opportunities.
5. Exhaust creative negotiation approaches.
6. Make mediation/arbitration efforts effective.
7. Create other ADR approaches appropriate for particular circumstances.

8. Develop an overall strategy to avoid litigation taking on a "life of its own."
9. Manage litigation and outside counsel from a workplan.
10. Work to prevent recurring disputes.

BRIEFING POINT 7.1

Contracts obligating parties to use ADR processes to resolves claims are normally enforceable. While there is some uncertainty about whether employees can be made to arbitrate civil rights and other federal statutory claims, courts have virtually always upheld agreements to use ADR in other types of claims.

While no ADR process is precluded from use, the process of choice for BP Amoco counsel is mediation. It is so because other processes, arbitration in particular, are in the judgment of BP Amoco legal leadership simply another form of litigation. As such they present relatively similar risks, delays and costs. BP Amoco makes use of both facilitative and evaluative mediation, employing the latter in cases of considerable technical complexity. It is, however, important to note that a major frustration conveyed by BP Amoco counsel is the shortage of genuinely qualified mediators of either type. Moreover, in cases where an expert determination can assist in settlement, an early neutral evaluation will be procured.

Training. Counsel at BP Amoco are trained by both ADR experienced BP Amoco counsel and experts in the field from outside the company. BP Amoco inside counsel are divided into seven "practice groups" to assure consistently high quality case analysis in specific areas of practice. The "practice groups" make use of ADR at differing levels, but all have received training in ADR. Training is supported by extensive written materials that carefully address case management, screening for ADR use, competence in ADR practice including negotiating skills and process details and contract preparation with respect to the use of ADR clauses. An BP Amoco intranet site provides additional training resources and information on the use of ADR in a variety of commonly encountered settings.

Pre-emptive efforts. Contracts prepared by BP Amoco attorneys often contain clauses requiring or suggesting that cases be submitted to ADR when they arise. BP Amoco hopes such clauses will expedite the use of ADR in cases arising under a given contract. In addition, such clauses convey to business partners a commitment to resolving differences arising under the contract in fashions that value the business relationship embodied in the contract.

In-house counsel are given the following points to guide them in drafting such clauses:

1. Follow the 'keep it simple stupid' principle. If the ADR clause is convoluted and complicated, it may be as time-consuming and confusing as to mimic litigation, defeating its purpose.
2. Specify a forum or a city where the ADR process will take place.

3. Include a choice-of-law provision in the contract. Not only is such a provision sometimes crucial to the substantive matters in the contract, it can affect an ADR provision.
4. If you plan in your ADR clause to incorporate by reference the written rules or procedures of an ADR provider, obtain and study those rules or procedures. Specify how the process will work procedurally.
5. The qualifications of the mediators, arbitrators, neutral fact-finders, or other neutrals (such as for a mini-trial procedure) must be considered.
6. Consider and address how the neutrals will be chosen.
7. Consider who will pay the neutrals' fees, and any administration fees.
8. An ADR clause should incorporate time limits or schedules.
9. By contract, the parties can specify what types of discovery they wish to pursue, perhaps limiting it to two or three depositions, or merely an exchange of statements of fact for the neutrals, and/or a specified number of key documents.
10. An ADR contract should contain a standard provision outlining the procedure to be followed if the dispute occurs at a time when irreparable damage might be suffered by a party while the ADR process is ongoing, or a statute of limitations is expiring. Normally the situation is handled by a provision which states that a party facing perceived irreparable harm may seek a temporary restraining order or preliminary injunction in court, but agrees to a stay of further litigation pending resolution of the ADR proceedings. For a statute of limitations problem, the parties can either draft in a tolling provision or a provision that suit may be filed, but will be stayed until the ADR process is completed. If the ADR procedure ultimately involves a binding procedure, the clause should recognize that the suit can only be filed for the limited purpose of protecting the statute of limitations.
11. A mediation clause should contain a reference to the Federal Rules of Evidence, or a state counterpart, recognizing that mediation is a form of negotiating, and statements or admissions made during the course of the mediation conference are not to be admissible in evidence. The contract also should include a provision that the mediator and his or her files or notes may not be subpoenaed at trial, and that such testimony and materials will not be admissible at trial.

BRIEFING POINT 7.2

Settlement conferences and the disclosures made in the course of those conferences are confidential under the Federal Rules of Evidence. Rule 408 of the federal rules provides: "Evidence of (1) furnishing or offering or promising to furnish, or (2) accepting or offering or promising to accept, a valuable consideration in compromising or attempting to compromise a claim which was disputed as to either validity or amount, is not admissible to prove liability for or the invalidity of the claim or its amount . . ."

---

12. In *all* mediation clauses, there should be a specific requirement that representatives with full authority to negotiate and settle must attend the mediation conference. The dynamics of mediation only work well when the clients and decision makers are present, not just their counsel or representatives.

Case evaluation. BP Amoco Counsel are expected to make a preliminary case evaluation in most matters within 60 days of receiving the matter to assure the possibility of early and cost-effective resolution. Counsel respond to three threshold questions regarding each case:

1. What are the real business objectives that the client is trying to achieve and what strategies will be used to achieve these objectives?
2. How will you begin the settlement effort?
3. What – at least at the present time – are the maximum concessions that could be offered to achieve a fair settlement, i.e., your walkaway position?

In addition to answering these three general questions, counsel have access to a comprehensive ADR screening form. This document, provided in the "BP Amoco Forms & Materials" section at the end of this chapter, helps the attorney thoroughly review the case for ADR suitability. Finally, BP Amoco Law Department has pioneered the use of quantitative risk assessment software to better evaluate complex legal disputes and to better communicate the spectrum of risk to their business unit clients.

Process selection. While mediation is the process of choice for BP Amoco, other ADR processes, including binding adjudicative processes like arbitration are used when appropriate. This determination is made by the in-house attorney managing the individual case. BP Amoco takes the position that mediation is appropriate in both large and small cases, and is "especially helpful for highly emotional disputes where parties need an opportunity to vent ... when there is a desire to maintain or resurrect a positive business relationship ... or when the dispute involves highly confidential or awkward information." BP Amoco also encourages counsel to select mediation to resolve highly technical issues and cases with merit on both sides.

BRIEFING POINT 7.3

Participation in a non-binding settlement process like mediation does not preclude adjudication of the case in the event that settlement discussions are unsuccessful. Companies frequently endeavor to negotiate settlement of some or all of the claims made in a particular case and arbitrate or litigate the remaining claims.

Using mediation successfully. BP Amoco attorneys are given resources to achieve maximum effectiveness in all ADR processes. These materials include not only the initial case screening device, but a variety of useful directions for employing mediation successfully.

Directions are provided for introducing mediation to the other side. These directions suggest that opposing counsel frequently are amenable to ADR use and simply need to be thoughtfully approached about ADR and mediation in particular. In addition, the mediator may be useful in making the initial offer to the opposing party to mediate in a neutral and well-informed way that does not convey any bias. The value of several pre-conditions to mediation such as confidentiality, finality and procedure that should be discussed early and in terms of the drafting of the agreement to mediate is considered as well. Finally, an early, voluntary exchange of relevant, discoverable documents which may facilitate an agreement to mediate with a party concerned that early resolution may be ill-informed and jeopardize a client is suggested.

Counsel are instructed in mediator selection as well. To that end, the thoughtful consideration and choice of an evaluative or facilitative mediator is encouraged. In addition, the need in some cases for a neutral with an understanding of the technical or substantive area in which the dispute arises is discussed. Sources of information on neutrals, both in print and on-line are outlined.[3] Counsel are advised to investigate the success rate of the potential mediator and to seek out mediators who request pre-conference submissions to promote settlement. Finally, an admonition to consider and avoid conflicts of interest is provided. A mediator interview form is provided to BP Amoco attorneys and is included in the "BP Amoco Forms & Materials" section of this chapter.

The "mediation agreement," the document signed by parties who have agreed to mediate and which describes the circumstances under which they have reached that agreement is carefully explained. Several tips for effectively drafting the agreement are provided:

1. Identify the neutral and establish how he or she is paid;
2. Establish who will attend the mediation conference for each party;
3. Make a statement that the entire process is confidential;
4. Establish in detail the mediation conference procedures;
5. Provide 'pause in litigation while mediating' language;
6. Disqualify the mediator as a witness in the underlying litigation and further disqualify him or her as an arbitrator if the dispute does not settle;
7. Provide for the exchange of documents and their return following the process;
8. Establish a schedule for the mediation and conference; and,
9. Set forth the nature of the written submissions and their due dates.

---

[3] A list of resources similar to those presented in the Amoco materials is included as appendix 2.

A discussion of the permissible participants at a mediation conference is provided and the possibility of including the list of agreed participants in the mediation agreement is raised. In addition to discussing the potential participants, the training materials describe the tactical advantages presented by some individuals over others as conference participants. Technical understanding of the underlying issues, for example, is important in a company representative. Balancing the role of in-house and outside counsel is also considered.

Preparation for the conference is explained. Describing the role each participant will have during the conference is strongly encouraged. Performing a mock run-through of the factual presentation of the case is suggested. Assisting participants to understand the role of the mediator and the type of interactions with the mediator they should anticipate is also suggested. Counsel are reminded that mediation, while not adversarial in the conventional sense of the word, is a forum in which persuasive skills are critical. A precise, focused, strong and creative presentation of the case is encouraged within the much broader procedural guidelines of mediation; evidence or materials not admissible in court may be useful and allowable in mediation. Lawyers are exhorted to "exercise the creativity that mediation permits," and advises that "[m]ediation provides you with a new 'poetic license' to use it."

Finally negotiation and advocacy strategies are covered. Understanding that mediation is a setting in which the persuasion of a jury or judge is irrelevant is stressed. Replacing that sort of advocacy with persuasion of the opponent and, perhaps, the mediator is explained. Agreements to settle are described and samples are provided to guide the creation of documents of closure. In short, a complete chronological set of resources guiding the company lawyer through the process of settlement has been constructed by BP Amoco to support their attorneys in the use of ADR.

BRIEFING POINT 7.4

Businesses can participate in ADR settlement processes with confidence in the outcomes reached in those processes. Caselaw supports the enforceability of negotiated agreements resulting from mediation and other non-adjudicative processes, even if the agreement is oral. See Sheng v. Starkey Labs, 117 F. 3d 1081 (1997).

ASSESSMENT

The BP Amoco PLC ADR approach is loosely structured to allow individual attorneys to pursue case specific settlement processes. It is a program with a number of best ADR practices:

1. It is a program organization that encourages individual initiative consistent with particular case circumstances, rather than an ADR case

quota or goal that artificially steers cases to ADR whether they are well
suited for it or not;

2.   The program encourages the use of pre-designed, enforceable ADR
contract clauses to preempt litigation when business disputes arise;

3.   It is a program that promotes a paradigm shift from case analysis
focussing on why to use ADR to one that asks why not use ADR;

4.   Early evaluation to achieve maximum savings is a stated goal of the
program;

5.   The creative use of supportive technology is embodied in the program
in the form of an intranet ADR resource center and proprietary case
evaluation software;

6.   The program focuses on private mediation that allows BP Amoco to
minimize cost, to preserve and enhance business relationships and to
solve legal disputes expeditiously; and,

7.   The recognition of the critical, but not easily quantifiable value of
business relationships and the likelihood that ADR will preserve them
is a cornerstone of the program.

There is, however, room for improvement. First, like many company ADR
programs, BP Amoco lacks clear indicia for measuring the tangible success of the
program. A metric that shows comparative time, economic and intangible savings
would improve the program substantially. It is important to note that the creation of
such a metric is something that no company has done in a completely satisfactory
fashion. While objective factors like cost to resolution and time to resolution are
measured with relative ease, intangible factors like preserved business relationships
and good will are far more difficult to quantify.

Second, one of the strengths of the program could, theoretically, be a
weakness. Programs that lack clear goals or expectations often fail to deliver results.
To the extent that BP Amoco relies on the judgment of each attorney to evaluate a
case for ADR suitability, it invites the possibility that lawyers will not use the
processes with regularity. While some lawyers have quite favorable attitudes toward
ADR, others regard it with considerable suspicion. As a result, BP Amoco runs the
risk of loosing valuable opportunities if lawyers are not meaningfully evaluated on
the regular and expected use they make of ADR.

BP Amoco Forms & Materials

The BP Amoco Early Case Evaluation Plan

Introduction

Effective litigation management includes early, accurate case evaluation. Early case
evaluation is a core competency of the BP Amoco Litigation Workplan. The

workplan methodology contemplates that such an evaluation be completed within the first 60 days of a case.

In some cases, our experience with similar cases allows us to formulate an evaluation without a great deal of additional work.   However, in most cases, an initial investigation must be undertaken before a case can be evaluated, and strategy established.

The checklist that follows is designed to assist you in conducting your initial investigation and evaluation.

BP AMOCO ADR CASE SUITABILITY SCREEN

CONFIDENTIAL AND PROPRIETARY

ATTORNEY WORK PRODUCT

I.		Factors favoring non-adjudicative ADR:	YES	NO
	a.	A significant business relationship could continue or be resumed.	_____	_____
	b.	The position of each side has merit, and a trial or binding arbitration could well result in either side prevailing.	_____	_____
	c.	Trial or binding arbitration preparations would be costly and protracted.	_____	_____
	d.	A speedy resolution is important to us.	_____	_____
	e.	The dispute raises highly technical or other complex factual or legal issues requiring expertise for resolution, as opposed to resolution by a judge, jury or arbitrator ("trier of fact").	_____	_____
	f.	This judge, jury or arbitrator should be avoided.	_____	_____
	g.	The law on the determinative legal issues is well settled.	_____	_____

h.   We need to avoid an adverse
precedent.   _____   _____

i.   Publicity about the case or its
outcome may be a significant threat
to the interests of the company and
should be avoided.   _____   _____

j.   No further discovery is required or
limited discovery will suffice for each
side to assess its strengths and
weaknesses.   _____   _____

k.   The case lends itself to settlement
before a binding decision.   _____   _____

l.   There is a reasonable basis to believe
that a case will settle at or prior to a
binding decision.   _____   _____

m.   A presentation by each side of its
best case will help promote a better
understanding of the issues.   _____   _____

n.   A strong presentation will give one
side or the other a more realistic
attitude about the case.   _____   _____

o.   A mediator could help diffuse the
emotion or hostility which may bar
a settlement of the dispute.   _____   _____

p.   The evaluation of a neutral advisor
could help break the stalemate.   _____   _____

q.   The risk of losing the litigation or
arbitration is unacceptable.   _____   _____

r.   Neither side really wants to litigate
or arbitrate.   _____   _____

s.   There is a need to keep the controversy
private, e.g. the dispute involves
sensitive information, disclosure of
proprietary information, etc.   _____   _____

t.   Resolution through ADR will not
encourage other claims and litigation. _____   _____

u. The factual issues do not turn on the
    credibility of key witnesses.   _____   _____

v. Other.   _____   _____

II. Factors weighing against non-adjudicative ADR:

a. The amount in controversy is extremely
    large.   _____   _____

b. A vital corporate interest is involved. _____   _____

c. The case can most probably be disposed
    of on a motion for summary judgment.   _____   _____

d. At least one side requires a judicial
    decision for its precedential value.   _____   _____

e. There is no bona fide dispute; the
    other side's case is without merit.   _____   _____

f. The advantages of a delay run heavily
    in favor of one side.   _____   _____

g. The case can most probably be settled
    in the near future through simple
    unassisted negotiations.   _____   _____

h. The other side has no motivation to
    settle, e.g. expectations of a large
    judgment, highly emotional stake in
    being vindicated, etc.   _____   _____

i. There is need for discovery first, e.g.
    need to first depose opponent's
    weakest link.   _____   _____

j. One side is refusing to settle so as to
    send a message to others who are not
    parties to the case.   _____   _____

k. The other side may not be forthright
    in its ADR presentation.   _____   _____

l. The negotiating abilities of the
    BP Amoco client are weak.   _____   _____

m. There is a need for continuing court
    supervision of one of the parties.   _____   _____

n.   Other.   _____   _____

III.   **Special factors influencing the use of ADR:**

A.   Summary of prior settlement discussions.

B.   Are there practical alternatives to a monetary settlement? (e.g., return of product, future business relationship, a discount on future goods or services)

Yes   _____   No   _____

1.   If so, what could BP Amoco offer which would respond to the other side's interest or needs?

2.   What practical alternatives could the other side offer which would respond to our interests or needs?

IV.   **Choice of ADR:**

A.   Does ADR seem generally appropriate for this case (or a portion of the case) at this time?

Yes   _____   No   _____

1.   If so, what is the most useful form of ADR in this instance? (Mediation, mini-trial, non-binding arbitration, summary jury trial, settlement conference, expert determination, other)

2.   What factors about that procedure have influenced your choice?

3.   Does the contract require ADR?

4.   What would be the estimated cost to BP Amoco of using that mechanism?

B.   Are there any other special factors (other than those cited above) which make ADR particularly inappropriate for this case at this time?

C.   Has ADR been discussed with the other side? If so, what has been its response?

BP Amoco Mediator Selection Guidelines

Introduction

Selecting a mediator can be the easiest step in litigation or it can be one of the hardest. The mediator works to improve communication across party lines, helps parties clarify their understanding of their own and their opponents interests, probes the strengths and weaknesses of each party's legal positions, identifies areas of agreement and generates options for a mutually agreeable resolution to the dispute. If you have a mediator you know and trust, selecting the mediator may be a matter of seconds for you. If you are new to mediation, new to an area (i.e. mediating in a city outside your normal practice area), or mediating in a special case, you should look for a mediator with appropriate experience in the area in conflict, not just "experience." You should match the type of training to the type of conflict.

All mediators will have vast sums of anecdotal experience upon which they base the theories they have for why and how mediation does (and should) work. There is great variety in mediator technique. Where one mediator considers separate caucuses a detriment to dispute resolution, another begins in them. One mediator handles all their cases on a contingent fee, another claims that it is an ethical breach. Where one mediator insists on extensive pre-session work, another mediator refuses to engage in it. One insists on a simple marathon session – refusing to break no matter how long it takes, another works the "session" into one hour increments stretching over several months and refuses to go over more than five minutes in any session.

Therefore, it is important to meet with and interview the mediator to determine whether the mediator will be appropriate for your case. The following are possible questions which may assist you:

QUESTIONS FOR POTENTIAL MEDIATORS

1. Are you a full-time or a part-time mediator?
2. Are you currently practicing law?
3. If yes, what areas of practice?
4. If no, when did you stop?
5. Are you a member of any professional organizations?
6. Do you have trial experience?
7. Do you have any professional relationship with either party? (affiliates, counsel)
8. Do you have any social relationship with either party? (affiliates, counsel)
9. What is your fee? What does it cover?

10.   Do you expect to be able to represent either party, in this case, if it should go to litigation? At any time in the future?
11.   Have you ever represented either party?
12.   What are your standard practices and procedures in handling a mediation?
13.   What advance documentation do you require?
14.   Do you impose any restrictions, such as confidentiality on the mediations which you oversee?
15.   What discovery, if any, is allowed during the mediation?
16.   Do you have a list of references?
17.   What is your success rate in assisting parties to resolve disputes as a result of the mediation?
18.   How open is your calendar? What is your availability to handle this case? (If a complex case, how much time can you set aside for this matter?)
19.   How much involvement/interaction will you expect from the business representative?
20.   If we don't settle during the first session, would you be willing to reconvene if the parties are interested?
21.   We don't plan to have our trial counsel attend. Is that a problem?
22.   Do you feel you have any expertise in _____ ?
23.   How open do you feel you are to creative solutions?
24.   Explain how you perceive your role as a mediator?
25.   What do you perceive your primary task to be as a mediator?
26.   Do you conduct separate caucuses?
27.   Do you issue evaluations of likely court outcomes?
28.   Do you consider your task to actively propose possible solutions?
29.   How much leeway do you assume you have to share what each side tells you?
30.   Do you establish ground rules for the mediation?

KEY DECISION

Effective mediation requires candor; candor is a product of privacy. The following case describes the creation of a federal mediation privilege allowing for a high level of confidence, beyond that provided by the rules of evidence, that the proceedings undertaken in a mediation conference are strictly confidential.

FOLB v. MOTION PICTURE INDUSTRY PENSION & HEALTH PLANS
16 F.Supp.2d 1164 (1998)
United States District Court C.D. California.

Folb contends that defendants discriminated against him on the basis of gender and retaliated against him because he objected when Directors of the Motion Picture Industry Pension & Health Plans violated fiduciary duties under the Employee

Retirement Income Security Act. Defendants allegedly relied on a complaint that Folb had sexually harassed another employee, Vivian Vasquez, as a pretext to discharge him for his whistle-blowing activities.

In approximately February 1997, Vasquez and the Plans attended a formal mediation with a neutral in an attempt to settle Vasquez' potential claims against defendants arising out of the alleged sexual harassment. Vasquez and the Plans signed a contract agreeing to maintain the confidentiality of the mediation and all statements made in it. Vasquez' counsel prepared a mediation brief and provided copies to opposing counsel and to the mediator. The parties apparently did not reach an agreement during the mediation. After the mediation, counsel presumably engaged in further settlement negotiations and the parties ultimately settled Vasquez' potential claims against the Plans. At some point, counsel for the Plans, Lawrence Michaels of Mitchell, Silberberg & Knupp provided Saxe [the mediator] with a copy of the mediation brief. Neither Vasquez nor her attorneys, Hadsell & Stormer, authorized the Plans to provide a copy of the mediation brief to Saxe.

Saxe refused to produce the mediation brief in response to Folb's subpoena, asserting that the confidentiality of the brief is protected under Fed. R. Evid. 408 and Cal. Evid. Code § 1119. Likewise, Hadsell & Stormer refused to produce either the mediation brief or documents relating to settlement negotiations with the Plans on behalf of Vasquez. Folb sought to compel production of (1) Vasquez' mediation brief; (2) correspondence between Vasquez' counsel and counsel for the Plans regarding mediation or other settlement discussions; and (3) notes to the file prepared by Vasquez' counsel regarding settlement communications. Folb argues that the Plans are trying to take a position in this litigation that is inconsistent with the position he believes they took in settlement negotiations with Vasquez. Folb suggests that the Plans will argue that he was properly terminated for sexually harassing Vasquez, despite the fact that they may have argued in mediation or settlement negotiations with Vasquez that she was never sexually harassed at all. Magistrate Judge Woehrle denied Folb's motion to compel production, and Folb filed the pending Objections.

Federal Rule of Evidence 501 provides: Except as otherwise required by the Constitution of the United States or provided by Act of Congress or in rules prescribed by the Supreme Court pursuant to statutory authority, the privilege of a witness, person, government, State, or political subdivision thereof shall be governed by the principles of the common law as they may be interpreted by the courts of the United States in the light of reason and experience. However, in civil actions and proceedings, with respect to an element of a claim or defense as to which State law applies the rule of decision, the privilege of a witness, person, government, State, or political subdivision thereof shall be determined in accordance with State law.

The federal courts are authorized to define new privileges based on interpretation of common law principles ... in the light of reason and experience. The general rule is that the public is entitled to every person's evidence and that testimonial privileges are disfavored. Consequently, we start with the primary assumption that there is a general duty to give what testimony one is capable of giving. Exceptions from the general rule disfavoring testimonial privileges may be justified, however, by a public good transcending the normally predominant principle of utilizing all rational means for ascertaining the truth. To determine whether an asserted privilege constitutes such a public good the Court must consider (1) whether the asserted privilege is rooted in the imperative need for confidence and trust; (2) whether the privilege would serve public ends; (3) whether the evidentiary detriment caused by exercise of the privilege is modest; and (4) whether denial of the federal privilege would frustrate a parallel privilege adopted by the states.

The existing Federal Rules provide an important backdrop against which to view the role of a mediation privilege in protecting confidentiality and trust between disputants. Federal Rule Civil Procedure 26(b) provides that it is not ground for objection that the information sought will be inadmissible at the trial if the information sought appears reasonably calculated to lead to the discovery of admissible evidence. Recognizing the broad sweep of Rule 26, several courts have looked to Federal Rule of Evidence 408 for protection of settlement negotiations, whether conducted with the assistance of a mediator or in private. Rule 408 provides that evidence of conduct or statements made in compromise negotiations is not admissible. Viewed in combination with Rule 26(b), Rule 408 only protects disputants from disclosure of information to the trier of fact, not from discovery by a third party. Consequently, without a federal mediation privilege under Rule 501, information exchanged in a confidential mediation, like any other information, is subject to the liberal discovery rules of the Federal Rules of Civil Procedure. No federal court has definitively adopted a mediation privilege as federal common law under Rule 501.

In one of the leading cases on the treatment of confidential communications in mediation, however, the Ninth Circuit approved revocation of a subpoena that would have required a Federal Mediation and Conciliation Service mediator to testify in a National Labor Relations Board enforcement proceeding. The Ninth Circuit's conclusion that requiring a federal mediator to disclose information about the mediation proceedings would inevitably impair or destroy the usefulness of the FMCS in future proceedings is equally applicable in the context of private mediation. Nonetheless, mediation in other contexts has clearly become a critical alternative to full-blown litigation, providing the parties a more cost-effective method of resolving disputes and allowing the courts to keep up with ever more unmanageable dockets. Focusing on the role of the mediator, the Macaluso court emphasized that the purpose of excluding mediator testimony is to avoid a breach of impartiality, not a breach of confidentiality. Nevertheless, rules protecting the confidentiality of mediation proceedings and rules protecting the actual or perceived impartiality of mediators serve the same ultimate purpose: encouraging parties to attend mediation and communicate openly and honestly in order to facilitate successful alternative dispute resolution. Whether information divulged in mediation proceedings is disclosed through the compelled testimony of a mediator or the compelled disclosure of documents conveyed to or prepared by the mediator, the side most forthcoming in the mediation process is penalized when third parties can discover confidential communications with the mediator. Refusing to establish a privilege to protect confidential communications in mediation proceedings creates an incentive for participants to withhold sensitive information in mediation or refuse to participate at all.

Today, the Court is faced with a somewhat more attenuated concern: whether the imperative need for confidence and trust that would support creation of a privilege protecting confidential communications with a mediator should extend so far as to protect all oral and written communications between the parties to a mediation. Given the facts presented by the parties before the Court, we need only consider whether communications between parties who agreed in writing to participate in a confidential mediation with a neutral third party should be privileged and whether that privilege should extend to communications between the parties after they have concluded their formal mediation with the neutral.

Several commentators have suggested that successful mediation requires open communication between parties to a dispute. Alan Kirtley argues that without adequate legal protection, a party's candor in mediation might well be 'rewarded' by a discovery request or the revelation of mediation information at trial. A principal purpose of the mediation privilege is to provide mediation parties protection against these downside risks of a failed mediation. In general, however, the academic literature provides little analysis of whether communications disclosed to the opposing party in the course of mediation proceedings should be accorded the same level of protection as private communications between one party and the mediator. At least one district court has concluded that confidential information disclosed in alternative dispute resolution proceedings is privileged.

New York district courts have impliedly approved a federal mediation privilege by sanctioning attorneys for disclosing information revealed during mediation proceedings conducted pursuant to the district court's mediation program. That court reasoned that: if any comments about the dispute made during the negotiation process were later to be construed as admissions, or even to be used to show bias, as permitted in Rule 408, the posturing of the parties in the negotiations could well reduce or eliminate any likelihood of settlement, or even serious negotiation, for the parties would be extremely cautious about advancing a settlement proposal that might be used against them. Thus, they may never get beyond their "positions," even if they both may genuinely want to settle their dispute. Likewise, several of the district court decisions relied upon by the magistrate judge and discussed above hold that settlement communications between parties should be privileged in one fashion or another, whether the information was communicated in the course of a formal mediation with a neutral or simply in private settlement negotiations between the parties.

Every state in the Union, with the exception of Delaware, has adopted a mediation privilege of one type or another. The District of Columbia's court rules on dispute resolution also provide that the mediation process is confidential. While some states provide only limited protection, a majority of the states go beyond protecting communications in private sessions with the mediator, requiring that the entire process be confidential. A number of states provide explicitly that information disclosed in mediation proceedings is not subject to discovery.

Taking the foregoing authorities en masse, the majority of courts to consider the issue appear to have concluded that the need for confidentiality and trust between participants in a mediation proceeding is sufficiently imperative to necessitate the creation of some form of privilege. This conclusion takes on added significance when considered in conjunction with the fact that many federal district courts rely on the success of ADR proceedings to minimize the size of their dockets.

The proliferation of federal district court rules purporting to protect the confidentiality of mediation and the ADR Bill now pending before the United States Senate indicate a commitment to encouraging confidential mediation as an alternative means of resolving disputes that would otherwise result in protracted litigation. Academic authors differ on the necessity of creating a mediation privilege, but most federal courts considering the issue have protected confidential settlement negotiations and mediation proceedings, either by relying on state law or by applying the confidentiality provisions of federal court ADR programs. Having carefully reviewed the foregoing authority, the Court concludes that the proposed blanket mediation privilege is rooted in the imperative need for confidence and trust among participants.

A new privilege must serve a public good sufficiently important to justify creating an exception to the general rule disfavoring testimonial privileges. The attorney-client privilege encourages observance of the law and facilitates the maintenance of an effective adversarial system of justice: the spousal privilege protects the public interest in marital harmony; the doctor-patient and psychotherapist- patient privileges serve the public interest in providing appropriate physical and mental health care. The proposed blanket mediation privilege would serve public ends by encouraging prompt, consensual resolution of disputes, minimizing the social and individual costs of litigation, and markedly reducing the size of state and federal court dockets.

In an early, broad-based critique of the ADR movement, Professor Owen Fiss argues against rules that promote settlement, contending that

> settlement is a capitulation to the conditions of mass society and should be neither encouraged nor praised.... [W]hen the parties settle, society gets less than what appears, and for a price it does not know it is paying. Parties might settle while leaving justice undone. The settlement of a school [desegregation] suit might secure the peace, but not racial equality. Although the parties are prepared to live under the terms they bargained for, and although such peaceful coexistence may be a necessary precondition of justice, and itself a state of affairs to be valued, it is not justice itself. To settle for something means to accept something less than ideal.

Similarly, Aseem Mehta, writing on confidential mediation of environmental disputes, suggests that confidential settlement of such disputes sometimes masks the true cost to society, allowing polluters to settle without alerting non-parties who will be affected by the clean-up plan, shielding producers of harmful products from public scrutiny, and allowing repeat offenders to avoid the creation of adverse precedent.

While this critique has merit and, in an ideal world, we might prefer to allocate all necessary resources to public adjudication of civil disputes, we live in a world of ever-expanding court dockets and limited judicial resources. A privilege that promotes conciliatory dispute resolution and alleviates the press of cases on the formal judicial system also allows the courts to devote those limited resources to fairly adjudicating those cases that do result in protracted litigation. Rather than the hasty judgments born of overcrowded dockets, the courts are able to provide more carefully considered decisions in matters of sufficient public concern that the parties submit their disputes to a court of law, having found it too difficult to reach a mutually agreeable settlement. Idealism aside, a mediation privilege would serve important public ends by promoting conciliatory relationships among parties to a dispute, by reducing litigation costs and by decreasing the size of state and federal court dockets, thereby increasing the quality of justice in those cases that do not settle voluntarily.

In assessing the necessity of adopting a new privilege, the courts must consider whether the likely evidentiary benefit that would result from the denial of the privilege is modest. Where, as here, an employer is sued by one employee claiming wrongful termination based on false allegations of sexual harassment and by another employee asserting a claim for sexual harassment perpetrated by the other employee, a blanket mediation privilege might permit an unscrupulous employer to garner the benefit of the two employees' opposing positions. In open mediation proceedings, the employer would be forced to strike a balance between the two parties positions rather than taking one employee's side in the first case and then shifting to the other side when defending against charges by the second employee. Despite the potential moral implications of fostering such duplicity, however, there is very little evidentiary benefit to be gained by refusing to recognize a mediation privilege.

First, evidence disclosed in mediation may be obtained directly from the parties to the mediation by using normal discovery channels. For example, a person's admission in mediation proceedings may, at least theoretically, be elicited in response to a request for admission or to questions in a deposition or in written interrogatories. In addition, to the extent a party takes advantage of the opportunity to use the cloak of confidentiality to take inconsistent positions in related litigation, evidence of that inconsistent position only comes into being as a result of the party's willingness to attend mediation. Absent a privilege protecting the confidentiality of mediation, the inconsistent position would presumably never come to light.

Despite the potential need to limit a federal mediation privilege in certain types of cases, the matter before the Court is directly in line with the Supreme Court's view that a new federal privilege results in little evidentiary detriment where the evidence lost would simply never come into being if the privilege did not exist.

In fact, this rationale applies even more strongly in the context of mediation proceedings than in a psychotherapeutic relationship because mediation is part of an overall litigation strategy while psychotherapy is a response to health care concerns. The decision to seek out a therapist is often made without considering the potential impact on pending litigation. By contrast, anyone who attends a mediation, or decides not to use mediation to attempt to resolve a dispute, will consider the effect of disclosures on the pending or potential litigation.

The fact that the states have not settled on the scope of protection to provide should not prevent the federal courts from determining that in light of reason and experience we should adopt a federal mediation privilege. While the contours of such a federal privilege need to be fleshed out over time, state legislatures and state courts have overwhelmingly chosen to protect confidential communications in mediation proceedings in order to facilitate settlement of disputes through alternative dispute resolution. Denial of the federal privilege ... would frustrate the purposes of the state legislation that was enacted to foster these confidential communications. Accordingly, this Court finds it is appropriate, in light of reason and experience, to adopt a federal mediation privilege applicable to all communications made in conjunction with a formal mediation.

The mediation underlying the instant dispute was a formal mediation with a neutral mediator, not a private settlement discussion between the parties. Accordingly, the mediation privilege adopted today applies only to information disclosed in conjunction with mediation proceedings with a neutral. On the facts presented here, the Court concludes that communications to the mediator and communications between parties during the mediation are protected. In addition, communications in preparation for and during the course of a mediation with a neutral must be protected. Subsequent negotiations between the parties, however, are not protected even if they include information initially disclosed in the mediation. To protect additional communications, the parties are required to return to mediation. A contrary rule would permit a party to claim the privilege with respect to any settlement negotiations so long as the communications took place following an attempt to mediate the dispute.

In short, the Court concludes that encouraging mediation by adopting a federal mediation privilege will provide a public good transcending the normally predominant principle of utilizing all rational means for ascertaining the truth.

CHAPTER 8

GEORGIA-PACIFIC CORPORATION[1]

Advance Planning and Active Management for Effective Business Dispute Resolution

Due Diligence[2]

Georgia-Pacific Corporation
133 Peachtree Street, NE
P.O. Box 105605
Atlanta, Georgia 30348-5605
404.652.4000
http://www.gp.com/

A.D. Correll, Chairman, Chief Executive Officer & President
James E. Bostic, Jr., Senior Vice President-Environmental, Government Affairs &
    Communications
James F. Kelley, Senior Vice President-Law & General Counsel

Total assets exceeding $11.5 billion
Net income of $98 million
Total liabilities of $2.38 billion
Total equity of $3.2 billion

Company Story

Georgia-Pacific Corporation was founded in 1927 in Augusta, Georgia by Owen R. Cheatham. The company was started with a $12,000 investment as the Georgia Hardwood Lumber Company, a wholesaler of hardwood lumber. By 1938, the company was operating five sawmills in the southern United States, and by 1945 was the largest supplier of lumber to the U.S. armed forces. The company was first listed on the NYSE in 1949.

Georgia-Pacific is now one of the world's leading manufacturers and distributors of building products, pulp and paper, manufacturing and distributing products used in virtually every environment. It is the largest producer of structural

---

[1] The author is deeply grateful to Phillip M. Armstrong, Georgia-Pacific Associate General Counsel-ADR & Litigation for his kind and invaluable cooperation in the preparation of this chapter.
[2] Year ended December 31, 1998

wood panels in the United States, with approximately 20 percent of total U.S. industry capacity and a leading producer of tissue products, with approximately 10 percent of total U.S. capacity in a variety of brands. Georgia-Pacific is also the leading U.S. supplier of wood resins, adhesives and specialty chemicals. It is, in addition, the second largest producer of gypsum products, containerboard, communication papers and lumber in North America. Finally, Georgia-Pacific is the world's second largest producer of market pulp.

The company has operating facilities in more than 400 locations in the United States and Canada and employs over 47,000 people; 1998 sales totaled $13.2 billion. It is responsible for maintaining more than six million acres of company-owned forestlands in the United States and Canada.

The building products Georgia-Pacific manufacturers include plywood, oriented strand board and other wood panels, lumber, chemicals and gypsum board at 139 facilities in the United States and Canada. The company is also the country's largest building products wholesaler, with a delivery network that serves markets throughout the U.S.

Georgia-Pacific's chemical business began in 1959, with the start-up of a plant in Coos Bay, Oregon, to supply the company's wood products operations on the West Coast. Soon after, the company pioneered the development of southern pine plywood adhesives and began resin production in the South. During the years that followed, the company expanded into industrial resins, paper and pulp chemicals, and specialty polyethylene films. Through internal growth and acquisition, Its Chemical Division now generates more than half a billion dollars in annual sales from producing plants, distribution facilities and laboratories at more than 30 locations across the nation.

The Pulp and Paperboard Group operates six mills with a combined annual capacity of 2.1 million tons, approximately 20 percent of domestic capacity. The corporation produces southern softwood and hardwood and northern hardwood pulps for use in the manufacture of many paper grades. Georgia-Pacific is also a major supplier of "fluff pulp," which is used primarily in the manufacture of disposable diapers and other sanitary items. The Corporation exports approximately 57 percent of its market pulp, primarily to Europe, Asia and Latin America. Georgia-Pacific can produce 400,000 tons of bleached paperboard each year for use in frozen food containers, food service items and other products.

The Group also produces containerboard, corrugated containers and packaging and craft paper. Containerboard is the brown paper from which most corrugated boxes are made. Annual capacity at Georgia-Pacific's four containerboard mills totals 3 million tons, representing approximately 10 percent of U.S. capacity. Georgia-Pacific is the largest U.S. supplier of containerboard to independent box makers. Approximately 72 percent of its containerboard production is used by the corporation's corrugated packaging plants. The company sells the remainder to independent converters in the United States, Central America and the Far East. During 1998, the corporation exported 520,000 tons of containerboard. In addition to standard corrugated containers, company packaging plants manufacture many specialty packaging products. These include double-wall and triple-wall boxes, bulk bins, water-resistant packaging and high-finish and preprinted packaging for point-of-sale displays. Georgia-Pacific operates a *Technology and Development Center*, to design and test packaging.

The Georgia-Pacific ADR program fits squarely within the company mission statement which commits the company to "... achieving excellence in operations and staff functions at all levels of the company in order to provide superior returns ... on shareholder investments."

ALTERNATIVE DISPUTE RESOLUTION PROGRAM

Overview. The Georgia-Pacific ADR program is a coordinated in-house effort to utilize a variety of ADR mechanisms to resolve its external civil legal disputes effectively. The company is sufficiently committed to the use of ADR that an Associate General Counsel oversees the implementation of its ADR initiatives. Following an overview of the program, we will consider four features of the program of particular importance to the reader:

- The use of ADR contract clauses;
- In-house technology and training;
- Supervision of outside counsel; and,
- An approach to measuring ADR savings.

Under normal business circumstances, when Georgia-Pacific is sued, an in-house attorney carries out an initial investigation and hires outside counsel to defend the company. Outside counsel would, at that point, file a responsive pleading, initiate discovery, and represent the company until the case was resolved. The result, usually after two to three years and the expenditure of many thousands of dollars in fees and costs, is that the vast majority of cases settle. Georgia-Pacific's experience in this regard is similar to that of most American businesses. Indeed, an historical analysis of Georgia-Pacific's docket revealed that it often settled cases for dollar amounts that could have been estimated much earlier in the litigation process, prior to incurring significant legal expenses. James Kelley, senior vice president and general counsel, decided in 1993 that early settlement for the estimated value of a case was a more efficient approach in many cases than protracted litigation.

BRIEFING POINT 8.1

"Even when the employer prevails on summary judgment, he has usually spent $50,000 or more in attorney's fees, in addition to the organization's time and resources. McDermott, E. & Berkeley, A., <u>Alternative Dispute Resolution in Workplace: Concepts and Techniques for Human Resource Executives and their Counsel</u>, Quorum Books (1996).

To realize the potential savings that early settlement offered, Kelley restructured the law department so that fewer lawyers were managing outside counsel and instead did more legal work in-house. He required lawyers to become actively involved in each case to which they were assigned. And, he created a separate in-house litigation group to manage the bulk of the company's lawsuits. Early case evaluation and stressing ADR consideration, were made standard procedures in cases filed against the company. Staff counsel received advanced training in ADR. Georgia-Pacific now endeavors to settle most cases in the first 60-90 days following the filing of suit.

To do so, the company program focuses very heavily on early settlement-oriented ADR procedures, primarily negotiation and private mediation. Georgia-Pacific sees these processes as both the fastest and the most cost-effective ones for case management. Phillip Armstrong, Georgia-Pacific's associate general counsel for ADR and litigation, believes in-house lawyers have the greatest success resolving disputes through "direct negotiation" with opposing parties – putting business people from each side together to determine whether they can negotiate a solution. Negotiation is the least complicated and most informal of the ADR settlement procedures the company uses.

Armstrong believes that face-to-face negotiation frequently results in a considerable difference in case valuation. "It proves ... that you can't always determine what the other side's opinion is of the value of their case. Often, they value cases far less than we had." After direct negotiation, Armstrong says, mediation ranks as the ADR process with the second highest rate of success and cost savings. Arbitration or litigation are processes of last resort. The company uses ADR only when a legitimate claim has been made against it, often in the context of an important business relationship worth preserving, and will litigate matters best resolved in a courtroom, perhaps to establish an important business or legal precedent. Kelley and Armstrong both stress that the use of ADR should not be interpreted as inferring fear of the courtroom and will exhaustively litigate when appropriate. In addition, neither believes that there is any reason to think that use of ADR encourages increased litigation against the company to recover nuisance value money.

Armstrong offers the following general pointers for business persons seeking to create ADR programs:[3]

1. **Get top management buy-in.** The executives in the company must be shown the economic benefits of early case resolution versus a winning-at-all-costs philosophy.
2. **Start training.** Although most lawyers today are at least familiar with ADR, few have had formal training. An interactive training session, complete with role-play, is money well spent.

---

[3] Phillip M. Armstrong. "Case Study: Georgia-Pacific's Aggressive Use of Early Case Evaluation and ADR." *ACCA Docket* 16, No. 6 (1998): 42-48

3. **Start small.** Don't try to change the corporate culture too quickly. Begin, perhaps, with a category of cases, such as product liability claims, and then expand.

4. **Incorporate the practice.** Require ADR clauses to be routinely incorporated into your commercial agreements. This provides a mutual, face-saving method of forcing the parties to use alternative means to resolve disputes before the battle lines are drawn.

5. **Grant authority.** Assign someone full-time responsibility for promotion and use of ADR. In-house expertise is essential to any successful program.

6. **Begin immediately.** When the existence of a dispute becomes known, promptly investigate the facts, objectively evaluate the case, and, when appropriate, initiate negotiation or ADR.

7. **Build a resource library.** Treatises and periodicals on alternative dispute resolution are both extensive and readily available.

8. **Fully litigate cases if necessary.** An aggressive program does not mean every case is suitable for ADR. Screen every case however, to determine its suitability for early settlement or ADR.

9. **Measure the results.** This can be somewhat tricky because one must necessarily estimate the cost of litigation. Yet most litigators have a sense for what a case will cost and, with some exceptions, can reasonably estimate the outcome. It's not a science, but the ability to properly evaluate a claim in its early stages is key to a successful program.

10. **Be patient.** It takes time to build a successful program and not every ADR experience will be positive. Over time the results will speak for themselves.

Use of ADR contract clauses. The first outstanding aspect of the Georgia-Pacific program is the use of well-crafted, multi-step ADR clauses in company contracts. Using such clauses assures the company that it will have the opportunity to avoid litigation and use ADR in matters in which it is appropriate to do so. Although the company provides four additional optional ADR clauses, its preferred clause does not obligate the parties to pursue arbitration in the event that settlement efforts fail.[4] Armstrong contends that clauses that culminate in arbitration when settlement efforts fail actually <u>reduce</u> the likelihood of settlement. He argues that it is the "cloud of costly and time-consuming litigation" that motivates parties toward settlement and without that cloud, parties will not make good faith efforts to agree. In addition, he believes that mediation is a preferable process to arbitration; the latter should be pursued only as a last resort. Finally, he notes that arbitration is often virtually indistinguishable from full-scale litigation in terms of time spent and costs incurred and therefore is not necessarily a preferable option to a trial.

---

[4] The "Forms & Materials" section at the end of this chapter sets forth three additional clauses.

> **BRIEFING POINT 8.2**
>
> State courts may also require ADR in a variety of cases. Many states have mandatory court annexed arbitration of cases in smaller dollar ranges. Illinois, for example, allows each court circuit to establish a mandatory arbitration program for civil cases with values up to $30,000; circuits may seek authority to mandate for arbitration for cases with greater dollar values as well.

The preferred Georgia-Pacific dispute resolution clause provides:

DISPUTE RESOLUTION

The parties will attempt in good faith to resolve any controversy or claim arising out or relating to this Agreement promptly by negotiations between representatives and Senior Executives of the parties who have authority to settle the controversy.

If a controversy or claim should arise, appropriate representatives of each party ("Managers") will meet at least once and will attempt to resolve the matter. The Managers will make every effort to meet as soon as reasonably possible at a mutually agreed time and place.

If the matter has not been resolved within twenty days of their first meeting, the Managers shall refer the matter to Senior Executives, who do not have direct responsibility for administration of this Agreement ("Senior Executives"). Thereupon, the Managers shall promptly prepare and exchange memoranda stating (a) the issues in dispute and their respective position, summarizing the evidence and arguments supporting their positions, and the negotiations which have taken place, and attaching relevant documents, and (b) the name and title of the Senior Executive who will represent that party. The Senior Executives shall meet for negotiations at a mutually agreed time and place within fourteen days of the end of the twenty-day period referred to above, and thereafter as often as they deem reasonably necessary to exchange relevant information and to attempt to resolve the dispute.

If the matter has not been resolved within thirty days of the meeting of the Senior Executives, or if either party will not meet within thirty days of the end of the twenty-day period referred to in the preceding paragraph, the parties will attempt in good faith to resolve the controversy or claim by mediation in accordance with the current model procedural rules of the [CPR Institute for Dispute Resolution.] [American Arbitration Association.]

Cont'd

If the matter has not been resolved pursuant to the aforesaid mediation procedure within thirty days of the commencement of such procedure, or if either party will not participate in a mediation, either party may initiate litigation or otherwise pursue whatever remedies may be available to such party.

All deadlines specified in this section may be extended by mutual agreement.

The procedures specified in this section shall be the sole and exclusive procedures for the resolution of disputes between the parties arising out of or relating to this Agreement; provided, however, that a party may seek a preliminary injunction or other preliminary judicial relief if in its judgment such action is necessary to avoid irreparable damage. Despite such action the parties will continue to participate in good faith in the procedures specified in this section. All applicable statutes of limitation shall be tolled while the procedures specified in this section are pending. The parties will take such action, if any, required to effectuate such tolling.

In-house Technology and Training. The second noteworthy feature of the Georgia-Pacific's ADR program is the effective transmission of program related knowledge to company personnel. The company intranet serves as a threshold source of information on ADR. The Law Department site provides a description of the company's ADR initiatives. Staff attorneys receive comprehensive, hands-on and systematic training in ADR, primarily in mediation advocacy. That training includes case and client preparation prior to the mediation conference, strategies for presenting a case in mediation, critical negotiation expertise, understanding the role of the mediator so as to use that process effectively and closing the deal or refusing to agree.

Supervision of Outside Counsel. A third noteworthy company innovation involves the supervision of private, outside legal counsel retained to represent company interests in civil legal matters. Georgia-Pacific has written careful *Guidelines for Outside Counsel* intended to clearly communicate the basis for retention and the expectations it has of outside counsel. Several provisions in the Guidelines support the efforts of the company to use ADR regularly and effectively.

> **BRIEFING POINT 8.3**
> We measured performance of our litigation group in part on the basis of early and cost effective case resolution by measurement of cycle time. This was done in a couple of ways, one just measuring cycle time from beginning to end of all case dispositions from year to year and tracking this and second, by means of a case cost resolution matrix. This chart plotted out the cost of litigation as it proceeded through its stages and, among other things, reflected where on the continuum the particular dispositions for a given year fell. This was a graphic means of demonstrating that early resolution avoided the mountainous transactional costs of discovery and, ultimately, pretrial preparation. **Hans Stucki, as counsel for Motorola, Inc.**

Under general guidelines, Georgia-Pacific preserves the opportunity, without compromising the skills or judgment of the outside attorney, to participate in litigation strategy planning. Doing so allows it to retain a meaningful role in dispute resolution process selection and use. Outside counsel do <u>not</u> have the same stake in the use of ADR processes that in-house counsel do, because ADR tends to reduce the total time to conclusion for case and therefore the fee earned in representation. As a result, the preservation of an in-house role in case management is critical and use of up-front retention guidelines is a very effective way to accomplish the preservation of that role.

> **GENERAL GUIDELINES:** The Georgia-Pacific legal staff and outside counsel are jointly responsible for planning and implementing a legal strategy for each matter (the "matter") in order to provide excellent representation of the Company. We want the best thinking, strongest advocacy, and greatest initiative, perseverance and steadfastness, from our outside counsel. We have joint responsibility for developing an effective strategy for each matter, which will include your support and input in preparing a plan that will bring us the desired objective for each matter.

Similarly, Georgia-Pacific initially places outside counsel on notice of its intention to manage cases through its proprietary database for the purpose analyzing them in the grand scheme of law department objectives. The effect of doing so is similar to the general guidelines provision above – it preserves a case management role for the in-house law department in case management, and at the same time conveys to outside counsel the intention of the company to track progress as measured by other cases.

> **CASE MANAGEMENT:** The Georgia-Pacific law department utilizes the latest technology available in case management. Upon your engagement, you will be provided with an LDIS (Law Department Information System) database record number that you should include with all correspondence relating to that specific matter. LDIS is used to manage all aspects of a case, including outside counsel

performance. We have found this to be an invaluable tool, providing analysis of individual cases and cross-functional analysis of the entire scope of legal matters managed by the law department. It also serves as a centralized communication tool within the department to share information on both active and historical legal matters.

Preparation of complete, though flexible litigation plans and budgets has several valuable outcomes. First, it allows Georgia-Pacific to understand early the long-term case objectives of outside counsel. Second, it permits the company to evaluate the competence of outside counsel by forcing the attorney to consider and communicate the long-term case resolution approach. Third, it creates an opportunity to suggest ADR to outside counsel if they do not address it in their initial plan. Fourth, it becomes a blueprint for the case, allowing Georgia-Pacific to assess the progress of outside counsel toward resolution of the matter. Finally, because it includes a budget, it provides the company with an early, but effective opportunity to practice cost containment.

LITIGATION PLAN: We believe the process of organizing your thoughts and preparing a litigation plan is beneficial to you and the Company. Accordingly, we expect you to prepare a plan for each litigated matter and to have it approved by the G-P attorney handling the matter. An initial litigation plan should be prepared during the first thirty days following the assignment of a new case and should closely follow the Budget you will submit.

LITIGATION BUDGET: A litigation budget should be prepared and submitted as soon as reasonably possible after you are retained, but in no event more than thirty days after your retention. The budget for a litigation matter should be prepared on a 12 month rolling basis, however, it must be detailed to match the Georgia-Pacific fiscal year January through December, and be revised every ninety days to accommodate developments as the case progresses. The initial budget also should include an estimate of the total fees and total disbursements required to carry the case to conclusion. The total budget estimate will likely include certain assumptions because of the uncertainties involved at the early stage of litigation. Please identify all assumptions on which your estimate is based.

Finally, a vigorous statement in support of <u>early</u> settlement places outside counsel on notice of the company's intention to manage the matter aggressively in that direction. Some private attorneys take cases and pay lip-service only to early settlement in the interest of pursuing the lucrative business of discovery and motion practice. Doing so in view of this unequivocal clause would jeopardize the possibility of future business from Georgia-Pacific.

SETTLEMENT: We strongly believe the exploration of settlement at early stages in litigation is often beneficial. We may discuss with you the advisability of obtaining settlement demands at very early stages of the litigation. You should not, however, undertake any discussions in this regard (or indirectly imply any interest in settlement) without our prior approval.

An approach to measuring ADR savings. Perhaps the most interesting feature of the Georgia-Pacific program is the highly effective and comprehensive fashion in which it accounts for savings garnered by the company through regular and effective ADR use. Mr. Armstrong says of the savings, "Just in routine matters, we're seeing savings in the seven figures over the course of one year." Some statistics on those savings: In 1996, the company's in-house lawyers settled nearly 50 cases through ADR, for an estimated $1.5 million of savings in legal fees and costs. In 1997, the number of cases settled increased to 75, resulting in savings of $6.5 million. (though one particularly large case was settled that year) These savings are primarily in attorney's fees, court costs, and related expenses. No "credit" is taken for avoided exposure, although Mr. Armstrong submits that virtually all cases are settled in amounts which are estimated to be equal to or less than the amount likely to be awarded had the case been litigated. If avoided exposure were included, the numbers would be substantially larger.

Armstrong creates the final calculations on ADR savings on an annualized basis. He does so by estimating the total cost of individual case resolution through an adjudicative mechanism and subtracts the actual cost of resolution through an ADR process for a savings value per case. A seven field database (Case name, Case Type, ADR Process Used, Final Settlement Value, Estimated Fees Saved, Estimated Liability Avoided and Estimated Total Savings) permits Armstrong to track savings by case type, ADR process type and settlement value range. It is important to note what is not included in the saving metric to understand the very conservative nature of the results. Armstrong does not calculate expenses associated with possible appeals of lost cases, or management time used to collect documents, respond to discovery or testify in depositions or court, all of which are substantial costs in full-blown litigation. Hence, the resulting figure, though estimated, is a conservative one, lending credibility to the numbers.

BRIEFING POINT 8.4

At GE, our management is receptive to any idea which can be proven to save the company money or otherwise contribute to the bottom line. This leads nicely into what I view as the bigger challenge: how do we change the way in which we evaluate the performance of our litigators so that cost effective early dispute resolution is valued over the kind of tough talk and saber rattling which may be emotionally satisfying but is, in most cases and in the long run, not in the shareholders' interest? **Elpidio Villarreal, Litigation & Legal Policy Counsel, General Electric Company**

Armstrong also tracks saving numbers by individual attorney on his staff and by practice group, e.g., Labor & Employment Law Group. Doing so not only allows for the assignment of cases to the department's staff in ways consistent with their abilities relative to ADR, but also permits judgments to be made about the performance of individual attorneys in terms of law department ADR goals.

Attorneys report more information than simply numbers. Case success stories are shared so that the salutary effect of ADR is clear. In one reported non-personal injury products liability claim against Georgia-Pacific, the case was settled in a single, one-day mediation session without outside counsel for a total payment of $75,000. The case was budgeted at $150,000 in legal fees and costs, <u>plus</u> exposure potential of $75,000, so the company realized a $150,000 ADR saving. A second case involving a breach of contract claim related to a price escalation provision generated further substantial savings for the company. The parties settled the matter, again in a single mediation session without outside counsel, by the execution of a contract amendment that saved an estimated $915,000 over the 18 months remaining on the contract as well as the $75,000 budgeted in legal fees and expenses; the total savings in the case approached 1 million dollars.

BRIEFING POINT 8.5

The Department of Labor, responding to federal law, is piloting a variety of ADR programs across the country. The Philadelphia Mediation Pilot Test had an 81% settlement rate in OSHA, Wage-Hour and MSHA claims with participants agreeing that the concluded settlements were at least as good as the likely outcomes of litigation.

ASSESSMENT

The Georgia-Pacific program in many ways speaks for itself. The economic returns provided by the program are substantial and sustained. Indeed, one expects that as company attorneys become increasingly adept at ADR use, those savings will continue to rise. The contract language used in the company clauses has proven effective in drawing parties into ADR and appears consistent with judicial expectations of such agreements, so that enforcement is likely should a party seek to avoid ADR. It is critical to note that the success of the program is largely a function of the commitment the company has made to making it work: a dedicated, high-level position overseeing the program; a strong and consistent message of support from general counsel; extensive use of internal technology to inform and professionally deliver training to help lawyers excel in their ADR practices; all constitute a very significant dedication to the ADR program.

Improving the program is arguably simply a matter of refining what already exists. For example, developing a precise method for calculating potential liability exposure, including punitive damages, for the purpose of sharpening the savings estimates would enhance the program. Developing in-house materials and training in effective early case evaluation for ADR applications are other avenues for improvement; a checklist like that provided in the Amoco "Forms & Materials" section might be suitable. Revising the already effective guidelines for outside counsel to discuss ADR overtly, perhaps in terms of a company expectation of expertise in and willingness to use the processes in matters referred, would be a favorable effort as well.

GEORGIA-PACIFIC FORMS & MATERIALS

Georgia-Pacific's Model ADR Contract Clauses

A Two-Step Dispute Resolution Clause:

Mediation-Arbitration or Litigation

The parties will attempt in good faith to resolve any controversy or claim arising out of or relating to this Agreement by mediation in accordance with the [Center for Public Resources] [American Arbitration Association] [other named organization] model procedures for mediation of business/commercial disputes.
If the matter has not been resolved pursuant to the aforesaid _____ days of the commencement of such procedure, or if either party will not participate in a mediation,

[Select one of the following alternatives.]

(i)   the controversy shall be settled by arbitration in accordance with the [Center for Public Resources Rules for non-Administered Arbitration of Business Disputes] [Commercial Arbitration Rules of the American Arbitration Association]. The arbitration shall be governed by the United States Arbitration Act, 9 U.S.C. 1-16, and judgement upon the award rendered by the arbitrators may be entered by any court having jurisdiction thereof. The place of arbitration shall be _____. The arbitrator(s) [are] [are not] empowered to award damages in excess of actual damages, including punitive damages.

(ii)   either party may initiate litigation [upon _____ days' written notice to the other party].

All deadlines specified in this Article may be extended by mutual agreement.

The procedures specified in this Article shall be the sole and exclusive procedures for the resolution of disputes between the parties arising out of or relating to this Agreement; provided, however, that a party may seek a preliminary injunction or other preliminary judicial relief if in its judgement such action is necessary to avoid irreparable damage.

Despite such action the parties will continue to participate in good faith in the procedures specified in this Article. All applicable statutes of limitation shall be tolled while the procedures specified in this Article are pending. The parties will take such action, if any, required to effectuate such tolling.

Three-Step Dispute Resolution Clause:

Negotiation-Mediation-Arbitration

The parties will attempt in good faith to resolve any controversy or claim arising out of or relating to this Agreement promptly by negotiations between senior executives of the parties who have authority to settle the controversy (and who do not have direct responsibility for administration of this Agreement).

The disputing party shall give the other party written notice of the dispute. Within twenty days after receipt of said notice, the receiving party shall submit to the other a written response. The notice and response shall include (a) a statement of each party's position and a summary of the evidence and arguments supporting its position, and (b) the name and title of the senior executives who will represent that party. The senior executives shall meet for negotiations at a mutually agreed time and place within thirty days of the date of the disputing party's notice and thereafter as often as they reasonably deem necessary to exchange relevant information and to attempt to resolve the dispute.

If the matter has not been resolved within sixty days of the disputing party's notice, or if the party receiving said notice will not meet within thirty days, the parties will attempt in good faith to resolve the controversy or claim by mediation in accordance with the [Center for Public Resources] [American Arbitration Association] [other named organization] model procedures for mediation of business/commercial disputes.

If the matter has not been resolved pursuant to the aforesaid mediation procedure within ____ days of the commencement of such procedure, or if either party will not participate in a mediation,

[Select one of the following alternatives]

(i)   the controversy shall be settled by arbitration in accordance with the [Center for Public Resources Rules for Non-Administered Arbitration of Business Disputes] [Commercial Arbitration Rules of the American Arbitration Association].   The arbitration shall be governed by the United States Arbitration Act, 9 U.S.C. 1-16, and judgement upon the award rendered by the arbitrator(s) may be entered by any court having jurisdiction thereof. The place of arbitration shall be _____. The arbitrator(s) [are] [are not] empowered to award damages in excess of actual damages, including punitive damages.

(ii)   either party may initiate litigation [upon _____ days' written notice to the other party.]

All deadlines specified in this Article may be extended by mutual agreement.

The procedures specified in this Article shall be the sole and exclusive procedures for the resolution of disputes between the parties arising out of or relating to this Agreement; provided, however, that a party may seek a preliminary injunction or other preliminary judicial relief if in its judgement such action is necessary to avoid irreparable damage.

Despite such action the parties will continue to participate in good faith in the procedures specified in this Article. All applicable statutes of limitation shall be tolled while the procedures specified in this Article are pending. The parties will take such action, if any, required to effectuate such tolling.

Four-Step Dispute Resolution Clause:

Two Stage Negotiation-Mediation-Arbitration or Litigation

The parties will attempt in good faith to resolve any controversy or claim arising out of or relating to this Agreement promptly by negotiations between representatives and senior executives of the parties who have authority to settle the controversy.

If a controversy or claim should arise, _____ of Owner [G-P or other] and _____ of _____ [Contractor or other], or their respective successors in the positions they now hold (herein called the "project managers"), will meet at least once and will attempt to resolve the matter. Either project manager may request the other to meet within fourteen days, at a mutually agreed time and place.

If the matter has not been resolved within twenty days of their first meeting, the project managers shall refer the matter to senior executives, who do not have direct responsibility for administration of this Agreement (herein called "the senior executives"). Thereupon, the project managers shall promptly prepare and exchange memoranda stating (a) the issues in dispute and their respective position, summarizing the evidence and arguments supporting their position, and the negotiations which have taken place, and attaching relevant documents, and (b) the name and title of the senior executive who will represent that party. The senior executives shall meet for negotiations at a mutually agreed time and place within fourteen days of the end of the twenty-day period referred to above, and thereafter as often as they reasonably deem necessary to exchange relevant information and to attempt to resolve the dispute.

If the matter has not been resolved within thirty days of the meeting of the senior executives, or if either party will not meet within thirty days of the end of the twenty-day period referred to in the preceding paragraph, the parties will attempt in good faith to resolve the controversy or claim by mediation in accordance with the [Center for Public Resources] [American Arbitration Association] [other named organization] model procedures for mediation of business/commercial disputes.

If the matter has not been resolved pursuant to the aforesaid mediation procedure within _____ days of the commencement of such procedure, or if either party will not participate in a mediation,

[Select one of the following alternatives]

(iii)   the controversy shall be settled by arbitration in accordance with the [Center for Public Resources Rules for Non-Administered Arbitration of Business Disputes] [Commercial Arbitration Rules of the American Arbitration Association]. The arbitration shall be governed by the United States Arbitration Act, 9 U.S.C. 1-16, and judgement upon the award rendered by the arbitrator(s) may be entered by any court having jurisdiction thereof. The place of arbitration shall be _____. The arbitrator(s) [are] [are not] empowered to award damages in excess of actual damages, including punitive damages.

(iv)   either party may initiate litigation [upon _____ days' written notice to the other party.]

All deadlines specified in this Article may be extended by mutual agreement.

The procedures specified in this Article shall be the sole and exclusive procedures for the resolution of disputes between the parties arising out of or relating to this Agreement; provided, however, that a party may seek a preliminary injunction or other preliminary judicial relief if in its judgement such action is necessary to avoid irreparable damage.

Despite such action the parties will continue to participate in good faith in the procedures specified in this Article. All applicable statutes of limitation shall be tolled while the procedures specified in this Article are pending. The parties will take such action, if any, required to effectuate such tolling.

KEY DECISION

The following case presents the interesting question of whether a court-appointed mediator or neutral case evaluator, performing tasks within the scope of his official duties, is entitled to absolute immunity from damages in a suit brought by a disappointed litigant.

JEROME S. WAGSHAL V. MARK W. FOSTER,
28 F. 3d 1249 (D.C. Circ., 1994)

In June 1990, Jerome S. Wagshal filed suit in D.C. Superior Court against Charles E. Sheetz, the manager of real property owned by Wagshal. In October 1991 the assigned judge, Judge Richard A. Levie referred the case to alternative dispute resolution pursuant to Superior Court Civil Rule 16 and the Superior Court's alternative dispute resolution ("ADR") program. While the program does not bind the parties (except when they agree to binding arbitration), participation is mandatory.

Judge Levie chose "neutral case evaluation" from among the available ADR options, and appointed Mark W. Foster as case evaluator. Pursuant to the order of appointment, the parties signed a "statement of understanding" providing (among other things) that the proceedings would be confidential and privileged, and that the evaluator, would serve as a "neutral party." Moreover, the parties were not allowed to subpoena the evaluator or any documents submitted in the course of evaluation, and "[i]n no event [could the] mediator or evaluator voluntarily testify on behalf of a party." Wagshal signed in January 1992 (under protest, he alleges).

After Foster held his first session with the parties, Wagshal questioned his neutrality. Foster then asked that Wagshal either waive his objection or pursue it: if Wagshal made no response warning the objection, Foster would treat it as a definite objection. Receiving no response by the deadline set, and later receiving a communication that he regarded as equivocal, Foster wrote to Judge Levie in February 1992 with copies to counsel, recusing himself. The letter also reported to the judge on his efforts in the case and recommended continuation of ADR proceedings. In particular, Foster said that the case was one "that can and should be settled if the parties are willing to act reasonably", and urged the court to order Wagshal, "as a pre-condition to any further proceedings in his case, to engage in a good faith attempt at mediation." He also urged Judge Levie to "consider who should bear the defendants costs in participating" in the mediation to date.

Judge Levie then conducted a telephone conference call hearing in which he excused Foster. Wagshal's counsel voiced the claim that underlies this suit - that he thought Foster's withdrawal letter "indicates that he had certain feelings about the case. Now, I'm not familiar with the mediation process but as I understood, the mediator is not supposed to say, give his opinion as to where the merits are." On that subject, Judge Levie said, "I don't know what his opinions are and I'm not going to ask him because that's part of the confidentiality of the process." Neither Wagshal nor his counsel made any objection or motion for Judge Levie's own recusal.

Judge Levie soon after appointed another case evaluator, and Wagshal and the other parties settled the *Sheetz* case in June 1992. In September 1992, however, Wagshal sued Foster and sixteen others (whom he identified as members of Foster's law firm) in federal district court, claiming that Foster's behavior as mediator had violated his rights to due process and to a jury trial under the Fifth and Seventh Amendments and seeking injunctive relief and damages under 42 U.S.C. § 1983. Besides the federal claims, he threw in a variety of local law theories such as defamation. invasion of privacy, and intentional infliction of emotional distress. His theory is that Foster's conduct as case evaluator forced him to settle the case against his will, resulting in a far lower recovery than if he had pursued the claim. The district court granted the defendants' motion to dismiss with prejudice, holding that Foster, like judges, was shielded by absolute immunity. We affirm.

Foster's first line of defense against the damages claim was the assertion of quasi-judicial immunity. The immunity will block the suit if it extends to case evaluators and mediators, so long as Foster's alleged actions were taken within the scope of his duties as a case evaluator.

Courts have extended absolute immunity to a wide range of persons playing a role in the judicial process. These have included prosecutors, law clerks, ... probation officers, ... a court-appointed committee monitoring the unauthorized practice of law, ... a psychiatrist who interviewed a criminal defendant to assist a trial judge, ... persons performing binding arbitration, ... and a psychologist performing dispute resolution services in connection with a lawsuit over custody and visitation rights. On the other hand, the Supreme Court has rejected absolute immunity for judges acting in an administrative capacity, ... court reporters charged with creating a verbatim transcript of trial proceedings, ... and prosecutors in relation to legal advice they may give state police. The official claiming the immunity "bears the burden of showing that such immunity is justified for the function in question."

We have distilled the Supreme Court's approach to quasi-judicial immunity into a consideration of three main factors: (1) whether the functions of the official in question are comparable to those of a judge; (2) whether the nature of the controversy is intense enough that future harassment or intimidation by litigants is a realistic prospect; and (3) whether the system contains safeguards which are adequate to justify dispensing with private damage suits to control unconstitutional conduct.

In certain respects it seems plain that a case evaluator in the Superior Court's system performs judicial functions. Foster's assigned tasks included identifying factual and legal issues, scheduling discovery and motions with the parties, and coordinating settlement efforts. These obviously involve substantial discretion, a key feature of the tasks sheltered by judicial immunity ... Further, viewed as mental activities, the tasks appear precisely the same as those judges perform going about the business of adjudication and case management.

Wagshal protests, however, that mediation is altogether different from authoritative adjudication, citing observations to that effect in radically dissimilar contexts. However true his point may be as an abstract matter, the general process of encouraging settlement is a natural, almost inevitable, concomitant of adjudication. Rule 16 of the Federal Rules of Civil Procedure, for example institutionalizes the relation, designating as subjects for pre-trial conferences a series of issues that appear to encompass all the tasks of a case evaluator in the Superior Court system: "formulation and simplification of the issues", "the possibility of obtaining admissions of fact and of documents", "the control and scheduling of discovery", and a catch-all, "such other matters as facilitate the just, speedy, and inexpensive disposition of the action." Fed.R.Civ.P. 16(c). Wagshal points to nothing in Foster's role that a Superior Court judge might not have performed under Superior Court Rule 16(c), which substantially. tracks the federal model. Although practice appears to vary widely, and some variations raise very serious issues, it is quite apparent that intensive involvement in settlement now by no means uncommon among federal district judges.

Wagshal does not assert that a case evaluator is performing a purely administrative task, such as the personnel decisions - demotion and discharge of a probation officer - at issue in *Forrester v White*. Because the sort of pre-trial tasks performed by a case evaluator are so integrally related to adjudication proper, we do not think that their somewhat managerial character renders them administrative for these purposes.

Conduct of pre-trial case evaluation and mediation also seems likely to inspire efforts by disappointed litigants to recoup their losses, or at any rate harass the mediator, in a second forum. ... Although a mediator or case evaluator makes no final adjudication, he must often be the bearer of unpleasant news - that a claim or defense may be far weaker than the party supposed. Especially as the losing party will be blocked by judicial immunity from suing the judge, there may be great temptation to sue the messenger whose words foreshadowed the final loss.

The third of the Supreme Court's criteria, the existence of adequate safeguards to control unconstitutional conduct where absolute immunity is granted, is also present. Here, Wagshal was free to seek relief from any misconduct by Foster by applying to Judge Levie. Alternatively, if he thought Foster's communications might prejudice Judge Levie, he could have sought Levie's recusal under Superior

Court R.Civ.P. 63-I, Bias or Prejudice of a Judge. The avenues of relief institutionalized in the ADR program and its judicial context provide adequate safeguards.

Wagshal claims that even if mediators may be generally entitled to absolute immunity, Foster may not invoke the immunity because his action was not taken in a judicial capacity, ... and because he acted in complete absence of jurisdiction. ... Neither exception applies.

Wagshal's argument that the acts for which he has sued Foster are not judicial (apart from the claim against mediators generally) rests simply on his claim that Foster's letter to Judge Levie, stating that he felt he "must recuse" himself and giving his thoughts on possible further mediation efforts and allocation of costs, breached Foster's obligations of neutrality and confidentiality. We assume such a breach for purposes of analysis. But "if judicial immunity means anything, it means that a judge will not be deprived of immunity because the action he took was in error . . . or was in excess of his authority." ... Accordingly "we look to the particular act's relation to a general function normally performed by a judge". Applying the same principle to case evaluators, we have no doubt that Foster's announcing his recusal, reporting in a general way on the past course of mediation, and making suggestions for future mediation were the sort of things that case evaluators would properly do.

Wagshal finally argues that Foster cannot be immune for the statements in his letter made after he stated that he "must recuse" himself. This is frivolous. Even if the letter alone effected a recusal (which is doubtful - Judge Levie clearly saw himself as later excusing Foster from service), the simultaneous delivery of an account of his work was the type of act a case evaluator could properly perform on the way out. In fact, we doubt very much if a modest gap in time between effective recusal and recounting of the events would take the latter out of the immunity..

Nor were Foster's actions "taken in the complete absence of all jurisdiction." Wagshal's claim to the contrary rests primarily on the theory that, although Superior Court Rule of Civil Procedure 16(j) requires parties to "attend ... any alternative dispute resolution session ordered by the court", there is no explicit authority to appoint case evaluators. This contrasts, says Wagshal, with explicit District law authorizing appointment of masters and hearing commissioners.

We hold that absolute quasi-judicial immunity extends to mediators and case evaluators in the Superior Court's ADR process, and that Foster's actions were taken within the scope of his official duties.

CHAPTER 9

SNAPSHOT ADR PROFILES:
WHIRLPOOL CORPORATION
BAXTER INTERNATIONAL INC.
NATIONAL ASSOC. OF MANUFACTURERS
JOHNSON & JOHNSON
HANFORD NUCLEAR SITE

The following five companies have ADR program components that round-out this survey very usefully. Each company has an ADR procedure, particular contract language or a method of ADR program administration worth considering.

WHIRLPOOL CORPORATION[1]

Whirlpool Corporation is a manufacturer of major home appliances in a highly competitive international industry. Three noteworthy features of the Whirlpool dispute resolution efforts worth considering briefly are: Management of Legal Staff, Pre-Litigation Negotiation Strategy and Mediation by Agreement.

Management of Legal Staff. Whirlpool evaluates its legal expenses by scrutinizing specific categories of legal work accomplished by in-house counsel as well as expenditures to secure outside counsel. Part of this evaluation includes an on-going effort to measure how effective in-house and outside counsel are in resolving disputes early and inexpensively. A further goal in Whirlpool's evaluation of counsel is to achieve as much financial predictability for management as possible regarding the resolution of legal issues.

To measure Law Department expenses accurately and meaningfully, work has been categorized into "key processes and projects." "Key processes" describes recurring work and routine legal services needed by the corporation including: commercial contract preparation, litigation management, environmental matters, antitrust and marketing oversight, and intellectual property protection. "Key projects" are one- time efforts, such as acquisitions or joint ventures. All employees in the Law Department allocate their time to both key projects and processes.

To further control litigation costs and product liability claims in particular, the Law Department has selected outside law firms to act as national product counsel

---

[1] For a far more complete description of the Whirlpool program, see the excellent article: Kenagy, Robert. "Whirlpool's Search for Efficient and Effective Dispute Resolutions." 59 Alb. L. Rev. 895 (1996)

for various categories of Whirlpool products. **These outside firms are paid a flat fee in addition to a performance bonus based on the average cost of resolving Whirlpool legal disputes.** Whirlpool hopes to create incentives for outside counsel to work with in-house counsel in a collaborative effort to reduce the cost of resolving product-related litigation through this fee structure. As a result, the outside firms are aggressively pursuing pre-litigation settlement and developing new and cost-effective practices in discovery, motion practice, and other particularly costly aspects of litigation.

Pre-Litigation Negotiation Strategy. Whirlpool has adopted a two-stage approach to pre-litigation negotiation which it endeavors to apply the approach in a wide range of significant commercial cases. At the first stage, mid-level management and company lawyers work together to settle the matter without high-level management participation. **When this effort is unsuccessful, Whirlpool suggests a formal negotiating session that is similar to a mini-trial.** Each company designates a high-level executive who has not been directly involved in either the underlying situation giving rise to the dispute or the initial attempts to resolve the dispute to act as a decision-maker on behalf of the company. The underlying facts of the dispute and the legal positions taken as a result are presented in a summary fashion to the executives by attorneys from each company. Whirlpool hopes that the executives are able to review the facts of the dispute and work together to develop a mutually satisfactory solution. Considerable effort is made to consider the logistics of the meeting prior to its commencement. As a result, a detailed schedule is developed for discovery and other procedural matters. Whirlpool believes this two-step approach is most successful when a period of interaction at lower levels of the organizations precedes the final mini-trial negotiation. These early attempts to settle permit the disputants to understand the facts and analyze the position of the other party. Moreover, some of the acrimony initially present in a dispute dissipates during this stage. In very substantial matters, Whirlpool has even used mock trials with juries to assess the strengths and weaknesses of its case and to stress to management the risks of taking a litigation approach. Because litigation is normally considered a last resort for Whirlpool, the company also is willing to use mediation as a second step alternative to the mini-trial approach; it will also consider binding arbitration as a third step in resolving significant business disputes as an alternative to litigation when settlement efforts fail.

Mediation by Agreement. Whirlpool, like many companies, builds mediation clauses into a variety of contracts. **Mediation under these conditions is triggered in one of two ways: a party may withdraw from negotiations, in which case the mediation begins within thirty days from the withdrawal _or_ mediation is required if the parties cannot successfully conclude negotiations within ninety days of their commencement.** The mediation is conducted by a mediator selected by the parties from a panel developed by a firm specializing in ADR or, if the parties are unable to agree on a mediator, the parties select the mediator by random drawing from the list of potential facilitators.

The mediation process required in Whirlpool contracts is strictly confidential and must be completed within sixty days after the mediator is formally selected. Within fifteen days from receiving the mediator's signed agreement to mediate the dispute, each party is required to submit to the mediator a statement summarizing the background and present status of the dispute, copies of expert reports, witness statements, and other relevant material. As in most mediation settings, parties may withdraw at any time after attending the first mediation session and prior to execution of a written settlement agreement. Unlike many conventional mediation conferences, Whirlpool obligates the mediator, before terminating the procedure, to submit to the parties a final settlement proposal that the mediator considers fair to both parties if they cannot reach a negotiated agreement. The parties are required to consider the mediator's proposal, and advise the mediator of the specific reasons that the proposal is unacceptable if it is rejected. Mediations continue until a settlement is reached, unless the mediator concludes that further efforts would not be useful, or one of the parties withdraws from the process. If a settlement is reached, a written settlement document including mutual general releases from liability is created and signed within thirty days of the conference. Many Whirlpool contract clauses obligate the parties to pursue binding arbitration with an outside provider like the AAA in the event mediation by agreement is not successful.

BRIEFING POINT 9.1

We at GE are also convinced of the need to involve business managers in the dispute resolution process. That's why our Early Dispute Resolution process calls for the formation of Dispute Resolution Teams composed of lawyers and business managers to resolve specific disputes. We have also emphasized training of business managers in Early Dispute Resolution techniques. Finally, we recently made Early Dispute Resolution a part of the standard business managers training curriculum at our corporate university in Crotonville, New York. As the savings of our program continue to add up, I believe getting business manager commitment/involvement in the process will be the least of our problems. **Elpidio Villarreal, Litigation & Legal Policy Counsel, General Electric Company**

BAXTER INTERNATIONAL INC.

Baxter International Inc. ("Baxter"), through its subsidiaries is a global leader in the development of critical therapy products for life-threatening conditions related to the blood and circulatory system. The company's blood therapies businesses make products that collect, separate and store blood, as well as therapeutic proteins derived from blood. Baxter renal products cleanse the blood and cardiovascular products keep blood pumping through the body. Finally, Baxter intravenous products infuse drugs and other solutions into the blood. Baxter is an international venture operating in nearly every type of political and health-care system in the world. Over 50 percent of Baxter sales come from outside the United States; Baxter products are sold in more than 112 countries. Baxter employs more than 42,000 people around the world.

Two features of the Baxter ADR program have particular merit for this survey text. First, Baxter has created a careful case-screening document. While it bears some similarity to the Amoco case evaluation checklist, it adds significantly to that document. In addition, Baxter has several very artfully drafted ADR contract clauses. While they are rooted in CPR language, they demonstrate nicely how companies can tailor ADR contract clauses to meet their individual needs. Both of the following sections are taken from the Baxter *ADR Manual*.

III.   Selecting Cases Suitable For ADR

A.   How to select which cases proceed through ADR.

Several vehicles may trigger the application of ADR. They include:

1.   **Attorney or client discretion** - this is based upon company's primary goal or business interests regarding the dispute. Sometimes early settlement or adjudication will best serve the company's goals or business interests. Settlement, with or without using some form of ADR, is usually preferable if any of the following exist:

   a.   no need for court precedent;
   b.   no need for court enforcement;
   c.   no need to create a public record;
   d.   a belief that litigation is not cost/time effective;
   e.   no need to "send a message" to other known potential plaintiffs

2.   **ADR contract clauses** - such clauses incorporate ADR into the process by design, removing the opportunity as well as the need to decide between litigation and ADR should a dispute later arise. This process requires careful preliminary analysis of the types of arrangements in which an ADR clause will be used, as well as careful structuring of the clause. Once negotiated, the clause virtually eliminates ADR case selection because the contract mandates ADR use in the event of a dispute.

3.   **Pre-selecting categories of cases** - this can occur in disputes arising in contractual or non-contractual areas. This creates a presumptive atmosphere for use in selected dispute categories. Common characteristics for cases falling in this category: disputes with persons in an ongoing

relationship or likely to have relationships periodically with the company; occurring in volume numbers; frequently resulting in pre-trial settlement; or cases with routine matters of fact and law, as opposed to pivotal business issues.

4. **Positive Case Indicators** - several indicators can be used to isolate specific cases from a larger body of claims to be considered for ADR submission. The goal is to seek cases where ADR would work best, and to evaluate whether negative indicators will exclude those cases from ADR submission.

Some factors to consider are:

a. Whether the parties may have an ongoing business relationship and want to preserve it;

b. Whether the parties need to resolve the dispute, but in a private, non-public fashion;

c. Whether legal fees have become, or are likely to become disproportionately high in relationship to the amount at stake;

d. Whether discovery has taken on a life of its own and no end appears in sight;

e. Whether the case is exceedingly complex in terms of technical or factual material and where an evaluation or determination by an expert party neutral would be useful;

f. Whether animosity has developed between the parties to the point where productive settlement discussions cannot take place because of communication breakdown.

Regardless of the method chosen for ADR case evaluation, it is beneficial to consider routine review of cases to determine ADR potential as cases mature so that ADR opportunities are not lost, except in those cases where ADR is mandated either by the court or by the parties. Such analysis is best performed at designated period intervals, including claim filing, after investigation, when litigation commences, during motion practice or at specified discovery levels, or when expenses have reached a predetermined level.

B.   Examples of disputes where ADR may be considered.

ADR is a versatile tool, and can be utilized in a variety of settings. Baxter has a broad base of ADR experience, and has used it in many of the categories noted below.

1. **Employment Related Claims**

   Wrongful termination
   Discrimination
   Harassment
   Workers Compensation

2. **Customer/Supplier Disputes**

   Bill disputes
   Breach of contract

3. **Competitor Disputes**

   Product dumping
   Employee raiding
   Theft of trade secrets
   Patent/copyright infringement

4. **Corporate Litigation**

   Product liability
   Taxes Environmental
   Regulatory Real Estate

C. Cases where ADR may be inappropriate.

   ADR may be inappropriate under certain circumstances. They are:

   1. When credibility is key (of product? of company?);
   2. When you need to establish a deterrent strategy by asserting a right through litigation in order to make a strong statement to a customer or competitor;
   3. When you need to establish a legal precedent which only the courts can provide; and
   4. When there are multiple parties.

   It is preferable that contracts involving Baxter contain the following, or some version of the following, ADR language, which has been approved by the Law Function. The language mirrors the CPR language and may be further revised to fit the particular circumstances of the case.

V.   Baxter Approved ADR Language

A.   PREAMBLE

Any dispute arising out of or relating to this Agreement shall be resolved in accordance with the procedures specified in Article which shall be the sole and exclusive procedures for the resolution of any such disputes.

B.   NEGOTIATION CLAUSES

Negotiation Between Executives

The parties will attempt in good faith to resolve any claim or controversy arising out of or relating to the execution, interpretation and performance of this Agreement (including the validity, scope and enforceability of this mediation and arbitration provision) promptly by negotiations between executives who have authority to settle the controversy and who are at a higher level of management than the persons with direct responsibility for the administration of this Agreement. Any party may give the other party written notice of any dispute not resolved in the normal course of business. Within fifteen (15) days after delivery of the notice, the receiving party shall submit to the other a written response. The notice and the response shall include (a) a statement of each party's position and a summary of arguments supporting that position, and (b) the name and title of the executive who will represent that party and of any other person who will accompany the executive. Within thirty (30) days after delivery of the notifying party's notice, the executives of both parties shall meet at a mutually acceptable time and place, and thereafter as often as they reasonably deem necessary, to attempt to resolve the dispute. All reasonable requests for information made by one party to the other will be honored. All negotiations pursuant to this clause are confidential and shall be treated as compromise and settlement negotiations for purposes of applicable rules of evidence.

C.   NON-BINDING DISPUTE RESOLUTION

Mediation with Designated Neutral

If any claim or controversy is not fully resolved through negotiation within [45] days of the notifying party's notice, or if the parties failed to meet within [20] days, the parties will attempt in good faith to resolve the controversy or claim in accordance with the Center for Public Resources (CPR) Model Procedure for Mediation of Business Disputes in effect on the date of this Agreement. Any such mediation shall be held in Northern Illinois unless the parties otherwise agree to another location. The parties agree to select a mediator listed on the CPR panel of approved neutrals.

D.   BINDING DISPUTE RESOLUTION

Arbitration

Any dispute arising out of or relating to this agreement or its breach, termination or validity which has not been resolved by the specified non-binding procedure within 90 days of the initiation of the date of delivery of notice shall be settled by binding arbitration in accordance with the CPR Non-Administered Arbitration Rules in effect on the date of this agreement, by three independent and impartial arbitrators, none of whom shall be appointed by either party. The arbitration shall be governed by the United States Arbitration Act, 9 U.S.C. Sec. 1-16, and judgment upon the award rendered by the arbitrator(s) may be entered by any court having jurisdiction thereof. The place of the arbitration shall be Northern Illinois. The Arbitrator(s) are not empowered to award damages in excess of compensatory damages [and each party hereby irrevocably waives any right to recover such damages].

E.   DISCOVERY

The following language may be applied in Mediation Or Arbitration Proceedings:

The parties agree that limited discovery shall be allowed in accordance with the Federal Rules of Civil Procedure for a period of 45 days after the initiation of the mediation or 120 days after the initiation of the arbitration process. See F.R.C.P. 26-37. All issues regarding compliance with discovery requests shall be decided by the [Arbitrator(s)/Mediator] pursuant to the Federal Rules of Civil Procedure.

The parties agree that the recipient of a discovery request shall have ten (10) business days after the receipt of such request to object to any or all portions of such request and shall respond to any portions of such request not so objected within thirty (30) business days of the receipt of such request. All objections shall be in writing and shall indicate the reasons for such objections. The objecting party shall ensure that all objections and responses are received by the other party within the above time periods; failure to comply with the specified time period shall be addressed as outlined in the F.R.C.P. 37. Any party seeking to compel discovery following receipt of an objection shall file with the other party and the [Arbitrator(s)/Mediator] a motion to compel, including a copy of the initial request and the objection. The [Arbitrator(s)/Mediator] shall allow ten (10) business days for the responses to the motion to compel before ruling. Claims of privilege and other objections shall be determined as they would be in United States federal court in a case applying Illinois law. The [Arbitrator(s)/Mediator] may grant or deny the motion to compel, in whole or in part, concluding that the discovery request is or is not appropriate under the circumstances, taking into account the needs of the parties and the desirability of making discovery expeditious and cost effective.

The statute of limitations of the State of Illinois applicable to the commencement of a lawsuit shall apply to the date of initial written notification of a dispute and shall be extended until commencement of arbitration if all interim deadlines have been complied with by the notifying party.

BRIEFING POINT 9.2

According to Tillinghast-Towers Perrin, wrongful injury litigation is unusually costly in the United States, reaching nearly 2.5% of the GDP in 1994. By way of contrast, Great Britain, Canada, France, Australia and Japan all hold that cost to under 1%.

NATIONAL ASSOCIATION OF MANUFACTURERS

The NAM, founded in Cincinnati, Ohio in 1895, began primarily as an association of associations. The emphasis has now shifted to individual manufacturers to better represent manufacturers' interests. The NAM's mission is "to enhance the competitiveness of manufacturers and improve living standards for working Americans by shaping a legislative and regulatory environment conducive to U.S. economic growth, and to increase understanding among policy-makers, the media and the general public about the importance of manufacturing to America's economic strength."

N.A.M. offers a mediation program to its members which can be a significant bonus for them. The following language is drawn from the N.A.M. website and describes why and how mediation fits into the N.A.M. member services portfolio. The language is brief, descriptive and sells mediation. The language could be useful to a company seeking to promote an existing in-house ADR effort, or to explain to a diverse external audience why the company seeks to use mediation in matters that could result in litigation.

**Resolve your disputes before they drain your resources:
Mediate, don't litigate.**

Disputes may be ugly, but they don't have to be costly – we've made sure of that. If you're involved in a dispute with a non-union employee or with another business, The Mediation Center for Business Disputes can help you resolve your differences without resorting to an expensive, time-consuming court battle. The NAM offers this valuable service in partnership with the non-profit CPR Institute for Dispute Resolution. The NAM uses the internet, among other venues, to describe the advantages of its program as follows:

Why Mediation Makes Good Sense:

You have lots of good reasons to choose mediation over litigation. With mediation, you:

- Save time. You resolve your dispute promptly instead of in court, where your case could drag on for years.
- Save money. In a five-year period, 652 companies using this service reported legal-cost savings averaging $300,000 per company.
- Preserve relationships and protect your company's privacy.
- Focus on how best to resolve your dispute – not worry about who will win.

How it Works:

In mediation, you and the other party-in-dispute meet with an experienced neutral party who:

- Examines the strengths and weaknesses of each party's legal position;
- Explores the consequences (legal and financial) of not reaching an agreement; and,
- Generates options for reaching a mutually satisfactory resolution.

Mediation Center staff help you and the other party agree on a mediator selected from a panel of eminent former judges, legal academics, outstanding attorneys and conflict-resolution specialists.

Other Benefits:

The mediation process is non-binding – both parties must agree on the terms recommended by the mediator. Once an agreement is reached, each party signs it, and it becomes enforceable, like any other contract. If mediation doesn't work, you can always go to court or arbitration.

> **BRIEFING POINT 9.3**
> ADR in business is becoming big business. More than 800 corporations with over 3200 subsidiaries have signed the CPR ADR "pledge" to consider ADR in any dispute with another signatory to the pledge; the list of signatories grows constantly.

JOHNSON & JOHNSON

Johnson & Johnson ("J&J") this year introduced a new employment dispute resolution program called "Common Ground" on a pilot basis at several operating companies. Designed to address and resolve employment disputes fairly, quickly and inexpensively, the Program supplements and enhances existing J&J procedures and provides a variety of options for resolving employment disputes.

Like the Darden and Dollar General programs covered earlier in this text, this is a multi-step, multi-process program. Excerpts from the language used to describe various aspects of the program to employees are quoted below. The language is provided to offer further drafting options to companies seeking to build in-house programs in areas in which the J&J language is particularly effective, or on which the Darden and Dollar General program guides are silent.

Common Ground
An Employee Dispute Resolution Program

Introduction

There are three parts to the program: Open Door, Facilitation and Mediation. We expect that the flexible procedures available under the Program will be highly successful at resolving disputes. However, if none of these steps resolves your dispute with the Company, you are free to pursue legal action in court. Your first option is Open Door. Under Open Door, you are encouraged to resolve the problem through discussions with your supervisor or with your supervisor's boss. Members of the Human Resources Department are also available to help you resolve the problem or complaint. If the problem remains unresolved, you can refer to your supervisor's manager or to whatever level of management is necessary to attempt to resolve the issue. If the Open Door procedure does not resolve your dispute, you can go to your next option, FACILITATION. The Company has designated a Facilitator to ensure that the Open Door process has been pursued fully. The Facilitator will review additional options for resolving the issue and help keep the lines of communication open. If your dispute remains unresolved, you can seek MEDIATION. Mediation is an informal process that uses a neutral third party to assist both sides in attempting to reach a mutually beneficial or satisfactory resolution of their dispute. We believe that the Common Ground program provides a better means to resolve problems, in a way that is efficient, flexible, and fair to both you and the Company. It is quicker and less costly than litigation. You are encouraged to use this Program and will not be subject to any reprisal or retaliation for doing so. These three dispute resolution methods, and the way they work, are described in more detail in this brochure and in the questions and answers that follow. If you have questions after reading these materials, or would like more information about the Program, please contact your Human Resources department.

Types of Disputes Covered By The Program

The Program applies to all employees of the Company except employees in units that are represented by labor organizations, unless permitted by the applicable collective bargaining agreement. The Program covers most, but not all, claims that you may have against the Company. Although almost any dispute can be raised through Open Door and Facilitation, only legally recognized claims may be submitted to Mediation. The following disputes are covered by all three methods available under the Program: wages or other compensation due; breach of contract; wrongful discharge; discrimination on the basis of race, color, sexual orientation, religion, national origin, disability or age; harassment; retaliation; defamation; infliction of emotional distress; whistleblowing claims; termination or violation or Company policies; and any other legally protected rights. In the case of a claim for denial of benefits under the Johnson & Johnson Employee Benefit Plan, any and all claim filings and appeal procedures must be undertaken and exhausted before the Program can be utilized.

The Program does not cover disputes relating to: claims for worker's compensation or unemployment benefits and claims by the Company for injunctive and/or other equitable relief for unfair competition, use of trade secrets or confidential information, or to enforce the terms of a Non-Compete, Secrecy, Non-Solicitation, or other employment-related agreement.

The Program does not affect the exclusive remedies provided under the applicable worker's compensation statute. The Program does not apply to challenges to the business decisions of the Company, such as decisions to restructure, reorganize, downsize or divest a business or to offer any Voluntary Separation or Early Retirement Programs, unless such decisions or programs violate the employee's legally protected rights.

Further Claims

Nothing in this Program prevents you from filing a claim with a federal or state administrative agency or from cooperating with a state or federal agency investigation. Nor does this Program prevent you from filing a lawsuit. However, if an employee notifies a federal or state agency of an employment-related issue or files a lawsuit, the Company will advise the agency or court of the existence of this Program and seek to stay or dismiss the agency or court proceeding until after the Program procedures are exhausted.

Impact of the Program on Employment

The Program does not establish any terms of your employment. It creates a mechanism for attempting to resolve your employment-related disputes. It does not create a contract of employment, express or implied, for any period of time or guarantee that your employment will end only under certain conditions. The Program does not alter or modify the "at will" employment relationship between you and the Company. By participating in the Program, you will not lose or compromise any substantive rights you have. The Program will not impair the right of the Company to make decisions regarding your compensation, benefits or continued employment.

Beginning on that date, it will become the exclusive means for attempting to resolve employment disputes between employees and the Company, including disputes for legally protected rights such as freedom from discrimination, retaliation or harassment. If you accept or continue employment with the Company after the date the Program goes into effect, you agree to process all employment-related legal claims against the Company through this Program. The Program will be evaluated periodically and may, in the future, be discontinued or offered by more Johnson & Johnson operating companies.

BRIEFING POINT 9.4

Line managers now list "managing conflict" as number 7 on their list of priorities according to research by Development Dimensions International. "It used to be much further down the list," says Alice Pescuric, Vice President and practice leader at Development Dimensions.

HANFORD NUCLEAR SITE

The Hanford Nuclear Site in southeastern Washington state is, perhaps, the largest toxic and radiological mess in the nation. It is a U.S. government-owned and private contractor-operated facility with more nuclear waste stored at it than at all other defense sites combined. Westinghouse-Hanford Company was the main contractor until recently when Fluor Daniel Hanford took over operation of the site. In addition, Hanford has the unpleasant distinction of having more leakage from its storage tanks than from all other site tanks combined, according to Tom Carpenter, director of the *Government Accountability Project*. Not surprisingly, Hanford has been the subject of a significant number of whistleblower lawsuits since 1988, many of which were brought by the *Accountability Project*. These suits are among the most acrimonious in American law.

The "Hanford Joint Council" is an attempt to manage these disputes more effectively. The Council is composed of seven chairs: two community/public interest seats, two seats held by contractor general managers, two seats filled by a former whistleblower and a whistleblower attorney, respectively; the Council chairman holds the final seat. Issues brought to the council involve health, safety, or environmental concerns that may lead to outside legal intervention. Any violation of the law that must be reported is still reported, but the Council is the forum of first resort for employees who believe they have been wronged or that the site is being managed or operated inappropriately. The process does not, however, cover collective bargaining grievances, or cases involving contractors who haven't signed on to the Council's charter.

The Council apparently has been a tremendous success. Since its creation in 1995, "no whistleblower case within its reach has resulted in litigation or been a subject of public controversy," says Jon Brock, chairman of the council and a public affairs professor at the University of Washington. Moreover, resolutions have come at less than a tenth of the cost of litigation. Carpenter, who was involved in much of the previous whistleblower litigation, says he joined the Council to reach resolutions without the "total warfare" of litigation. "Often, our clients won in name only, their careers ruined, their families split asunder, and their lives effectively destroyed. Plus, the safety issues employees raised were lost in litigation over who said what, when, to whom, and why."

Brock believes that "once you get people discussing in a professional manner the best ways to fix a given issue, many options are generated, and extreme statements and claims normally give way to reasoned professional dialogue." He continues, "by getting the conflict early, and protecting the person, we slow the polarizing of the problem and the smirching of reputations. If it turns out a beef is legitimate, we deal with it via recommendations that only go forward by the consensus of the council." "By the final stages of the mediation process, if you close your eyes and listen to the voices, you wouldn't know who is talking," he says. The former lead contractor, Westinghouse-Hanford Company, continues to support the Council. A. LaMar Trego, Westinghouse's President, calls the Council "a fundamentally new management technique that will surely become the approach of choice by forward-thinking organizations."

KEY DECISION

This final case addresses an area of ADR not covered before – building ADR into customer contracts to obligate them to use ADR in external lawsuit settings. While the approach taken by Gateway 2000, a major domestic computer manufacturer, leaves much to be desired, the opinion demonstrates the common sense judicial approach to enforcement of these clauses and provides a measure of assurance to companies seeking to employ them.

HILL v. GATEWAY 2000, Inc., 105 F.3d 1147 (7th Cir. 1997)

A customer picks up the phone, orders a computer, and gives a credit card number. Presently a box arrives, containing the computer and a list of terms, said to govern unless the customer returns the computer within 30 days. Are these terms effective as the parties' contract, or is the contract term-free because the order-taker did not read any terms over the phone and elicit the customer's assent?

One of the terms in the box containing a Gateway 2000 system was an arbitration clause. Rich and Enza Hill, the customers, kept the computer more than 30 days before complaining about its components and performance. They filed suit in federal court arguing, among other things, that the product's shortcomings make

Gateway a racketeer, leading to treble damages under RICO for the Hills and a class of all other purchasers. Gateway asked the district court to enforce the arbitration clause; the judge refused, writing that "[t]he present record is insufficient to support a finding of a valid arbitration agreement between the parties or that the plaintiffs were given adequate notice of the arbitration clause." Gateway took an immediate appeal.

The Hills say that the arbitration clause did not stand out: they concede noticing the statement of terms but deny reading it closely enough to discover the agreement to arbitrate, and they ask us to conclude that they therefore may go to court. Yet an agreement to arbitrate must be enforced "save upon such grounds as exist at law or in equity for the revocation of any contract." 9 U.S.C. sec. 2. Doctor's Associates, Inc. v. Casarotto, 116 S. Ct. 1652 (1996), holds that this provision of the Federal Arbitration Act is inconsistent with any requirement that an arbitration clause be prominent. A contract need not be read to be effective; people who accept take the risk that the unread terms may in retrospect prove unwelcome. Terms inside Gateway's box stand or fall together. If they constitute the parties' contract because the Hills had an opportunity to return the computer after reading them, then all must be enforced.

ProCD, Inc. v. Zeidenberg, 86 F.3d 1447 (7th Cir. 1996), holds that terms inside a box of software bind consumers who use the software after an opportunity to read the terms and to reject them by returning the product. Likewise, Carnival Cruise Lines, Inc. v. Shute, 499 U.S. 585 (1991), enforces a forum-selection clause that was included among three pages of terms attached to a cruise ship ticket. ProCD and Carnival Cruise Lines exemplify the many commercial transactions in which people pay for products with terms to follow; ProCD discusses others. 86 F.3d at 1451-52. The district court concluded in ProCD that the contract is formed when the consumer pays for the software; as a result, the court held, only terms known to the consumer at that moment are part of the contract, and provisos inside the box do not count. Although this is one way a contract could be formed, it is not the only way: "A vendor, as master of the offer, may invite acceptance by conduct, and may propose limitations on the kind of conduct that constitutes acceptance. A buyer may accept by performing the acts the vendor proposes to treat as acceptance." Id. at 1452. Gateway shipped computers with the same sort of accept-or-return offer ProCD made to users of its software. ProCD relied on the Uniform Commercial Code rather than any peculiarities of Wisconsin law; both Illinois and South Dakota, the two states whose law might govern relations between Gateway and the Hills, have adopted the UCC; neither side has pointed us to any atypical doctrines in those states that might be pertinent; ProCD therefore applies to this dispute.

Plaintiffs ask us to limit ProCD to software, but where's the sense in that? ProCD is about the law of contract, not the law of software. Payment preceding the revelation of full terms is common for air transportation, insurance, and many other endeavors. Practical considerations support allowing vendors to enclose the full legal terms with their products. Cashiers cannot be expected to read legal documents to customers before ringing up sales. If the staff at the other end of the phone for direct-sales operations such as Gateway's had to read the four-page statement of terms before taking the buyer's credit card number, the droning voice would anesthetize rather than enlighten many potential buyers. Others would hang up in a rage over the waste of their time. And oral recitation would not avoid customers' assertions (whether true or feigned) that the clerk did not read term X to them, or that they did not remember or understand it. Writing provides benefits for both sides of commercial transactions. Customers as a group are better off when vendors skip costly and ineffectual steps such as telephonic recitation, and use instead a simple approve-or-return device. Competent adults are bound by such documents, read or unread. For what little it is worth, we add that the box from Gateway was crammed with software. The computer came with an operating system, without which it was useful only as a boat anchor. Gateway also included many application programs. So the Hills' effort to limit ProCD to software would not avail them factually, even if it were sound legally - which it is not.

For their second sally, the Hills contend that ProCD should be limited to executory contracts (to licenses in particular), and therefore does not apply because both parties' performance of this contract was complete when the box arrived at their home. This is legally and factually wrong: legally because the question at hand concerns the formation of the contract rather than its performance, and factually because both contracts were incompletely performed. ProCD did not depend on the fact that the seller characterized the transaction as a license rather than as a contract; we treated it as a contract for the sale of goods and reserved the question whether for other purposes a "license" characterization might be preferable. 86 F.3d at 1450. All debates about characterization to one side, the transaction in ProCD was no more executory than the one here: Zeidenberg paid for the software and walked out of the store with a box under his arm, so if arrival of the box with the product ends the time for revelation of contractual terms, then the time ended in ProCD before Zeidenberg opened the box. But of course ProCD had not completed performance with delivery of the box, and neither had Gateway. One element of the transaction was the warranty, which obliges sellers to fix defects in their products. The Hills have invoked Gateway's warranty and are not satisfied with its response, so they are not well positioned to say that Gateway's obligations were fulfilled when the motor carrier unloaded the box. What is more, both ProCD and Gateway promised to help customers to use their products. Long-term service and information obligations are common in the computer business, on both hardware and software sides. Gateway offers "lifetime service" and has a round-the-clock telephone hotline to fulfil this promise. Some vendors spend more money helping customers use their products than on developing and manufacturing them. The document in Gateway's box includes promises of future performance that some consumers value highly; these promises bind Gateway just as the arbitration clause binds the Hills.

Next the Hills insist that ProCD is irrelevant because Zeidenberg was a "merchant" and they are not. Section 2-207(2) of the UCC, the infamous battle-of-the-forms section, states that "additional terms [following acceptance of an offer] are to be construed as proposals for addition to a contract. Between merchants such terms become part of the contract unless. . .". Plaintiffs tell us that ProCD came out as it did only because Zeidenberg was a "merchant" and the terms inside ProCD's box were not excluded by the "unless" clause. This argument pays scant attention to the opinion in ProCD, which concluded that, when there is only one form, "sec. 2-207 is irrelevant." 86 F.3d at 1452. The question in ProCD was not whether terms were added to a contract after its formation, but how and when the contract was formed - in particular, whether a vendor may propose that a contract of sale be formed, not in the store (or over the phone) with the payment of money or a general "send me the product," but after the customer has had a chance to inspect both the item and the terms. ProCD answers "yes," for merchants and consumers alike. Yet again, for what little it is worth we observe that the Hills misunderstand the setting of ProCD. A "merchant" under the UCC "means a person who deals in goods of the kind or otherwise by his occupation holds himself out as having knowledge or skill peculiar to the practices or goods involved in the transaction", sec. 2-104(1). Zeidenberg bought the product at a retail store, an uncommon place for merchants to acquire inventory. His corporation put ProCD's database on the Internet for anyone to browse, which led to the litigation but did not make Zeidenberg a software merchant.

At oral argument the Hills propounded still another distinction: the box containing ProCD's software displayed a notice that additional terms were within, while the box containing Gateway's computer did not. The difference is functional, not legal. Consumers browsing the aisles of a store can look at the box, and if they are unwilling to deal with the prospect of additional terms can leave the box alone, avoiding the transactions costs of returning the package after reviewing its contents. Gateway's box, by contrast, is just a shipping carton; it is not on display anywhere. Its function is to protect the product during transit, and the information on its sides is for the use of handlers ("Fragile!" "This Side Up!") rather than would-be purchasers.

Perhaps the Hills would have had a better argument if they were first alerted to the bundling of hardware and legal-ware after opening the box and wanted to return the computer in order to avoid disagreeable terms, but were dissuaded by the expense of shipping. What the remedy would be in such a case - could it exceed the shipping charges? - is an interesting question, but one that need not detain us because the Hills knew before they ordered the computer that the carton would include some important terms, and they did not seek to discover these in advance. Gateway's ads state that their products come with limited warranties and lifetime support. How limited was the warranty - 30 days, with service contingent on shipping the computer back, or five years, with free onsite service? What sort of support was offered? Shoppers have three principal ways to discover these things. First, they can ask the vendor to send a copy before deciding whether to buy. The Magnuson-Moss Warranty Act requires firms to distribute their warranty terms on request, 15 U.S.C. sec. 2302(b)(1)(A); the Hills do not contend that Gateway would have refused to enclose the remaining terms too. Concealment would be bad for business, scaring some customers away and leading to excess returns from others. Second, shoppers can consult public sources (computer magazines, the Web sites of vendors) that may contain this information. Third, they may inspect the documents after the product's delivery. Like Zeidenberg, the Hills took the third option. By keeping the computer beyond 30 days, the Hills accepted Gateway's offer, including the arbitration clause.

The Hills' remaining arguments, including a contention that the arbitration clause is unenforceable as part of a scheme to defraud, do not require more than a citation to Prima Paint Corp. v. Flood & Conklin Mfg. Co., 388 U.S. 395 (1967). Whatever may be said pro and con about the cost and efficacy of arbitration (which the Hills disparage) is for Congress and the contracting parties to consider. Claims based on RICO are no less arbitrable than those founded on the contract or the law of torts. The decision of the district court is vacated, and this case is remanded with instructions to compel the Hills to submit their dispute to arbitration.

CHAPTER 10

CONCLUSION

The emergence of alternative dispute resolution is one the most significant legal developments of the last decade. While ADR remains a field in relative infancy when compared with the traditional litigation approach to dispute resolution, it has been embraced, in varying degrees, by the courts, businesses and individuals, as a way to avoid the cost, delays and acrimony of litigation. There is, no doubt, additional work to be done in defining and applying the many facets of ADR. This chapter begins that work by summarizing the major lessons learned from the programs reviewed. In addition, it predicts trends in dispute resolution, both legal and business related, and offers several final suggestions for effective program design and case management.

Lessons Learned

The variety of successful ADR efforts undertaken by the companies reviewed in this text suggests five cardinal rules for effective corporate ADR use, whether internal or external. Companies with successful ADR programs engage in careful predispute planning, insist on thorough ADR training, provide multiple process options, designate ADR leadership and manage outside legal work very carefully.

Pre-Dispute Planning. In every program reviewed, considerable effort is made to plan for disputes <u>before</u> they occur. Indeed, we could suggest that ADR implies 'anticipatory dispute resolution.' Anticipatory dispute resolution planning includes, perhaps primarily, obligatory employee handbook descriptions of dispute resolution mechanisms required of employees and the company for internal programs. Contract clauses describing a required sequence of dispute resolution processes are critical in external programs.

In addition, we have learned that establishing a network of in-house and external ADR providers in advance of a dispute allows for a timely, efficient and predictable response when the dispute occurs. A component of maintaining that provider network is the creation of hiring guidelines and interview questions for use when a particular case presents itself, as in the BP Amoco and Air Products programs. Further, we have seen in the best ADR programs, including the Baxter effort, that case screening methodology must be created to quickly and accurately determine the best course of dispute resolution action on a case-by-case basis. In short, companies that leverage ADR for maximum advantage do so by planning in advance for employee and external difficulties and preparing a careful system for responding to such cases when they arise.

Training and continuing education in ADR. Programs that succeed are programs that encourage a thorough understanding of the range of alternative dispute resolution options available, the advantages and disadvantages of each, and the proper method of participating in each process. Every program covered in this text makes an effort to train the users and providers of the program. In addition, Air Products maintains a substantial *Mediation Resource Center* toward that end. Darden Restaurants and Dollar General both train employee neutrals carefully as well as provide extensive information to the entire workforce on dispute resolution program options and use. The U.S. Postal Service has retained private professional trainers to prepare external mediators for Postal Service cases. Clearly, creating a broad base of understanding is critical to program success.

Multiple ADR options. The most effective internal and external programs utilize the full range of facilitative and adjuducative dispute resolution processes.   While mediation has become the process of choice for many companies, at least at the outset of a dispute, the best programs offer other ADR options as well. Darden and Dollar have created internal programs with several process options. All four external efforts profiled in this text use not just mediation, but the mini-trial, the summary jury trial and arbitration when the case calls for it. Additionally, the best programs sequence process responses so that less formal, less costly, less time-consuming methods are tried first, and more elaborate, formal and intensive efforts follow. Air Products, for example, always builds in a direct negotiation option before pursuing more formal methods of dispute resolution.

Leadership. There is considerable value in identifying a high-level executive to provide leadership for and oversight of the company ADR effort. Even with the upper management support present in each company profiled in this text, without an individual or identifiable committee responsible for ADR program coordination, success would be far less dramatic. In addition, while non-hierarchical, voluntary methods are the most popular external programs, they fail in at least one crucial respect: the absence of oversight, coordination and accountability.   To realize maximum company-wide benefits, a deliberate, organized effort directed by an individual with authority to expect ADR results is advisable in both internal and external ADR programs.

Managing outside counsel. The joke in many law firm hallways is that ADR stands not for 'alternative,' 'accelerated,' 'anticipatory,' or even 'appropriate' dispute resolution,' but for '**A**larming **D**rop in **R**evenue.' Designers of corporate efforts to use ADR to resolve employee or external disputes would do well to appreciate the extent to which lawyers see ADR as a threat to their bottom line. Indeed, as businesses look to reduce expenditures on dispute resolution, lawyers are the principal source from which those savings are created. As a result, there is increasing effort from the bar to curtail or control the use of alternative dispute resolution.

Companies may, for example, observe state bar associations endeavoring to classify functioning as a neutral as a legal activity. Doing so allows the bar to limit the practice to lawyers, and to punish non-lawyer neutrals with unauthorized practice of law sanctions which normally carry criminal penalties. Companies also confront law firms who 'front-load' billing, working intensively on a case very early, before settlement efforts are made, to assure a sizable fee even if the case is ultimately directed to an ADR process. Finally, companies may encounter law firms that consistently suggest the use of ADR, so long as the ADR process employed is arbitration, which presents the firm with the opportunity to bill for virtually the same amount of time and effort as a full-blown trial.

Management of outside counsel to avoid loss of ADR savings can take many forms:

1. The **legal audit**, a critical, line-by-line review of each invoice sent by a law firm, has become nearly universal in application. Active, on-going billing review allows a company to insist on appropriate and less costly methods of preparation in the context of sustained ADR use.

2. **Up-front billing** has also begun to grow in popularity. This scheme pays set fees for certain activities, motions, hearings, discovery preparation, etc., rather than the far less predictable hourly billing rate. Again, companies are able, in this way, to negotiate, control and anticipate the cost of moving a matter through any dispute resolution process, including litigation.

3. Companies have assuaged law firm fears of reduced revenue by offering **increased case volume** in exchange for greater use of ADR to reduce per case spending. Adopting such a practice makes both sides winners: the company reduces overall law-related spending by reducing per case billing, while the law firm maintains an income status quo by handling more cases, with greater economy.

4. Companies also have seen success with an **annual retainer** against which the firm works, in exchange for a pledge to use facilitative ADR in an agreed percentage of cases referred to the firm.

5. Companies have reduced reliance on outside counsel by building **larger in-house legal staffs**. When a larger in-house staff is created and trained in ADR advocacy and given caseloads to resolve through ADR, sizable economic gains can be realized.

6. Many companies have simply indicated to law firms that they are prepared to let the **market work** by hiring only firms that exhibit a meaningful commitment to ADR use that translates into bottom-line savings for the client. Very few U.S. legal markets have an undersupply of lawyers; companies are in a buyer's market for legal services as a result. In that buyer's market, businesses are in the advantageous position of driving a very hard bargain on the terms of

the representation they purchase from their outside counsel, and insisting that ADR use be incorporated in the terms of representation.

7. Finally, companies are taking advantage of **private firm ADR expertise**. With increasing regularity, firms are building departments and practice groups devoted to and specializing in ADR advocacy. While businesses would do well to remain guarded in their fee review practices, there is considerable value in hiring a firm the holds itself out as expert in and willing to use ADR to resolve legal disputes. When a company pursues such a firm, it is critical to inquire of the lawyers doing the ADR advocacy during the initial interview what their ADR philosophy is. Some ADR departments are simply clusters of litigators who, without any particular ADR expertise, take the combative, take-no-prisoners litigation approach to ADR. Doing so fails to take advantage of the benefits of ADR and increases the likelihood that such an approach will likely result in added legal fees and litigation, subsequent to the failed ADR.

Whatever form the outside counsel management efforts of a company take, it is clear to most ADR experts that private law firms, primarily hourly-fee defense firms, represent both the most substantial obstacle to ADR use and the greatest potential for economic savings.

BRIEFING POINT 10.1

Litigation prompts 36% of companies to discontinue products, 15% to lay-off workers and 8% to close plants, according to a 1988 Conference Board survey.

ADR Trends

ADR users are likely to see several trends in ADR development in the near future. Virtually all of these trends represent positive change for the business consumer of ADR.

Process standardization & clarity and uniformity of legal authority. The current law, both statutory and common, on ADR practice remains in its infancy. There are virtually no cases, for example, on the question of neutral malpractice; the odd disparity presented by the <u>Kientzy</u> and <u>Carman</u> ombudsman cases presented in this text is another example of incomplete or conflicting law. Moreover, while all states have statutory authority of some sort regarding ADR, typically some version of the Uniform Arbitration Act, none of the state statutes regulates all aspects of ADR practice. Private facilitative mediation, for example, is regulated in less than half of the states, and while recognized in federal law, is not regulated there at all.

Businesses using ADR should expect to see various efforts to standardize ADR practice in the interest of enhancing consumer trust in it. State statutes certifying or registering neutrals and obligating them to certain forms of ADR practice are moving through several state legislatures at the time of this writing. In addition, the growing body of case law suggests consistent and general judicial support for ADR efforts made in good faith and even-handedly. There is every reason to expect that courts, still faced by crushing dockets, will support the use of both private and court-annexed ADR to assist them in managing their caseloads.

Businesses play a crucial role in the development of ADR law. As the principal consumers of ADR services, business interests are well-advised to seek an ADR regulatory scheme that remains relatively permissive in terms of neutral credentialing and process oversight. The practice of ADR will not be improved by making it a lawyers-only arena, and the input of in-house counsel and management could prove critical in shaping the future of ADR law.

Development of meaningful standards of practice for neutral practitioners. Related to the development of legal standards is the development of practice standards for neutrals. This text provides an overview of the Ombudsman Association ethics standards in Chapter 3. Several other ADR professional associations have also promulgated rules of professional conduct. None of these codes has any disciplinary component beyond dismissal from the professional organization. While state statutes eventually will subsume some of these codes of conduct, and likely add more meaningful disciplinary schemes, business ADR consumers are advised to become involved now in the development and application of the private codes of conduct. To the extent that they are likely to form the basis for state and/or federal legislation on neutral ethics, there is a benefit in having them created and applied well now.

Development of effective assessment mechanisms. There is a growing understanding of the wide range of benefits offered by regular ADR use. In addition, users have become increasingly attracted to the intangible benefits ADR can provide, such as increased employee loyalty and productivity, preserved or enhanced business relationships and privacy. For example, companies have begun to scrutinize their accounting practices to assess and report these savings. Measuring average reduced time to case resolution or reduced litigation and law-related expenses is only part of the formula. Accordingly, it is very likely that more sophisticated accounting for intangible benefits will be developed and applied by enterprises eager to quantify the total effect ADR use has on the bottom line.

BRIEFING POINT 10.2
The *Center for Public Resources Institute for Conflict Resolution* estimates that 95 percent of all lawsuits settle outside of court.

Final Suggestions for a Successful ADR Program

Create comprehensive internal/external ADR programs. The single most striking aspect of the research that accompanied the writing of this text was the finding that very few companies operate both internal and external ADR programs. Perhaps this is a function of the division of responsibilities for external lawsuits and internal employee disputes. Normally, internal ADR programs originate in and function out of the Human Resources Department, while the Law Department is virtually always responsible for external litigation. The absence of comprehensive internal/external efforts may also be a function of the heightened effort required to create and coordinate the programs. Still, given the savings realized from each type of program, as demonstrated in the preceding company discussions, this area calls for greater attention. Many of the forms and clauses used in one type of program may be applied in the other. Moreover, the training of employees in ADR for an internal program cannot help but prepare the company for better external ADR use and the benefits reaped by comprehensive application of ADR could be exponentially increased.

Create incentives for use. The Air Products fee and bonus structure suggests an approach to ADR use that has a far greater application than simply to outside counsel. Companies should consider offering managers and employees economic and/or performance review-related incentives to use ADR. Forcing principle into practice likely will require tangible inducements.

Pursue creative uses of technology to further ADR program goals and objectives. The BP Amoco proprietary decision-making software and the use of company intranets for distribution of forms and program information counsel the more intensive use of technology to enhance company ADR use, particularly in large companies. Software packages are presently available to assist in negotiation preparation and decision-making. There is, in addition, a wealth of on-line material related to ADR available, including internet ADR discussion lists, and professional organization sites that include practitioner codes of conduct, referral services and private provider sources offering contract clauses, process overviews and training modules.

Leverage ADR success with important stakeholders. Many constituencies have a stake in corporate success, and communicating to them the successes of ADR use is a worthwhile endeavor. While each of the companies profiled in this text claimed sizable dollars savings from ADR use, none discussed those savings in its recent annual reports. Investors clearly are interested in company efforts to control the costs of litigation, and should be told when those attempts are made and savings are realized. Suppliers and vendors seeking long-term relationships with economic value and who already use ADR may also be attracted to a company by the promise of a less acrimonious approach to dispute resolution. Going public with a description of the ADR program and the benefits it delivers has considerable value.

Create a budget that reflects a commitment to ADR. Businesspeople know that to make money, one must spend money. Undoubtedly, to <u>save</u> money in the long-run, one must spend money in the short-run. Hiring ADR practitioners of national repute, designing ADR programs with multiple steps and multiple processes, conveying a professional image with excellent ADR program materials and undertaking continuous and effective program evaluation, perhaps with an outside consultant, are all expensive. However, the contribution to program success these practices offer more than offsets the expenditures.

Benchmark the program. To measure savings, an accurate assessment of current and past spending on dispute resolution is critical. Companies already normally collect data on case types, case sources, win/lose percentages, average court judgments, and annual law firm fees paid. It does not take a considerable additional effort to collate these figures to provide a benchmark against which to compare the company's future ADR results. A further suggestion is to reflect in the data national and regional trends. Companies may, for example, be realizing a decline in overall law firm spending because hourly rates have been compressed, as opposed to through ADR use. Certain types of legal actions may be eliminated or curtailed by changes in the law, and not by in-house efforts to control the number of suits filed by employees.

In a recent study of 1000 of the largest U.S. corporations, nearly 100 percent of those responding to the survey reported trying ADR some of the time, but fewer that 20 percent reported that they try to use ADR all of the time.[1] It is clear, based on the profiles of the companies in this text, that ADR can and does save time, money and business relationships while reducing the risk of unnecessary exposure in the courtroom. In an intensely competitive business world, companies that succeed do so by vigorously pursuing opportunities to improve their business practices. Using ADR to resolve company disputes, whether inside the business or out, is one way to improve those practices.

---

[1] Lipsky, David & Seeber, Ronald, "The Use of Alternative Dispute Resolution in U.S. Corporations" (1997)

APPENDIX 1: ADR SYSTEM DEVELOPMENT CHECKLISTS FOR BUSINESS

The following materials summarize several prominent authors' approaches to ADR system design. Each author has produced a text that provides very helpful information for those seeking to create business ADR systems.

Cronin-Harris, Catherine. *Building ADR into the Corporate Law Department: ADR Systems Design.* **New York: CPR Institute for Dispute Resolution, 1997**

The potential ADR program and its applications should be considered in a deliberate design process, rather than a disorganized development of the practices of ADR. The following steps should be taken to implement a successful corporate ADR program:

- **Assess current disputes for ADR potential** by looking at the existing patterns of disputes in a company, and the costs of the current resolution paths (which includes those actions that are taken even before a dispute reaches the legal department), and selecting goals for an ADR program that are appropriate for relevant dispute categories.

- **Review effective ADR programs** which are used by corporations that have already established ADR programs. This "benchmarking" process will identify those practices and tools that have been proven effective and can most easily be worked into newly proposed programs.

- **Create a team** of managers, lawyers, and consultants to examine and predict the course of the ADR program. It will be important to involve any identifiable in-house opponents who might potentially be involved in the process.

- **Generate corporate motivation to pursue ADR** by focussing on the crucial goals of minimizing the costs of litigation such as excessive time and business disruption.

- **Designate "ADR Counsel" to implement the program** who reports to general counsel, is a senior legal staff member and who will be able to serve as a knowledgeable ADR resource, a proponent of ADR and an ongoing program coordinator.

- **Conduct limited pilot programs** or projects to demonstrate and refine the process that is to be employed company-wide. Doing so will also create successful experiences to aid in promoting the ADR program to the company.

- **Develop "Upward Loop-Back" practices to avoid future disputes** by insuring that communication links will be established between lawyers and business personnel. Lawyers will be able to identify defects in manufacturing or conduct that may have been a factor in a dispute but may be preventable.

Trantina, Terry L. "One Clause Doesn't Fit All." *Business Law Today* **(March/April 1999): 42-46**

Trantina offers an extensive checklist of items to consider in the development of a corporate ADR program:

- Specify the types or combinations of types of ADR that are desired (mediation only, arbitration only, negotiation or any combination of the three).

- Specify the skill set of the ADR panel (one mediator or additional expert mediator to assist, one arbitrator which is less expensive or three arbitrators which would perhaps be appropriate for larger more complex cases).

- Specify the requirements for skill set and background of a mediator, arbitrator or negotiator. (Lawyer? Former judge? Nonlawyer professional such as an accountant, architect or engineer?). What knowledge of specific legal areas, what educational background, licenses or ADR neutral training and experience should he possess.

- Specify the location of ADR proceedings (site, state, selection process).

- Specify the scope of the issues and parties subject to ADR. (All inclusive or only specific issues? Third party beneficiaries? Claims arising under prior or related contracts?).

- Specify who should determine how or whether certain statutes of limitations and issue preclusion apply. (Court? Arbitrator?).

- Specify the arbitrator's ethical obligations and restrictions.

- Specify the extent of confidentiality and the permitted scope and methods of discovery.

Mazadoorian, Harry N. "Establishing and Implementing a Corporate ADR Program." *Business Law Today* **(March/April 1999): 37-40**

Mazadoorian establishes six preliminary steps to beginning a corporate ADR program:

- **Assess the dispute resolution need** to establish the scope, nature and volume of disputes along with the existing methods used to resolve them. The company must examine the shortcomings of its current methods of resolving disputes and set goals for what it hopes to accomplish with an ADR system.

- **Build support** from the top of the organization. This is most easily accomplished by becoming a signatory to the CPR policy statement on ADR, which requires the signature of both the CEO and the general counsel.

- **Anticipate and deal with resistance** which can come in many forms including resistance based upon policy objections, lack of familiarity and lack of understanding of ADR, or financial or personal considerations.

- **Include the basic elements of a successful program.** There are certain foundational blocks that are likely to prove useful to most corporate ADR programs such as: appointing an **ADR Coordinator** to oversee the program's design, implementation and evaluation; **communicating the ADR message well to critical constituencies** such as the legal department and business personnel who are likely to be involved; and, **developing educational and resource materials**.

- **Ensure a good ADR program by** starting on a limited basis, exploring ADR contract clauses and other agreements, using court-annexed ADR procedures, developing case-specific ADR strategies, knowing the ADR providers, learning from past experiences with ADR and building from the successful practices and procedures that have been developed.

- Finally, **Institutionalize ADR** with clear guidelines and policies.

Ury, William, Brett, Jeanne, & Goldberg, Stephen. *Getting Disputes Resolved: Designing Systems to Cut the Costs of Conflict.* **San Francisco: Jossey-Bass Publishers, 1988**

Ury and collaborators believe that dispute resolution systems are designed to handle disputes in a more cost-effective way as well as to provide more satisfying and long-lasting resolutions. In order to establish a successful system they present six basic design principles:

- The first of these basic principles, **putting the focus on interests**, is the most fundamental yet most difficult of the six. It involves creating or strengthening methods by which the interests of disputants can be reconciled. One of the design procedures that insures this is conducting negotiations as early as possible in the dispute.

- **Build in "Loop-Backs" to negotiation.** "Loop-back" procedures are those designed to cause disputants to turn back to ADR rather than become embroiled in contests of rights or power in adjudicative settings.

- **Provide low-cost rights and power backups.** Low-cost procedures to determine rights include conventional arbitration, which can come in a few different forms but is generally a far less expensive method of dispute resolution than formal litigation. Low-cost procedures to determine power include voting or limited strikes in which both employees and employers continue to work with salaries and profits placed into escrow so parties can continue to struggle over control while continuing to be productive.

- **Build in consultation before and feedback after the ADR process.**

- **Arrange ADR procedures in a low-to-high cost sequence.**

- **Provide the necessary motivation, skills, and resources to make the program work.**

APPENDIX 2: RESOURCES FOR BUSINESS ADR SYSTEM DESIGN

American Arbitration Association:

The American Arbitration Association, which handles roughly 80,000 cases annually through its network of over 18,000 expert neutrals, has regional offices in all fifty states as well as in Washington, D.C. Their very comprehensive website is located at the following address: **http://www.adr.org**.

In addition to extensive information on how to reach all regional offices to obtain service from an AAA neutral, the AAA's website offers a wealth of practical resources including focus areas on commercial ADR, developing a corporate ADR policy, construction, employment, labor, insurance and international ADR, selected federal and state ADR statutes, and *The Federal Center for Dispute Resolution*.

The site also offers extensive information regarding ADR education & research, ADR law, and links to their four specialized publications as well as dozens of related sites. Finally, this web page provides the rules and procedures for the various types of arbitrations that the AAA conducts, as well as sample copies of all forms related to AAA arbitration. Guides to ADR and Model Neutral Ethics & Standards are also provided. Contact the Washington, D.C. regional office at:

> Arnold B. Crews
> Regional Vice President
> 1150 Connecticut Avenue NW
> Floor 6
> Washington, D.C. 20036-4104
> 202.296.8510
> Facsimile 202.872.9574

CPR Institute for Dispute Resolution:

The CPR Institute for Dispute Resolution, a comprehensive, not-for-profit resource in ADR, can be found at: **http://www.cpradr.org**.

The CPR website offers links to numerous publications regarding ADR. Some of them are conventional periodical publications while others are one-time publications or pamphlets on subjects such as "Building ADR into the Law Firm." The site also provides wide-ranging ADR practice tools. For example, the CPR "Program for Resolving Employment Disputes," describes in detail the complete CPR employment dispute resolution program. The very useful "ADR Suitability Screen" provides a series of questions to be answered in order to determine the likelihood of resolving a specific matter through ADR.

The ADR clauses section, which not only addresses concerns about the precise language used in ADR contracts, but provides a "Drafters Guide to CPR Dispute Resolution Clauses," is the most comprehensive ADR drafting resource available. This section treats, among others, the following topics: "Why Use Pre-Dispute ADR Clauses?," "Detailed ADR Clauses for Business Agreements," "Abbreviated Clauses for Standard Business Agreements," "Optional Clauses to Protect Rights," and "Legal Concerns" (such as enforceability and confidentiality).

> James F. Henry
> President
> CPR Institute for Dispute Resolution
> 366 Madison Avenue
> New York, NY 10017-3122
> 212.949.6490
> Facsimile 212.949.8859
> Email: info@cpradr.org

Society of Professionals in Dispute Resolution:

The Society of Professionals in Dispute Resolution is "an international membership association committed to the advancement of the highest standards of ethics and practice for dispute resolvers." Their website can be found at **www.spidr.org** and has a number of very helpful resources.

The website includes several special features such as online articles and a lengthy section describing the ethical standards of the organization and its members. These rules of professional conduct cover topics ranging from general practitioner responsibilities to unrepresented interests and advertising and solicitation. Several ADR related publications may be ordered directly through the site. There are member and non-member prices for these publications. They include special committee and special sector reports, as well as an occasional ADR paper series.

SPIDR's website also offers a link to the *Mediation Information & Resource Center* and contact information and e-mail links to all of SPIDR's regional chapters located in most major U.S. cities. The international office can be reached at:

> 1527 New Hampshire Avenue, NW
> Third Floor
> Washington, D.C. 20036
> Phone: 202-667-9700
> Fax: 202-265-1968
> E-mail: spidr@spidr.org

Ombudsman Association:

The Ombudsman Association provides support to those practicing as both public and private ombudsmen. While the Association does not maintain a website, they do sponsor an annual conference, offer twice yearly ombudsman training, publish a variety of newsletters and bulletins as well as *The Ombudsman Handbook*, and staff several committees on ombudsman-related matters. The ethical standards promulgated by the group are the standard for all ombud practitioners. The Association can be reached at:

> Executive Office
> 5521 Greenville Avenue
> Suite 104-265
> Dallas, Texas 75206
> 214.553.0043
> Facsimile 214.348.6621
> Email CompuServe id=73772.1763

The Federal Mediation & Conciliation Service:

The FMCS was created by the 1947 United States Labor-Management Act. In 1978, the Labor-Management Cooperation Act expanded the services offered by the FMCS to include economic development, job security and organizational effectives initiatives. The principal role of the Agency, however, remains mediation of disputes in the collective bargaining context.

FMCS is an independent agency of the United States Government, and provides a variety of dispute resolution services to the nation's labor-management community, including mediation assistance in contract negotiation disputes between employers and their unionized employees. The Mission Statement of the FMCS provides five key objectives for the agency:

- Promoting the development of sound and stable labor-management relations;
- Preventing or minimizing work stoppages by assisting labor and management in settling their disputes through mediation;
- Advocating collective bargaining, mediation and voluntary arbitration as the preferred processes for settling issues between employers and representatives of employees;
- Developing the art, science and practice of conflict resolution; and,
- Fostering the establishment and maintenance of constructive joint processes to improve labor-management relationships, employment security and organizational effectiveness.

FMCS mediators operate out of over 75 Field Offices throughout the country. These Field Offices are administered by five Regional Offices. The FMCS National Office will provide contact information for individual mediators as well as the Regional Offices.

>Federal Mediation & Conciliation National Office
>2100 K Street, NW
>Washington, DC 20427
>202.606.8100

Mediation Council of Illinois:

State ADR organizations have proliferated over the past decade and are splendid resources on state specific ADR practice rules and law. A representative example is the Mediation Council of Illinois, which can be located at the following address: **http://www.mediate.com/illinois/**.

The website includes primarily membership information. However, one can also review the ethical standards of practice for mediators established by MCI, mediator referral information, annual conference information and MCI's newsletter *Mediation Works*. The site also provides answers to commonly asked ADR questions, as well as a link for direct inquiry to the ethics committee on specific ADR practice questions. The site also provides applicable state and federal statutes and caselaw. The substantive committees operated by MCI can be accessed with the following addresses, numbers and locations:

>### *ETHICS COMMITTEE:*
>Margaret S. Powers, Chair
>120 W. Eastman Street
>Suite 106
>Arlington Heights, IL
>312.943.2155
>Facsimile 847.670.0036
>Email mspowers09@aol.com

>### *LEGISLATION & PROFESSIONAL LIAISON COMMITTEE and LONG-RANGE PLANNING COMMITTEES:*
>Jerry Kessler, Chair
>1950 Sheridan Road
>Suite 1010
>Highland Park, IL 60035
>847.433.2323
>Facsimile 847.433.2349

CONFERENCE and FINANCE COMMITTEES
Dave Stone, Chair
804 Front Street
McHenry, IL 60050
815.385.8888

SELECTED BIBLIOGRAPHY IN DISPUTE RESOLUTION

General Dispute Resolution:

Auerbach, Jerold S. *Justice Without Law? Resolving Disputes Without Lawyers*. New York: Oxford University Press, 1983

Axelrod, Robert M. *The Evolution of Cooperation*. New York: Basic Books, 1984

Blalock, Hubert M. *Power and Conflict: Towards a General Theory*. Newbury Park, CA: Sage Publications, 1989

Bobo, L. "Prejudice and Alternative Dispute Resolution." *Studies in Law, Politics & Society* 12 (1992): 147

Boulding, Kenneth. *Three Faces of Power*. Newbury Park, CA: Sage Publications, 1989

Bunker, B., and J. Rubin, eds. *Conflict, Cooperation and Justice: Essays Inspired by the Work of Morton Deutsch*. San Francisco, CA: Jossey-Bass Publishers, 1995

Burton, John, *Conflict: Human Needs Theory*. New York: St. Martin's Press, 1990

Burton, John, and Frank Dukes. *Conflict: Readings in Management and Resolution*. New York: St. Martin's Press, 1990

Burton, John, and Frank Dukes. *Conflict: Practices in Management, Settlement and Resolution*. New York: St. Martin's Press, 1990

Burton, John W. *Conflict: Resolution and Prevention*. New York: St. Martin's Press, 1990

Bush, Robert A. Baruch. "Defining Quality in Dispute Resolution: Taxonomies and Anti-Taxonomies of Quality Arguments." *Denver University Law Review* 66 (1989): 335-80

Costello, Edward. *Controlling Conflict: Alternative Dispute Resolution for Business*. Chicago: CCH, Incorporated, 1996

Crum, T. *The Magic of Conflict: Turning a Life of Work Into a Work of Art*. New York: Simon & Schuster Inc., New York, NY., 1987

De Bono, Edward. *Conflicts: A Better Way to Resolve Them*. Middlesex: Penguin, 1985

Deutsch, Morton. *The Resolution of Conflict: Constructive and Destructive Processes*. New Haven, CT: Yale University, 1973

Emond, D.P., ed. *Commercial Dispute Resolution: Alternatives to Litigation*. Aurora, ON: Canada Law Book, Inc., 1989

Felstiner, William L.F. "Influences of Social Organization on Dispute Processing." *Law and Society Review* 8 (1974): 63-94

Felstiner, William L.F., Richard L. Abel, and Austin Sarat. "The Emergence and Transformation of Disputes: Naming, Blaming and Claiming..." *Law and Society Review* (1980-81): 631- 54

Fisher, Roger, Elizabeth Kopelman, and Andrea Kupfer Schneider. *Beyond Machiavelli: Tools for Coping with Conflict*. Cambridge, MA: Harvard University Press, 1994

Fiss, Owen. "Against Settlement." *Yale Law Journal* 93 (1964): 1073-90

Folger, J.P. et al. *Working Through Conflict: Strategies for Relationships, Groups, and Organizations*. New York: Harper Collins College Publishers, 1993

Galanter, M., and M. Cahill. "Most Cases Settle: Judicial Promotion and Regulation of Settlement." *Stanford Law Review* 46 (1993-94): 1339

Galanter, M., and J. Lande. "Private Courts and Public Authority." *Studies in Law, Politics & Society* 12 (1992): 393

Gleason, Sandra. *Workplace Dispute Resolution: Directions for the Twenty-First Century*. East Lansing, MI: Michigan State University Press, 1997

Goldberg, Stephen B., Eric D. Green, and Frank E.A. Sander. *Dispute Resolution*. Boston, MA: Little, Brown, 1999

Goss, Joanne H. "An Introduction to Alternative Dispute Resolution." *Alberta Law Review* 34 (1995): 1

Hocker, Joyce L., and William W. Wilmot. *Interpersonal Conflict*. Dubuque, IA: William C. Brown, 1991

Kolb, D.M., and Bartunek, J.M. *Hidden Conflict in Organizations: Uncovering Behind-the-Scenes Disputes*. Newbury Park, CA: Sage Publications, 1992

Leeson, Susan M., and Bryan M. Johnston. *Ending It: Dispute Resolution in America* Cincinnati, OH: Anderson Publishing 1988

Lipsky, David B. and Seeber, Ronald L. *The Appropriate Resolution of Corporate Disputes: A Report on the Growing Use of ADR by U.S. Corporations*. Ithaca: Cornell/PERC Institute on Conflict Resolution, 1998

Menkel-Meadow, Carrie. "Pursuing Settlement in an Adversary Culture: A Tale of Innovation Co-opted or The Law of ADR'." *Florida State University Law Review* 19(6) (1991): 1- 46

Morrill, Calvin. *The Executive Way: Conflict Management in Corporations*. Chicago, IL: The University of Chicago Press, 1995

Muldoon, Brian. *The Heart of Conflict*. New York: G.P. Putnum's Sons, 1996

Nolan-Haley, Jacqueline. *Alternative Dispute Resolution*. St. Paul, MN: West Publishing Company, 1992

Pirie, Andrew. "Manufacturing Mediation: The Professionalization of Informalism." In *Qualifications for Dispute Resolution: Perspectives on the Debate*, edited by Catherine Morris and Andrew Pirie, 165-91. Victoria, BC: UVic Institute for Dispute Resolution, 1994

Pirie, Andrew. "The Lawyer as a Third Party Neutral: Promise and Problems." In *Commercial Dispute Resolution: Alternatives to Litigation*, edited by D.P. Emond, 27-54. Aurora, ON: Canada Law Book, Inc., 1989

Ponte, Lucille & Cavenagh, Thomas. *Alternative Dispute Resolution in Business*. Cincinnati, OH: West Publishing Company, 1999

Rahim, M. Afzalur. *Managing Conflict in Organizations*. Second edition. Westport, CT: Praeger Publishers, 1992

Rahim, Afzalur, ed. *Theory and Research in Conflict Management*. New York: Praeger, 1990

Riskin, Leonard L., and James E. Westbrook. *Dispute Resolution and Lawyers*. St. Paul, MN: West Publishing Co., 1987

Riskin, L. "The Lawyer's Standard Philosophical Map." In "Mediation and Lawyers." *Ohio St Law Journal* 42 (1982): 41

Roberts, S. "ADR and Civil Justice: An Unresolved Relationship." *Minnesota Law Review* 56 (1993): 450

Ross, M.H. *The Management of Conflict: Interpretations and Interests in Comparative Perspective*. New Haven, CT: Yale University Press, 1993

Ross, M.H. *The Culture of Conflict: Interpretations and Interests in Comparative Perspective*. New Haven, CT: Yale University Press, 1993

Rubin, Jeffrey Z., Dean G. Pruitt, and Song Hee Kim. *Social Conflict: Escalation, Stalemate and Settlement*. New York: McGraw Hill, 1994

Sandole, J.D., and Herbert C. Kelman. *Conflict Resolution and Theory and Practice: Integration and Application*. New York: St. Martin's Press, 1993

Schelling, T.C. *The Strategy of Conflict*. Cambridge, MA: Harvard University Press, 1960

Silbey, Susan, and Austin Sarat. "Dispute Processing in Law and Legal Scholarship." *Denver University Law Review 66* (1989): 437-98

Singer, Linda R. Settling Disputes: Conflict Resolution in Business, Families, and the Legal System. Boulder: Westview Press, 1990

Strong, Elizabeth. "Nuts and Bolts of ADR for Business Disputes," New York Law Journal. March 6, 1997.

Stulberg, Joseph B. *Taking Charge/Managing Conflict*. Toronto, ON:, D.C. Heath & Co., 1987

Tillett, G. *Resolving Conflict: A Practical Approach*. Sydney, Australia: Sydney University Press, 1991

Tjosvold, D. *The Conflict-Positive Organization: Stimulate Diversity and Create unity*. Don Mills, ON: Addison-Wesley Publishing Company, 1991

Trachte-Huber, E. Wendy & Huber, Stephen. *Alternative Dispute Resolution: Strategies for Law and Business*. Cincinnati, OH: Anderson Publishing Company, 1996

Trubek, D., A. Sarat, W. Felstiner, H. Kritzer, and J. Grossman. "The Costs of Ordinary Litigation." *UCLA Law Review* 31 (1983): 72

Tyler, T. "The Quality of Dispute Resolution Procedures and Outcomes: Measurement Problems and Possibilities." *Denver University Law Review* 66 (1989): 419

Wehr, P. *Conflict Regulation*. Boulder: Westview, 1979

Younger, S. "Effective Representation of Corporate Clients in Mediation." *Albany Law Review* 59 (1996): 951

Negotiation:

Bazerman M., and M. Neale. *Negotiating Rationally*. New York: Free Press, 1991

Breslin, J.W., and J.Z. Rubin, eds. *Negotiation Theory and Practice*. Cambridge, MA: Program on Negotiation Books, 1991

Craver, Charles B. *Effective Legal Negotiation and Settlement*. Third edition. Charlottesville, VA: Michie, 1997

Cutcher-Gershenfeld, Joel, Robert B. McKersie, and Richard E. Walton. *Pathways to Change: Case Studies of Strategic Negotiations*. Kalamazoo, MI: W.E. Upjohn Institute for Employment Research, 1995

Druckman, Daniel, ed. *Negotiation: Social-Psychological Perspectives*. Beverly Hills, CA: Sage Publications, 1977

Fang, Tony. Chinese Business Negotiating Style. Thousand Oaks: Sage Publications, 1998

Fisher, Roger, and Scott Brown. *Getting Together: Building Relationships As We Negotiate*. New York: Penguin Books, 1989

Fisher, Roger, and William Ury, with Bruce Patton, ed. *Getting to Yes: Negotiating Agreement Without Giving In*. Second edition. New York: Penguin Books, 1991

Freund, James C. *Smart Negotiating: How to Make Good Deals in the Real World*. New York: Simon & Schuster, 1993

Gifford, D. *Legal Negotiations: Theory and Applications*. St. Paul, Minnesota: West Publishing Co., 1989

Gulliver, P.H. *Disputes & Negotiations: A Cross-Cultural Perspective*. New York, N.Y: Academic Press, 1979

Hendon, Donald W. and Hendon, Rebecca Angeles. *World-Class Negotiating: Dealmaking in the Global Marketplace*. New York, N.Y.: John Wiley and Sons, Inc., 1990

Jandt, Fred E. *Win-Win Negotiating: Turning Conflict into Agreement*. New York, N.Y.: John Wiley & Sons, Inc., 1987

Kritek, Phyllis Beck. *Negotiating at an Uneven Table: Developing Moral Courage in Resolving our Conflicts*. San Francisco, CA: Jossey-Bass Publishers, 1994

Lax, D.A., and J.K. Sebenius. *The Manager as Negotiator*. New York: Free Press, 1976

Lewicki, Roy J. et al. *Negotiation: Readings, Exercises, and Cases*. Third edition. Homewood, IL: Richard D. Irwin, 1999

Lewicki Roy J. et al. *Essentials of Negotiation*. Homewood, IL: Richard D. Irwin, 1999

Lewicki, Roy J. et al. *Negotiation*. Third edition. Burr Ridge, IL: Irwin, 1998

March, Robert, *The Japanese Negotiator: Subtlety and Strategy Beyond Western Logic*. New York: Kodansha International, 1989

Menkel-Meadow, Carrie. "Lawyer Negotiations: Theories and Realities - What do we learn from Mediation?" *Minnesota Law Review* 56 (1993)

Menkel-Meadow, Carrie. "Toward Another View of Legal Negotiation: The Structure of Problem-Solving." *UCLA Law Review* 31 (1984): 754-842

Putnam, L.L., and M.E. Roloff. *Communication and Negotiation.* Newbury Park, CA: Sage Publications, 1992

Raiffa, Howard. *Lectures on Negotiation Analysis.* Program on Negotiation at Harvard Law School, 1996

Raiffa, Howard. *The Art and Science of Negotiation.* Cambridge, MA: Belknap Press, 1982

Ury, William. *Getting Past No: Negotiating With Difficult People.* New York: Bantam Books, 1991

Walton, Richard E., and Robert B. McKersie. *A Behavioral Theory of Labor Negotiations: An Analysis of a Social Interaction System.* Second edition. Ithaca, N.Y.: ILR Press, 1991

Walton, Richard E., Joel Cutcher-Gershenfeld, and Robert B. McKersie. *Strategic Negotiations: A Theory of Change in Labor-Management Relations.* Boston, MA: Harvard Business School Press, 1994

White, J.J. "The Pros and Cons of *Getting to Yes.*" *Journal of Legal Education* 34 (1984):115-24

Mediation:

Bush, Robert A. Baruch, and Joseph Folger. *The Promise of Mediation: Responding to Conflict Through Empowerment and Recognition.* San Francisco, CA: Jossey-Bass Publishers, 1994

Bush, Robert A. Baruch. *The Dilemmas of Mediation Practice: A Study of Ethical Dilemmas and Policy Implications.* Washington, DC: The National Institute for Dispute Resolution, 1992

Cavenagh, Thomas. "A Quantitative Analysis of the Use and Avoidance of Mediation by the Cook County, Illinois, Legal Community." *Mediation Quarterly* 14(4) (1997): 353

Dunlop, John & Zack, Arnold. *Mediation and Arbitration of Employment Disputes.* San Francisco, CA: Jossey-Bass Publishers, 1997

Folberg, Jay, and Alison Taylor. *Mediation: A Comprehensive Guide to Resolving Conflict Without Litigation.* San Francisco, CA: Jossey-Bass Publishers, 1984

Goss, J.H., and D.C. Elliot. *Grievance Mediation: Why and How it Works.* Aurora, ON: Canada Law Book, 1994

Golann, Dwight. *Mediating Legal Disputes: Effective Strategies for Lawyers and Mediators.* New York: Aspen Law Publishers, 1996

Greenstone, J., S. Leviton, and C. Fowler. "Mediation Advocacy: A New Concept in the Dispute Resolution Arena." *Mediation Quarterly* 11(3) (1994): 293

Kolb, Deborah. *When Talk Works: Profiles of Mediators.* San Francisco, CA: Jossey-Bass Publishers, 1994

Kolb, D.M. *The Mediators.* Cambridge, MA: MIT Press, 1995

Kramer, Henry. *Alternative Dispute Resolution in the Workplace*. New York: Law Journal Seminars-Press, 1998

Kressel, Kenneth, and Dean Pruitt, eds. *Mediation Research: The Process and Effectiveness of Third-Party Intervention*. San Francisco, CA: Jossey-Bass Publishers, 1989

Leviton, Sharon & Greenstone, James. *Elements of Mediation*. Cincinnati, OH: International Thompson Publishing Co., 1997

Mennonite Conciliation Service. *Mediation and Facilitation Manual: Foundations and Skills for Constructive Conflict Transformation*. Third edition. Akron, PA: Mennonite Conciliation Service, 1995

Moberley, Robert. "Ethical Standards for Court-Appointed Mediators and Florida's Mandatory Mediation Experiment." *Florida State University Law Review* 21 (1994): 702- 27

Moore, Christopher W. *The Mediation Process: Practical Strategies for Resolving Conflict*. Second edition. San Francisco, CA: Jossey-Bass Publishers, 1996

Noone, M. "Mediation." In *Essential Legal Skills Series*, edited by Julie Macfarlane. London, UK: Cavendish Publishing, 1996

Phillips, Barbara. *Finding Common Ground: A Field Guide to Mediation*. Austin: Hells Canyon Publishing, 1994

Picker, Bennett. *Mediation Practice Guide: A Handbook for Resolving Business Disputes*. Bethesda, MD: Pike & Fischer, Inc. for the ABA, 1998

Pirie, Andrew. "The Lawyer as Mediator: Professional Responsibility Problems or Profession Problems?" *Canadian Bar Review* 63 (1986): 378-411

Potter, Beverly. *From Conflict to Cooperation: How to Mediate a Dispute*. Berkeley, CA: Ronin Publishing Company, 1996

Schwarz, R., *The Skilled Facilitator: Practical Wisdom for Developing Effective Groups*. San Francisco, CA: Jossey-Bass Publishers, 1994

Umbreit, M.S. *Mediating Interpersonal Conflicts: A Pathway to Peace*. West Concord, MN: CPI Publishing, 1995

Arbitration:

Boyd, S.C., and Mustill, M.J. *The Law and Practice of Commercial Arbitration in England*. Second edition. London, ENG: Butterworths, 1989

Brown, Laura F., ed. *The International Arbitration Kit*. Fourth edition. New York: American Arbitration Association, 1993

Casey, J.B. *International and Domestic Commercial Arbitration*. Scarborough, ON: Carswell, 1993

Continuing Legal Education Society of B.C. (CLE). *Commercial Arbitration: Advanced Practice Materials*. Vancouver, BC: CLE, 1991

Cooley, John & Lubet, Steven. *Arbitration Advocacy*. NITA Practical Guide Series. South Bend, IN: NITA, 1997

Craig, W. Lawrence, William W. Park, and Jan Paulsson, eds. *International Chamber of Commerce Arbitration.* Second edition. Dobbs Ferry, NY: Oceana Publications, 1990

Dore, Isaak I. *Arbitration and Conciliation Under the UNCITRAL Rules: A Textual Analysis.* Boston, MA: Marinus Nijhoff, 1986

Eijsvoogel, Peter V., ed. *Evidence in International Arbitration Proceedings.* London, ENG: Kluwer, 1995

Holtzmann, Howard M., and Joseph E. Neuhaus. *A Guide to the UNCITRAL Model Law on Commercial Arbitration: Legislative History and Commentary.* London, ENG: Kluwer, 1989

Hunter, Martin et al. *The Freshfields Guide to Arbitration and ADR Clauses in International Contracts.* London, ENG: Kluwer, 1993

Jacobs. *International Commercial Arbitration in Australia: Law and Practice.* Sydney, Australia: Law Book Company, 1992

Kaplan, Neil, et al. *Hong Kong and China Arbitration: Cases and Materials.* Butterworths, 1994

McLaren, R.H., and E.E. Palmer. *The Law and Practice of Commercial Arbitration.* Scarborough, ON: Carswell, 1982

Mustill, M.J., and S.C. Boyd. *Commercial Arbitration.* Second edition. Stoneham, MA: Butterworths, 1991

Powell-Smith, Vincent, Sims, John, and Dancaster, Christoper. *Construction Arbitrations: A Practical Guide,* 2d ed. Oxford: Blackwell Science, Osney Mead, 1998

The Ombudsman:

Reif, Linda, Mary Marshall, and Charles Ferris. *The Ombudsman: Diversity and Development.* Edmonton, AB: International Ombudsman Institute, 1993

Rowe, Mary P. "The Corporate Ombudsman: An Overview and Analysis." *Negotiation Journal* 3(2) (April, 1987): 127-40

Rowe, Mary P. "Helping People Help Themselves: An Option for Complaint Handlers," *Negotiation Journal* 6(3) (July, 1990): 239-48

Rowe, Mary P. "Options, Functions, and Skills: What the Organizational Ombudsperson Might Want to Know." *Negotiation Journal* 11(2) (April 1995): 103-14

Rowe, Mary P. "The Ombudsman's Role in a Dispute Resolution System." *Negotiation Journal* 7(4) (October, 1991): 353-61

Rowe, Mary P. "An Overview of Client and Internal Ombudsmen." *Journal of Health and Human Resources Administration* (Winter, 1993): 259-60

Rowe, Mary P., with John Reddy. "The Ombudsman as an Ounce of Prevention." *Industry* 51(3) (March, 1987): 42-44

Rowe, Mary P. with Mary Simon and Ann Bensinger, "Ombudsman Dilemmas: Confidentiality, Neutrality, Testifying, Record-Keeping." Proceedings of the Annual Conference of SPIDR, 1989. Washington, DC: SPIDR, 1990, 282-

93. Also reprinted in *Journal of Health and Human Resources Administration* (Winter 1993): 329-40

Rowe, Mary P., with James T. Ziegenfuss. "Corporate Ombudsmen: Functions, Caseloads, Successes and Problems." *Journal of Health and Human Resources Administration* (Winter 1993): 261-80

Rowe, Mary P., with James T. Ziegenfuss, Gary Hall, Anthony Perneski, and Marshall Lux. "Perspectives on Costs and Cost Effectiveness of Ombudsman Programs in Four Fields." *Journal of Health and Human Resources Administration* (Winter 1993): 281-312

System Design:

Blake, R.R., and J.S. Mouton. *Solving Costly Organizational Conflicts: Achieving Intergroup Trust, Cooperation, and Teamwork.* San Francisco, CA: Jossey-Bass Publishers, 1985

British Columbia Commission on Resources and Environment. *The Provincial Land Use Strategy: Dispute Resolution, Volume 3.* Victoria, BC: Commission on Resources and Environment, 1995

Costantino, C.A., and C.S. Merchant. *Designing Conflict Management Systems: A Guide to Creating Productive and Healthy Organizations.* San Francisco: Jossey Bass Publishers, 1996

Gray, Barbara. Collaborating: *Finding Common Ground for Multiparty Problems.* San Francisco, CA: Jossey-Bass Publishers, 1989

Rowe, Mary P. "The Non-Union Complaint System at MIT: An Upward-Feedback Mediation Model." In *Alternatives to the High Cost of Litigation* 2(4) (April, 1984): 10-18

Rowe, Mary P. "Dispute Resolution in the Non-union Environment: An Evolution Toward Integrated Systems for Conflict Management?" In *Frontiers in Dispute Resolution in Labor Relations and Human Resources*, edited by Sandra Gleason. East Lansing, MI: Michigan State University Press, 1997

Rowe, Mary P. "Options and Choice for Conflict Resolution in the Workplace." In *Negotiation: Strategies for Mutual Gain*, edited by Lavinia Hall. Newbury Park, CA: Sage Publications, 1993, 105-19

Rowe, Mary P. "People Who Feel Harassed Need a Complaint System with both Formal and Informal Options." *Negotiation Journal* 6(2) (April, 1990)

Rowe, Mary P., "Dealing with Harassment: A Systems Approach." In *Sexual Harassment: Perspectives, Frontiers, and Response Strategies, Women & Work, Vol. 5*, edited by Peggy Stockdale. Newbury Park, CA: Sage Publications, 1996

Rowe, Mary P., "The Post-Tailhook Navy Designs an Integrated Dispute Resolution System." *Negotiation Journal* 9(3) (July 1993): 203-13

Rowe, Mary P. "Specifications for an Effective Integrated Complaint System." In *Sexual Harassment on Campus*, edited by Robert Shoop et al. New York: Simon and Schuster, 1997

Mary P. Rowe with Michael Baker. "Are You Hearing Enough Employee Concerns?" *Harvard Business Review* 62(3) (May-June, 1984): 127-136

Ury, William, J.M. Brett, and S.B. Goldberg. *Getting Disputes Resolved: Designing Systems to Cut the Costs of Conflict.* San Francisco, CA: Jossey-Bass Publishers, 1988

Internet Articles and Useful Sites:

"Alternative Dispute Resolution: It's More Than Just Good Business."
http://www.hsba.org/ADR/ADRcontents.htm

Better Business Bureau and Alternative Dispute Resolution
http://www.buffalo.bnbb.rog/complaints.alternat.html

Boskey, James. The Alternative Newsletter:
http://www.mediate.com/tan/currentissue/index.htm

Braun, Robert. "Mandatory Arbitration Agreements.
http://www.uslaborcourt.com/bytes.htm

"Key Elements to Implementing a Successful ADR Program."
http://adrr.com/adr4/tenkeys.htm

Newman, Lawrence W. and Burrows, Michael, Arbitration Of Antitrust Disputes,
http://www.ljextra.com/practice/interna t/0519intarb.html

INDEX

A

Administrative Dispute Resolution Act of 1990, 42

ADR, *See* Alternative dispute resolution.

Air Products & Chemicals, Inc. (APC), 101–123
  ADR contract clauses, 108–112
  Agreement to Mediate, 112–114
  Confidentiality Agreement, 117–118
  forms and materials, 108–118
  key decision, 118–123
  Mediation Agreement, 114–116
  Mediation Resource Center, 103, 106, 108

Alternative dispute resolution (ADR), v, 1, 7–14
  advantages of, 10–12
    confidentiality, 11
    control, 11
    cost, 10
    flexibility, 11
    individually tailored outcomes, 10–11
    internationalization, 11–12
    speed, 10
  disadvantages of, 12–14
    enforcement, 12–13
    equal protection, 12
    public access, 13
    regulation, 13
  lessons learned, 185–188
    leadership, 186
    managing outside counsel, 186–188
    multiple options, 186
    pre-dispute planning, 185

    training and continuing education in, 186
  overview, 7–9
    arbitration, 9
    mediation, 8
    mediation-arbitration, 9
    mini-trials, 8
    negotiation, 8
    private judging, 9
    summary jury trial, 8–9
  program, 103–108
    assessment of, 108
    case successes, 107
    fee structuring for, 105–106
    preference for mediation, 104–105
    structured negotiation, 106–107
    trial and ADR team, 105
  suggestions for successful program, 190–191
    create comprehensive internal/external ADR programs, 190
    create incentives for use, 190
    pursue creative uses of technology to further goals and objectives, 190
    leverage success with important stakeholders, 190–191
    create a budget that reflects a commitment, 191
    benchmark the program, 191
  system development checklists for business, 193–196
  trends, 188–189
    development of effective assessment mechanisms, 189

development of meaningful standards of practice for neutral practitioners, 189
process standardization and clarity and uniformity of legal authority, 188–189
Alternative Dispute Resolution Act of 1998, 22
American Arbitration Association (AAA), 65, 197
  website, 197
American civil lawsuit
  cost, 6
  different interests, 7
  loss of the business relationship, 7
  risk, 7
  stages of, 1–7
    post-trial phase, 1, 5–7
    pre-trial phase, 1, 2–4
    trial, 1, 4–5
  time, 6
Answer, 2
Appeal, 5–6
Arbitration, 9
Armstrong, Phillip, 150, 156–157

B

Baxter *ADR Manual*, 170–175
Baxter International Inc., 169–175
Bench trial, 4
Bingham, Lisa, 22–26
Boeing, v
BP Amoco PLC, 125–146
  ADR program, 127–134
    assessment of, 133–134
    case evaluation, 131
    pre-emptive efforts, 129–131
    process selection, 131
    training, 129
    using mediation successfully, 131–133
  Early Case Evaluation Plan, 134–138

forms and materials, 134–140
Guide to Alternative Dispute Resolution, 127
key decision, 140–146
Mediator Selection Guidelines, 139–140
mid-level civil case, *chart*, 128
Brett, Jeanne, *Getting Disputes Resolved: Designing Systems to Cut the Costs of Conflict*, 196
Brock, Jon, 180
Browning-Ferris, v
Business dispute resolution programs
  designing, 14–16
    implementation, 15–16
    planning, 14–15

C

Carman v. McDonnell Douglas Corporation, 56–58
Carnival Cruise Lines, Inc. v. Shute, 181
Case investigation, 2
Closing arguments, 5
Code of Ethics of the Corporate Ombudsman Association, 43
Complaint, 2
Confidentiality, 11
CPR Institute for Dispute Resolution, v, 197–198
  website, 197
Cronin-Harris, Catherine, *Building ADR into the Corporate Law Department: ADR Systems Design*, 193–194

D

Darden Restaurants, 59–78
  ADR program, 61–69
    assessment of, 69
    fees and costs, 68
    hearing, 67–68

requirements for, 66–67
summary, *table*, 68
Dispute Resolution Procedure
(DRP), 61
    arbitration, 66–68
    how to use, 62
    mediation, 65
    open door, 63
    peer review, 64
    what is covered, 62–63
    forms and materials, 70–73
    key decision, 74–78
    mediation, summary, *table*, 65
    open door meetings, 63
        summary, *table*, 63
    peer review panel, summary,
    table, 64
    Peer Review/Mediation/
    Arbitration request form, 73
Darden, Bill, 60
Defendant presents a case in chief, 5
Discovery, 3
Dispositive, motions, 3
Doctor's Associates, Inc. v.
Casarotto, 181
Dollar General Corporation, 79–100
    ADR program, 81–91
        assessment of, 89–91
        option 1, open door tradition,
        83
        option 2, human resources
        support, 83
        option 3, conference, 84
        option 4, internal facilitation,
        84–85
        option 5, internal mediation,
        85–86
        option 6, peer review, 86–88
        option 7, external mediation,
        STEPS program, 88–89
        program manager, 82, 88
    conference, 84
    Dispute Resolution Program
    Contact Form, 93

Dispute Resolution Program
Request for Internal Facilitation,
94
external mediation, the STEPS
Program, 88–89
forms and materials, 91–95
human resources support, 83
internal facilitation, 84–85
internal mediation, 85–86
key decision, 96–100
Mission Statement, 81
open door tradition, 83
peer review, 86–88
Peer Review Request Form, 86, 95
sample letters, 91–92
STEPS Program, 88–89
Due process, 12

E

Employment Dispute Resolution Rules
of the American Arbitration
Association, 66
Employment Mediation Rules of the
American Arbitration Association, 65
Enforcement, 12–13
Equal protection, 12
Expert witnesses, 3

F

*Federal Center for Dispute
Resolution*, 197
Federal Mediation & Conciliation
Service, 199–200
Flexibility, 11
Folb v. Motion Picture Industry
Pension & Health Plans, 140–146
Forrester v. White, 164

G

Georgia-Pacific Corporation, 147–
165
    ADR program, 149–158

assessment of, 157–158
in-house technology and
training, 153
measuring ADR savings, 156–
157
overview, 149–153
use of ADR contract clauses,
151–153
supervision of outside counsel,
153–156
contract clause, 152
forms and materials, 158–162
Guidelines for Outside Counsel,
153–157
key decision, 162–165
Model ADR contract clauses, 158–
162
Goldberg, Stephen, *Getting Disputes
Resolved: Designing Systems to Cut
the Costs of Conflict*, 196
Government Accountability Project,
179
Graphic Communications
International Union, Local 735-S v.
North American Directory
Corporation II, 96–100

H

Hanford Nuclear Site, 179–184
key decision, 180–184
Hill v. Gateway 2000, Inc., 180–184
Hooters of America, Inc. v. Annette
R. Phillips *et al.*, 74–78

I

Individually tailored outcomes, 10–11
Internationalization, 11–12

J

Jerome S. Wagshal v. Mark W.
Foster, 162–165
Johnson & Johnson, 176–179

Common Ground, 176, 177–179
Jurisdiction, 2
Jury deliberations, 5
Jury selection (*voir dire*), 4

K

Kelley, James, 149–150
Kientzy v. McDonnell Douglas, 42,
54–56
Kummetz v. Tech Mold, Inc. 36–38

L

Labor-Management Cooperation Act,
199
Lande, John, 6–7
Legal counsel, 2
Loop-back, 194, 196
upward, 194

M

Managing outside counsel
annual retainers, 187
increased case volume, 187
larger in-house legal staffs, 187
market work, 187–188
private firm ADR expertise, 188
the legal audit, 187
up-front billing, 187
Mazdoorian, Harry N. "Establishing
and Implementing a Corporate ADR
Program," 195
Mediation, 8
Mediation-arbitration (med-arb), 9
Mediation Council of Illinois, 200–
201
conference and finance
committees, 201
ethics committee, 200
legislation and professional liaison
committee, 200
website, 200

Mediation Information and Resource Center, 198
Mini-trials, 8
Motion for a judgment notwithstanding the verdict, 5
Motion for summary judgment, 3
Motion to dismiss, 3
Motions *in limine*, 3–4

N

National Association of Manufacturers, 175–176
    website, 175–176
Negotiation, 8
Nuclear Posture Review, 40

O

Olive Garden, 59, 60
Ombudsman Association, 43, 44, 199
Ombudsman Handbook, The, 199
Opening statements, 4

P

Perfection or enforcement of judgment, 6
Plaintiff presents a case in chief, 4
Postal Reorganization Act, 18
Postal Service Settlement Agreement Form, 34–35
Post-trial phase, 1, 5–7
    appeal, 5–6
    motion for a judgment notwithstanding the verdict, 5
    perfection or enforcement of judgment, 6
Pre-trial phase, 1, 2–4
    answer, 2
    case investigation, 2
    complaint, 2
    discovery, 3
    dispositive motions, 3
    expert witnesses, 3

legal counsel, 2
    trial preparation, 3–4
Prima Paint Corp. v. Flood and Conklin Mfg. Co., 184
Private judging, 9
ProCD, Inc. v. Zeidenberg, 181
Public access, 13

R

Red Lobster, 59, 60
REDRESS program (Resolve Employment Disputes Reach Equitable Solutions Swiftly), 18–27
    assessment, 26–27
    detailed program analysis, 22–26
    extensive dispute resolution training, 21–22
    facilitative mediation approach, 22
    process employee satisfaction, *figure*, 24
        with mediator, *figure*, 25
        with outcome, *figure*, 26
    process First Quarter National Closure Rate, 1999, *figure*, 23
    process overview, 20–21
    process supervisor satisfaction, *figure*, 24
        with mediator, *figure*, 25
        with outcome, *figure*, 26
Resources for Business ADR system design, 197–201

S

Sandia National Laboratory, 39–58
    ADR program, 41–50
    ombudsman, 41–50
        assessment of, 50
        comparison of ethics and ombudsman programs, *figure*, 48
        comparison of ethics and ombudsman tasks, *figure*, 48

corporate compliance
perspective, 44
employee's perspective, 45
ethics, 43–44
forms and materials, 50–54
history of, 41–43
interpersonal conflict cases,
figure, 47
key decisions, 54–58
laboratory interests perspective,
44
managerial perspective, 45
number of management conflict
cases, *figure*, 47
reason to establish, 44–45
use of, 45–50
strategic objectives, 40–4
Society of Professionals in Dispute
Resolution, 198
website, 198
Standards of Practice of Postal
Service Mediators, 27–32
mediation process and mediator's
role, 27–28
purpose, 27
Standard I, competency, 28
Standard II, impartiality, 28–29
Standard III, confidentiality, 29
Standard IV, consent, 29–30
Standard V, self-determination,
30–31
Standard VI, separation of
mediation from counseling and
legal advice, 31
Standard VII, promotion of respect
and control of abuse of process,
31–32
Standard VIII, conflicts of interest,
32
Summary jury trial, 8–9

T

Thermos Company v. Starbucks
Corporation, 118–123
Trantina, Terry L., "One Clause
Doesn't Fit All," 194–195
Trial, 1, 4–5
closing arguments, 5
defendant presents a case in chief, 5
jury deliberations, 5
jury selection (*voir dire*), 4
opening statements, 4
plaintiff presents a case in chief, 4
preparation, 3–4

U

United States Postal Service, 17–38
REDRESS program, 18–26. *See
also* REDRESS.
Standards of Practice, 19
United States v. Orr Construction Co.,
123
Up-front billing, 187
Ury, William, *Getting Disputes
Resolved: Designing Systems to Cut
the Costs of Conflict*, 196

V

Voir dire (jury selection), 4

W

Whirlpool Corporation, 167–169
management of legal staff, 167–
168
mediation by agreement, 168–169
pre-litigation negotiation strategy,
168
Whitney, Bruce, 104, 105